Where the Creosote Blooms

Where the

Creosote Blooms

A Memoir by

Mary King Rodge

Number Nineteen in the Chisholm Trail Series

Copyright © 1999 by Mary King Rodge

Library of Congress Cataloging-in-Publication Data

Rodge, Mary King, 1914-
Where the creosote blooms / by Mary King Rodge.
P   cm. ñ (The Chisholm Trail series : no. 19)
ISBN 0-87565-193-3 (paperback : alk. paper)
Rodge, Mary King, 1914-   —Childhood and youth. 2. El Paso
(Tex.)óBiography.   3. El Paso (Tex.)óSocial life and customs.
Title   II. Series
F394.E4R63   1999
976.4í96062-0926dc21
[b]   98-14193
CIP

Book design by Barbara M. Whitehead

Acknowledgments

This book was made possible by my enrollment in the Master of Liberal Arts Program at the University of North Carolina, Asheville. Thanks to all my professors who stimulated my interest in creative writing and especially to Peggy Parris, Sandra Obergfell and David Hopes, who served on my MLA Project Committee.

Thanks to my editor, Tracy Row, who early on spotted a few grains of wheat among the bushels of chaff and helped me sort it out.

Finally, thanks to my sister, Rebekah King Conrad of New Orleans, for sharing the memories and insisting I could do it.

The story of the pigeon raising fiasco was first published in *The Journal of Graduate Liberal Studies* (Vol. II, No. 1, Fall 1996).

For Becky

Prologue

I wasn't born in El Paso. We moved there from California during the summer of 1924 just before my tenth birthday. I remember that move very well, how we settled down in our brick bungalow on Mountain Avenue and thought it would be forever. Mama was so happy about that little house; and after all our moving around in California Papa felt good about his permanent job as overseer of the dye house at The Lone Star Cotton Mills. Of course my little sister Becky and I loved it, all that blue sky and open space. That's the word that describes El Paso best: openness.

That move was a long time ago. Years have passed and I have lived in many different places, but to this day when someone asks me where I am from, I respond happily, "Well, I grew up in El Paso." Just the sound of that musical name, El Paso, and the years roll away and I am transported back to that sunny, desert city. The adolescent years are important to all of us; but with me it's more than the years, more than time passing. It's the place. It's the desert and the mountains, the cloudbursts and sandstorms, and the sun, always the sun.

Looking back, way back before World War II and even before the Depression, I see an eager, impulsive little girl, growing up in the sun-baked city. Her brown curls, cut short in the new boyish bob, are blown almost straight by the dry desert wind, and her naturally blue eyes look even bluer against her suntanned face. In spite of Mama's warnings she can never remember to wear a sun hat. In her sleeveless, sun-back dresses and brown sandals she roams the desert, watches the sunrise, the sunset, the ever-changing shadows, gathers odd-shaped pods and seeds, and unconsciously, day after day, puts down her own roots as tough and enduring as those of the desert plants she loves.

Mountain Avenue was the last paved street on the northern rim of the city. The black asphalt pavement started at the foothills of Mount Franklin on the west and ran downhill in a straight line all the way to Fort Bliss on the east. Our block, on the steep, upper end of the hill, consisted of seven or eight look-alike red-brick bungalows. Each house had a wide front porch shaded by Virginia creeper which against all odds managed to flourish in the dry, desert air. The only exception to the brick bungalows was the small flat-roofed, Spanish-style stucco building on the lower corner of the block next to Copia Street. Its white walls glistened in the sun like a spatter of rhinestones. The large letters, scratched with Bon Ami on the plate glass window facing Mountain Avenue, announced the building's useful purpose: HAIR CUTS 25 CENTS.

On across Copia, with plate glass windows facing both Copia and Mountain, was Quinn's Grocery and Market. The plainness of its red brick walls was broken by the brown canvas awnings that Kerry Quinn let down every morning to protect the fresh produce behind the windows from the merciless sun. A truck, bearing the sign "Quinn's Grocery and Market," and beneath that, in smaller letters, "Free Delivery," was parked on the Copia side of the store, if Kerry didn't have it out on delivery. Mrs. Quinn worried about the way Kerry drove, always cutting around corners on two wheels, and even sneaking the truck out at night and taking it to Juarez. She tried to caution him, telling him the truck would be confiscated at the International Bridge if he didn't quit smuggling liquor home. But Kerry didn't listen. He was enjoying life too much.

Our house was in the middle of the block. We were lucky, because there were no houses across the street from us, just the open school grounds. Rusk School stood on the lower end of the block, facing Copia, so we could look straight across the rocky school grounds to the mesa—we called it the desert—which spread out like an open fan all the way to Sugar Loaf, the mountain to the north, then curved a little uphill and to the left across the mouth of McKelligon Canyon and on around to the foothills of Mount Franklin on the west.

At least at first, the days passed gently on Mountain Avenue, one much like another, just as the look-alike houses resembled each other. I remember the winter mornings when Mama asked me to run out front and pick up the *Times* so that Papa could glance at the headlines before he left for the cotton mill. Without taking time to put on a robe—I don't think I even had one—I dashed out in my nightgown and picked up the paper from the sidewalk. The air was so cold my breath froze and floated away like a misty cloud; but in the dry atmosphere the cold didn't penetrate my flannel gown, and I hardly noticed it. As I started back up the steps, my ear caught that first clear bugle note, the sound of reveille out at Fort Bliss. Quick as a flash I tucked the folded paper under my arm, turned around, and ran out to the edge of the street. Standing on the high white curbing I leaned forward and gazed down the long hill, trying to get a glimpse of the flag, a tiny speck at that distance, silhouetted against the sun rising over Hueco Mountains far beyond the eastern plains:

> I can't get 'em up, I can't get 'em up,
> I can't get 'em up in the morning . . .

Every child in the neighborhood knew those words. I tapped my blue felt bedroom slipper in time and repeated the words to myself:

> Coffee, coffee, coffee,
> Sugar never seen,

Bacon, bacon, bacon,
And nota streak of lean.

I stood there until the last note had floated up the hill and died out against the steep sides of Mount Franklin, the brown cliffs now turning watermelon pink in the early dawn.

Mama was at the front door calling, "Mafra, do come in. Papa is ready to leave and wants his paper. You'll catch your death out there."

Hurrying back into the warmth of the kitchen, I sat down to my own breakfast of grits and black-eyed peas fried in bacon grease. Sitting next to the chair Papa had just vacated, I mixed my peas into the buttered grits, stirred them around until the grits cooled and, putting a large forkful into my mouth, closed my eyes and sighed blissfully. When I did it that way, the peas tasted just like nuts.

I remember summer mornings, playing in the backyard and watching Mama work in her flower garden, especially after she gave up on the exotic plants she had known in California and decided to go native. She gathered all sorts of dried seeds and even roots from the desert, planted them with loving care in the sandy, rocky soil, and gloried in their endurance. "So tough and so lovely," she would say. "Just look at this purple verbena, and the blue of that wild aster. Did you ever see such a heavenly blue?"

And I remember Mama bending over the creosote bushes by the back fence after a quick shower, sniffing audibly in appreciation of the fresh, clean aroma, as she admired the tiny golden blooms or woolly little seeds. Nothing grows under creosote, and more than one neighbor had urged Mama to get rid of the bushes. She had a spirited defense. "It's a native plant," she argued, "and makes the yard look natural. The soil is so poor, actually caliche, and the creosote can't tolerate other plants because it needs all the nourishment itself. It's just survival instinct." She emphasized her affection for the straggly bush by stroking the sticky leaves, then surreptitiously wiping her fingers on her skirt, trying to rub off the resin.

And I remember the long summer afternoons when it was too hot to play on the parched Bermuda lawn and Becky and I sat on the shady porch, waiting for the sun to drop behind Mount

Franklin's long serrated ridge. At last the sun disappeared, and the shadows slipped down the mountain and scooted on down the black asphalt pavement, block after block, faster than a child could run, or even skate for that matter. In just moments the whole street was in shadow, then Fort Bliss, the plains beyond, and the sky above the Hueco Mountains burst into color.

I would call to Mama. "Come out for a minute and see the sunset over the Hueco Mountains. It's all pink and orange and red. Hurry, Mama. It's the brightest I've ever seen.

Mama left her half-kneaded biscuit dough on the kitchen table and came out, wiping her flour-covered hands on her apron. Yes, she agreed, it was indeed the best sunset ever.

And I remember the long summer evenings when Becky and I sat on the porch steps playing jacks, and Mama and Papa settled themselves comfortably in the wicker rockers behind the Virginia creeper. As long as it was light they read the paper, talked about politics and laughed about Will Rogers' latest joke: "Coolidge didn't do nothing, but that's what the people wanted done."

When it got too dark to read or play jacks Becky put the jacks and ball away in the little drawstring bag, and we both leaned back against the brick pillars, one on either side of the steps. We usually sat quietly, listening to Mama tell some bit of neighborhood news. She had a pleasant voice, a full voice. Her years in California had modified her southern drawl, but people hearing her talk could usually guess she came from Georgia. Our neighbors—privately Mama referred to them as "Yankees"—often told Mama they loved to hear her voice. Sometimes Becky and I tried to imitate her, but we couldn't do it. We had both learned to talk in California.

If Mama wasn't giving us some neighborhood news, Papa talked about the cotton mill. He told about the Mexicans crossing the river every morning to work in the mill or about giving a job to some old friend who had turned up unexpectedly from Georgia. Papa was manager of the dye house, but he could run any machine in the mill, and they often called on him to straighten out some problem in the weave room or spinning room. The dry air—static electricity he called it—was always making the threads break.

Around eight o'clock street noises began to quiet down. Our

own conversation had ceased, and up and down the street lights were going out. Mama said she knew it was late but she wanted to hear just one song before she went to bed, and she sent me inside to put a record on the Victrola. I usually picked "Good-Bye Sweet Day," because I knew it was her favorite. After giving the Victrola a good winding and placing the needle on the record, I hurried out to sit on the steps and listen to the music:

> Good-bye, sweet day. I have so loved thee,
> But cannot, cannot hold thee.
> Fading like a dream. . .

It was so pleasant just sitting there, leaning against the pillar, listening to the music and watching the stars twinkle over the desert. The song faded away, and Mama said again that it really was late. She went inside; I could soon hear the clatter of pans in the kitchen. She was soaking the grits in the double boiler for breakfast.

Papa yawned, got out of his chair, and stretched himself. He was a tall man with dark wavy hair. Winding his watch, he came over to the steps for a better look at the night sky. "Yeah, there's the Big Dipper," he said, as though he were surprised to find it right up there in its usual place over McKelligon Canyon, pointing to the North Star directly over Sugar Loaf. "The drinking gourd—that's what they used to call the dipper down South when I was a boy. Some old slave song about following the drinking gourd to freedom. I don't remember the song anymore, but I think I remember how to tell time by the stars. I'll figure it out sometime and teach you girls."

Papa had promised that so many times, we didn't bother to answer. He opened the screen door to go inside, and Becky and I stood up to follow him. Suddenly a heavy fragrance filled the air. Mama's night-blooming angel-trumpet in the side yard had opened its pink throat, inviting a visit from some nocturnal moth or butterfly. Papa went ahead, letting the door slam behind him; but Becky and I lingered, filling our lungs with the cloying sweetness of the angel-trumpet. It was like being covered with a dash of baby powder, but we both liked it, at least that first whiff.

Even now, I always try to have a potted angel-trumpet on my

patio, just for the aroma. I still live in the mountains—the Smokies now, much softer than the austere southern Rockies—and when the sun drops behind the western peaks and twilight falls, I like to sit there in the fading light and catch the first fragrant whiff of angel-trumpet, and I am a little girl in a sun-back dress and brown sandals, sitting on the porch on Mountain Avenue.

1

We had been living in Redlands about a year when Papa got the letter from El Paso. Its arrival turned out to be one of those before-and-after events in life from which everything else can be dated.

The letter arrived on a typical California morning, warm but breezy. Becky and I, playing hopscotch in the sandy yard under the palm trees, didn't even notice the postman when he turned up our walk. Mama happened to be standing in the doorway, not waiting for the mail but trying to catch a breath of fresh air after her kitchen exertions. Her fluffy brown hair, recently bobbed for the very first time in her life, stuck in tiny ringlets to her damp forehead. She wasn't accustomed to the short strands and was brushing them back rather impatiently when the postman handed her the long white envelope.

Mama started to chat with the postman in her friendly fashion, but when she noticed the El Paso return address on the envelope, she cut herself short mid-sentence, held the envelope in both hands, and stood quite still, scrutinizing it carefully. In a moment she stepped to the edge of the porch and called to me, interrupting the interminable hopscotch game: "Come, here, Mafra, I need you. It's a business letter for Papa. It's from El Paso."

The strange name had no meaning for me, but I caught the urgency in Mama's voice and responded without my usual dawdling. As I went up the porch steps, she was holding the envelope up to the light in a vain attempt to peek through the heavy paper and decipher a word or two of its contents.

"Well, I can't read it," she complained. "But I can tell it's urgent. You'll have to go down to the factory right away, Mafra, and give it to Papa."

The little family-owned towel factory where Papa was the dyer was just a few blocks down the street, and I always welcomed an excuse to go down there. The factory only ran part-time, and Papa was never too busy to talk a while or maybe show me a new batch of towels. Now, sweaty from my morning play, I wanted a minute to go inside to put on a clean dress and comb my hair.

Mama was strangely impatient. "Oh, just go as you are, Mafra." She ran her fingers through my dark hair and wiped the dust from my hands on her apron. "Carry the letter under your arm where nobody will notice. Don't actually run but walk as fast as you can, and be sure Papa is alone when you give it to him. As soon as he reads it, come back and tell me what it says. Hurry, now."

I had caught Mama's excitement and didn't argue. Proud to be entrusted with this mysterious mission, I concealed the envelope under my arm as Mama had ordered, walked sedately, and waited until I was out of sight of the house before slipping the envelope out for a closer look. Papa's name was spelled out in full, Habersham King. It took a minute to figure that out. I knew he had been named Habersham for his grandfather back in Georgia, but out here in California everybody just called him Hab, and I had forgotten he really had a longer name. Well, the same thing had happened to my own name. I had been baptized Mary Frances, but when my little sister Becky was about two, just learning to talk, she cut it down to Mafra, and that's what everybody called me now, except, of course, my teachers.

After spelling out Papa's name I examined the return address: The Lone Star Cotton Mill, El Paso, Texas. I remembered studying about Texas in geography class, but I wasn't sure about El Paso. I was so busy examining the envelope and trying to recall something about El Paso that I arrived at the towel factory without realizing I was there.

Suddenly I looked up and saw the sign, "Redlands Towel Factory," just across the street. I put the envelope back under my arm and stood on the curbing while I waited for a truckload of oranges headed for the packing shed to pass. I knew if I waved at the driver he would toss me an orange, but I didn't want to get juice all over the envelope so I missed the opportunity and just let the truck go by.

The dye house was quiet, the dye vats empty. Papa in his white shirt and tie was standing in the open door. I thought he was a fine looking man with broad shoulders, dark wavy hair and blue eyes, and I was always pleased when people said I looked just like him. I liked his white shirt and tie, too. Mama washed, starched, and ironed the shirts herself. She had explained to me how she had learned to be very good at ironing and it was worth the trouble because wearing a white shirt and tie showed Papa was an overseer and not an ordinary, blue-collared mill hand running some noisy machine.

Seeing Papa was alone, I held out the envelope. That El Paso return address seemed to mean as much to him as it had to Mama. He ripped the envelope open, glanced at the contents, and let out a loud whistle. "El Paso, Texas," he exclaimed. "How about that, Mafra? How are you going to like living in Texas? That's it. We're moving to El Paso. Come on, let's go tell your mother."

Papa walked so fast I could hardly keep up with him, but I managed to gasp out a few questions as we rushed along. The letter, he explained, was from Fred Mae, a man he had worked for back in Georgia. Mr. Mae was going to be general manager of the new Lone Star Cotton Mill in El Paso. Papa had heard they were building a new mill in El Paso, but he didn't know until he got the letter that Mr. Mae was going to be general manager. Now Mr. Mae had written and asked Papa to come at once to help set up the dye house and then to be head dyer.

"How did he know where to find you out here in Redlands?"

"Oh, that's the way the cotton mill business works. People move around a lot, but there's sort of an underground network. Somebody can always tell you where to find a friend of a friend. You know, it goes like that."

Mama was on the porch waiting for us. When I saw how over-joyed she was at the news, I realized that we had really been having a hard time in Redlands: Papa working only part time and always complaining that California cotton mills would never be able to compete with the low wages in southern mills. Mr. Mae's letter, which Mama and Papa read aloud in their enthusiasm, even explained that the El Paso mill could count on cheap Mexican labor. Rushing ahead with moving plans, Papa joked that he might have to learn Spanish.

We tore a map out of my old geography book, and Papa drew a red line for our route through Indio, Brawley, Yuma, and Phoenix, checked off possible campsites, and ended with a big star at El Paso, hoping aloud that the old Overland could make it. He bought an extra secondhand tire, spent an afternoon tuning up the engine, and crated the few pieces of furniture we were shipping by train.

Mama packed boxes and suitcases, and while she worked she talked about the move. She admitted California was a beautiful state and people were moving out there in droves, just like she and Papa had moved out from Georgia when they were first married. But you can't live on scenery, she kept saying. She thought it was really funny we were going the other direction, crossing the desert from west to east. But that's what we were doing—and in August, too.

On the second day after we got the letter we were packed and ready. We tried to get an early morning start, but at the last minute there was trouble about the furniture. The drayman from the rail-road didn't like the way Papa had crated the highchair and refused to take it. He drove off with the rest of the load, and Mama didn't know about the highchair until she came out to get into the car and saw it standing there, half-crated, under one of the palm trees. Well, she wasn't going to leave the highchair. Both of her girls had used it, she said proudly, as though we were going to grow up to be famous and the highchair would be a valuable museum piece.

Papa said we sure couldn't take it in the car, and just a glance at the old Overland proved he was right. We already had a mattress and tent strapped on top, suitcases on the running boards, two spare tires on the back, and so many boxes, blankets, and camping supplies inside there wasn't going to be any room in the back seat for Becky and me to stretch our legs.

While the argument about the highchair was going on, a gray-haired man I vaguely recognized from down the street happened by, listened to the dispute, and said he would give Mama fifty cents for the highchair. Mama's blue eyes flashed angrily, but she was a practical person and knew she was beaten. Without a word she held out her hand for the half-dollar, thrust it into her purse, snapped the purse shut, and climbed into the car.

Even then we didn't make a speedy takeoff. The Overland had a bad habit of reflecting family moods, always choking and flooding when it sensed a crisis. True to form, it chose this moment to balk, and Papa had to do a lot of grinding on the starter before the engine finally sputtered into action. By that time the old man had knocked the shoddy crate off and heisted the highchair up on his back. I started to say it looked funny, but just a glance at Mama, her jaunty little black sailor hat jammed down over her short hair, her shoulders squared, and her eyes straight ahead, convinced me this was no time for joking.

Papa pulled the car away from the curb, and as we chugged along the palm-lined street, I craned my neck, looking backward for a final glimpse of my highchair bobbing along the sidewalk on the old man's back.

We camped the first night at Indio, and the next morning we skirted south around the Salton Sea. At noon, the temperature well over a hundred degrees, we arrived in Brawley where Papa went into a tiny building marked "Chamber of Commerce" and got the bad news about the road across the desert to Yuma. Just east of Brawley, they told him, the pavement ended and the road was a single width of railroad ties, but we could make it all right if we observed the courtesy of the road. Papa liked that phrase and kept repeating it as he pointed to the little diagram the men had given him showing how oncoming cars could pass each other, each car keeping center wheels on the ties and letting outside wheels go in the sand. If we did happen to get all four wheels off in the sand and got stuck, we should stay by the car and at daybreak the Dawn Patrol would come pull us back onto the ties.

Worst of all, it was too hot to cross during the daytime, and we would have to wait until sunset to start. Though the Chamber of Commerce had been generous in advice, Brawley offered no hospitality for passing the scorching afternoon except a central plaza with a few scrawny Chinese elms and some withered grass. Papa parked near one of the trees, and Mama spread an army blanket so we could sit in the little spot of shade which was about the size of the blanket. The only point of interest was a rock pillar supporting a drinking fountain in the center of the plaza. During the course of the long afternoon Becky and I made many trips to the fountain and tried to cool off by squirting each other with the brackish, tepid water. Although we soaked our hair and clothes, by the time we got back to the blanket we were completely dry, as hot as ever, and ready to go again. When we ran across the parched grass we stirred up hordes of tiny yellow butterflies. Papa said they were migrating to Mexico and as our paths had crossed we should not step on them but observe the courtesy of the plaza. I tried to smile at his weak attempt at humor, but I was too hot to care. Finally the sun was almost down to the low buildings on the west side of the plaza. Mama handed out the last sandwiches and the oranges we had brought from Redlands, and at last we were ready to go.

On the edge of town we made a final stop at a dingy, little, one-pump filling station topped by an impressive sign, "Last Chance Filling Station—No Service Beyond this Point." Papa bought gas and oil, checked the battery water and tires, and filled our two canvas water bags and hung them on the front of the car where the wind would keep them cool. We were the only customers, and the station owner seemed reluctant to see us go. He stood next to the car, his scuffed boot resting on the running board, and gave us final instructions: "No matter what happens, don't never put your last water in the radiator. You ain't gonna believe it, but people do that fool thing, and they die. You're lucky though. This time of year you don't have to worry none about the cold. We done found people got stuck out there in the winter time and burned their cars trying to keep from freezing. Didn't help. They died. If it ain't too dark, you might see some of them skeleton cars out there. There ain't no reason to move them—sort of a warning to other people, you might say."

Papa shrugged off the unwanted advice and asked once more the way to Yuma. "Straight ahead," the man said, pointing east. "Right on down this here road. You can't miss it. There ain't no other way."

Once the sun was down the light faded quickly, and it was already dark when we hit the railroad ties. Papa was a good driver, but it was hard to hold to the middle of the ties and his hands were clenched tight around the steering wheel. I leaned forward for a while, glimpsing the red tail light of a car far ahead, but it soon gained distance on us and disappeared. After that there was only darkness and our weak headlamps lighting a few ties at a time in front of us. I felt each bump, wishing it was over, wishing for daylight, but we had hardly started.

On long drives Becky was in the habit of lying on a blanket and pillow on the floor of the car and taking a nap, but we were so tightly packed there was no room at all. With a resigned sigh she rested her head against the back of the seat and impatiently pushed her blond hair back from her gray eyes. Being restless and unable to sleep, she was the first to notice the orange glare ahead, over to the right on her side of the road. "What's that?" she exclaimed, and we all echoed her wonderment. There wasn't anything to burn out there, no town or trees, not even cacti. What could it be? Becky soon made out the symbol. "A cross!" she gasped. "Oh, Mama, it's a burning cross. Are they crucifying somebody?"

Before Mama could answer, we were close enough to see for ourselves. A fiery cross, maybe twelve feet high, was burning brightly, the orange flames leaping up into the dark sky. At the base of the cross a group of white-robed figures milled about.

"Why, it's the Ku Klux Klan!" Mama exclaimed. "Here in the middle of the desert. How dreadful! I can't believe it!"

But it was true. One of the hooded figures, waving a flashlight, approached the car and stood on the railroad ties directly ahead of us. Papa put on the brakes and brought the slow-moving car to a dead stop. The white-robbed figure silently came closer and shone the light on each of us in turn. Nobody spoke. I could feel his eyes peering through the narrow slit in his hood. It seemed a long moment, but apparently he was satisfied that we were of no importance to the Klan, and he waved us on.

It was past midnight when we began meeting cars from the other direction—cars that had left Yuma at sundown. To Papa's delight the other drivers all seemed to be aware of the courtesy-of-the-road custom. They shared the ties, and passed easily. Papa was so pleased he would call out, "Courtesy of the road, thank you, pardner," chuckling to himself at how well it was all going. We were driving so slowly we could read the sign on the front of one of the cars we met: California or Bust.

It must have been after one o'clock, maybe close to two, when a car approached out of the darkness ahead, traveling at a fast rate and showing no signs of slowing down. Papa honked, but the car came straight on, right in the middle of the ties. Papa had already pulled his outside wheels off onto the sand, and to avoid being hit head-on he pulled off the center wheels. The speeding car whizzed by and must have been out of earshot when Papa yelled after it, "You unmitigated jackass. Didn't you ever hear of the courtesy of the road?" The only answer was the disappearing tail lights.

Papa revved up the engine and tried to rock the car forward and backward, but it only sank deeper into the sand. We all climbed out, and he struck a match for light and kneeled down by the back wheel. Sand was up over the hubcap. He scooped up a handful, stood up slowly, and let the sand dribble through his fingers. "End of the trail," he said, and just to be sure we heard it he repeated the hopeless phrase, "end of the trail."

Watching Papa, I panicked. My throat was dry, and I remembered the old man at Last Chance Filling Station warning us to save our water. I took a quick glance at the bags on the front of the car but resolved not to be the first one to ask for a drink. Becky leaned against Mama, pulled at her skirt and tearfully demanded to know if we were all going to die right there in the middle of the desert.

In a matter of seconds Mama took charge, patted Becky reassuringly on the head and reminded us this was just another adventure—could happen to anybody. While she was talking, she pulled our two army blankets from the back seat and spread them by the side of the car. Becky and I could sleep there, she said, and she and Papa would try to doze in the front seat. We must get what rest we could. Morning was just a few hours away, and we would have the fun of being rescued by the Dawn Patrol. "That's what they're paid to do," she said, cinching the argument.

Becky, reassured by Mama's optimism, lay down on one blanket, pulled the other up to her shoulders, and was soon sleeping. Mama and Papa settled down in the car, and I lay beside Becky. But I was too tense. I could feel my heart beating against my chest, and I looked at the millions and millions of stars and heard the silence, the enormous silence, ringing in my ears. I wished I could sleep like Becky. Most of all I wished time would pass, that morning would come.

Mama was restless too. After a while she got out of the car, said she wanted to look at the stars, and lay on the blanket beside me. I was glad to have her close, but so many thoughts were spinning in my head I still couldn't sleep. I was worried about the rest of the trip and even uneasy about arriving in El Paso. When I could stand the tension no longer, I whispered softly. "Mama, when we get there—if we make it all right—do you think we'll like El Paso?"

"Well, of course, we'll make it all right, and we'll like El Paso," she answered, her voice growing sleepy. "Think how nice it will be: Hab with a permanent job, our own home like I've always wanted. We moved around so much in California we could never get our own place. Couldn't even build on that lot we bought in Los Angeles. Maybe we can trade the lot for something in El Paso. Now Papa has a good job, and it'll be different. You and Becky can make friends and put down roots. Of course we'll like it. I can hardly wait."

On that note of confidence, I went to sleep.

At daybreak we were awakened by the Dawn Patrol, a truck with a winch mounted on the rear, approaching from the east. We barely had time to fold our blankets and toss them into the back of the car when the driver stopped his truck, hitched up the Overland, and hoisted it back onto the ties. His routine job completed, he asked

Papa to test the engine to be sure the carburetor wasn't chocked with sand. The Overland, with no more than its usual coughing and sputtering, chugged into action. We shouted our thanks as the Dawn Patrol continued on its rescue mission towards Brawley, and we headed east towards the sunrise and Yuma.

We rested that day and night at a tourist court in Yuma, and the next day followed the red line Papa had drawn on the map across Arizona and New Mexico. The last night we camped in a cotton-wood grove next to the Rio Grande, just outside Las Cruces, still in New Mexico but only forty miles from El Paso.

The next morning we broke camp early and headed southeast, the last lap of our trip. The sun had not yet touched the Organ Mountains on our left, their smooth, round peaks, jutting up straight and tall like so many organ pipes. On our right, flat, irri-gated fields of cotton stretched from the road to the Rio Grande, its banks marked by groves of light green cottonwoods and darker clumps of tamarisks. The cotton bolls were dazzling white in the morning sun. Papa said cotton was not that white in Georgia and wondered if irrigation or the dry desert air made the difference.

Mama, after a few remarks about the mountains, was concen-trating on the real-estate page of an El Paso newspaper she had bought in Las Cruces. We couldn't camp out in El Paso and we sure couldn't afford tourist court rates, so she was determined to find a house right away.

After a few miles the Organ Mountains gave way to the Franklin Range, bare and rocky. The highway curved toward the river, giving us a better view of the mountains: the foothills studded with yucca, the rocky outcroppings, barren slopes crisscrossed with horizontal ridges, the long narrow crest running in a straight line north to south, brown against the brilliant desert sky. That was my first view of Mount Franklin, and I sat on the edge of the seat, looking care-fully, and wanting to remember.

If I had given it a lot of thought, I couldn't have found a better symbol for El Paso than Mount Franklin. It was more than a sym-bol. It was an actual presence, always there—pale lavender in the sunrise, parched brown in the noonday sun, purple in the twilight, occasionally dusted by light snow in the winter, often obliterated by raging sandstorms in the spring—but there, a towering presence. Even now I can't think of El Paso without feeling the dominance of Mount Franklin.

A sign at the city limits pointed to Scenic Drive climbing up over the southern tip of Mount Franklin and advised us to enter by the mountain route and enjoy a panoramic view of the city. I was thrilled when Papa said since we had the day before us we might as well make a proper entrance. He turned the car left and headed up the steep road blasted out of sheer rock. It swung out around boulders and skirted steep precipices with no protection between us and eternity but the scrawled warning on the white boulders: Prepare to Meet God.

The Overland was steaming like a teakettle when we reached the high point of the drive, and Papa pulled off onto a belvedere to let it cool. We got out and looked over a low rock wall that gave a little protection from the sheer precipice dropping down to the city below. We were wishing we could locate some landmarks when a wizened old man wearing a broad sombrero approached Papa, said he had noticed our California license and wondered if we were moving to El Paso. Papa assured him that we were, and his weather-beaten face broke into smiles. "Well, you come to a good city, pardner. El Paso—Where Sunshine Spends the Winter. I spent sixty winters here myself, and I got no complaints."

He continued to chat with Papa about our trip and then invited us all to step over to the little rock wall so he could point out a few landmarks. Resting one foot on the wall and nodding appreciatively at his attentive audience, he told us to think of the city as a long, skinny cat, curled around the southern tip of Mount Franklin. The cat's belly was directly below us, pressed close against the mountain. I peered straight down over the little rock wall, imagining the cat's pink belly just as he indicated. The green spot, a little farther out, he identified as San Jacinto Plaza, the center of town. The cat's rear—its tail—extended straight up the valley, between the river and the west side of the mountain, the area we had travelled that very morning, which he referred to as "up the valley."

Sure that we were following his directions, he invited us to turn and look straight to the west to an outcropping that would be the cat's haunches. Those cream colored buildings we could barely see were the Texas State School of Mines and Metallurgy. That, he assured us, was the best mining school in America. The buildings were trapezoid in shape, he said, and while I wondered about that word he went on to explain that the style, the slight slant of the walls, was Bhutanese, copied from Tibet, and he thought it fitted into the mountains just right—once you got used to it. The huge whitewashed "M" half way up the mountain directly above Scenic Drive was painted each year by the Mines freshmen.

We followed the scene as he made a wide arc with his arm, embracing smokestacks that marked the cement plant and the smelter. A sudden red glow verified the location of the smelter—they were dumping slag at that very moment. A little farther to the south, the brick building with a silver steeple was the international depot accommodating trains to and from Mexico. The depot boasted a Harvey House Restaurant with a national reputation, and travelers coming through El Paso often arranged stopovers just to eat at that Harvey House. The old man took a personal pride in the Harvey House, although he admitted, rather regretfully, he had never eaten there himself. He pointed out the Paso del Norte Hotel near the green plaza in the center of town, claiming it was the finest hotel west of the Mississippi.

In the distance, the silver thread wrapping around the city like the cat's spine, was the Rio Grande. The International Bridge crossed the river to La Ciudad Juarez. I wanted to know more about Juarez, but he skimmed over it, saying it didn't amount to much except for saloons and gambling at the Tivoli. If it wasn't for prohibition in this country, he told us in a rather confidential tone, he doubted Juarez would have any business at all.

Across the plains to the east we could see the Hueco Mountains. Returning to the notion of the sleeping cat, our guide said its head would be Fort Bliss, probably the biggest cavalry post in the world. Close to Fort Bliss was William Beaumont, the military hospital, and out beyond that the Baptist Sanatorium for tuberculosis.

Finally, as far as the cat's paws can stretch, the old man pointed to Sugar Loaf, not quite as high as Mount Franklin, its smooth white slopes and peaked top perfectly described by its name. He stood back, hands on hips, pleased with his description. "Well, that's the story, friends. You'll get to know it all in no time. Friendly town, El Paso. Sleepy town, just a lazy cat laying in the sun."

The car was almost cool now. Papa released the cap and filled the radiator with water from one of our canvas bags. I recalled the warning from the owner of the Last Chance filling Station and sighed with relief. We had made it all right.

The old man tipped his sombrero and was about to leave, when Mama stopped him and asked if he had any idea where Mountain Avenue was. "I've been looking at house ads," she explained, "and there's something interesting here, a five-room, brick bungalow on Mountain Avenue. Do you happen to know where that is?"

Glad to prolong the conversation, the man took off his sombrero, scratched his head, and squinted his eyes at the city below as though he expected to read a street sign from that distance. He was about to give up when he suddenly recalled Mountain Avenue was north of town, almost as far as Sugar Loaf. Mama thanked him, said she liked the name Mountain Avenue, and would call about the house as soon as she had a chance. It surprised me how easily she talked about the house, as though we already had some claim on it.

We climbed back into the car and followed Scenic Drive down the eastern side of the mountain. In south El Paso, not far from the Lone Star Cotton Mill, we signed in at Camp Grande, a pink stucco tourist court.

That same afternoon Papa reported to his new job, and Mama, Becky, and I went to the office of the tourist court so Mama could call about the house ad. Becky and I, sitting on a little couch near the phone, listened to Mama and exchanged knowing glances. She introduced herself to the seller, a man by the name of Mitchelmore, talked about our trip, and casually mentioned the California lot as a possible down payment. Mr. Mitchelmore was apparently receptive to the idea. While he considered it, Mama put her hand over the mouthpiece and whispered in an aside to Becky and me: "People always want to go to California. There's just something about it."

Mama's hunch was right. If we wanted the house, Mr. Mitchelmore agreed to take the California lot and arranged to show us the house the next day.

We all liked the red-brick bungalow, the shady porch covered with Virginia creeper, Rusk School right across the street, and the view of the desert and mountains. Mr. Mitchelmore, happy with some private dreams about owning property in California, helped arrange a mortgage on the Mountain Avenue house and offered to lend us a little furniture so we could move in right away and not wait for our own furniture to come from Redlands.

On August 15, 1924, we moved into our own home—3320 Mountain Avenue.

2

Our house, in the middle of the block, was a natural stopping-off place for people toiling up the steep hill, especially housewives carrying groceries from Quinn's Grocery and Market. Of all the people who paused for a few moments rest and a chat with Mama on our shady porch, I remember Mrs. McCabe the best, maybe because she complained the most. A dumpy little woman, short and fat, she lived up in the next block. No matter what dress Mrs. McCabe wore, her petticoat always showed, hanging down an inch or two below her skirt in the back.

Setting her sack of groceries on the concrete floor, leaning back in the wicker rocker, and mopping the perspiration from her florid face, Mrs. McCabe invariably began the conversation by assuring Mama that she was never one to complain. But, she'd go on, Mrs. Quinn was certainly taking advantage of her good nature, always giving her a sweet smile and saying she lived just a block away and could carry her own groceries instead of tying up the delivery truck. Mama usually came to Mrs. Quinn's defense, pointing out that the store was busy and Kerry who drove the truck couldn't always be out on deliveries because he had to help Mr. Quinn at the meat counter. Mama was trying to be conciliatory, but her remarks only served to launch Mrs. McCabe into her favorite subject: Kerry Quinn.

Later on, after Becky and I got to know Kerry pretty well, we thought he was funny and we liked to go into the store just to hear his crazy jokes. But we first heard about him from Mrs. McCabe, and she didn't have a good word to say. He had worked in the store since he was a little kid—she wasn't quite sure if he had finished high school—and she could even remember when Gladys, now his wife, came to help out at the store. She was a pretty little thing, probably about seventeen, and did Kerry ever fall in love with her!

At this point in the story, Becky and I, playing jacks on the top step, stopped bouncing our ball, the better to appreciate the oft-told tale of Kerry's romance. Well, Mrs. McCabe assured us with a nod of her little round head, Kerry was head-over-heels for Gladys. But he already was too fond of drink, and Gladys would have none of him—even quit the store.

We should have seen Kerry then, Mrs. McCabe went on, relishing this part of the story. Into deep mourning, he was. Dyed all his shirts black and vowed he'd never, ever love again. And all this time Mrs. Quinn was blaming Kerry, saying it was all his fault and he better quit drinking and taking the truck over to Juarez and smuggling liquor over the bridge. God knows if the truck was confiscated how they could keep the store going. And so it went on that way, back and forth, until finally Gladys—fool that she was—married Kerry.

At this point Mama usually made a kind remark about Kerry and Gladys, now living two doors up the street from us and having such a cute little girl.

This only provided Mrs. McCabe with fresh ammunition. "Ha! Clarabow! Did you ever hear of such a name for a child?"

"Oh, you mean Clara Bow for the movie star?" Mama asked.

"Clarabow. All one word. Gladys says she is raising her to be a movie star and wants her to think of herself as a movie star. She is to have dancing lessons and singing lessons, if you please, and not even go to school if she doesn't want to."

Mama repeated rather lamely that Clarabow was a cute little thing and tried to turn the subject back to the store. "I don't always shop at Quinn's because I find things a little cheaper at Safeway over on Fort Boulevard. But I send the girls to Quinn's frequently, and I think it's very nice of them to have the Library Bookmobile at the store on Fridays. When I go down to get some books, I buy a few things to show my appreciation."

Mrs. McCabe gave Mama a superior look and piously remarked that she herself certainly had no time for reading. Then, having exhausted the subject of Kerry and recovered her breath, she braced her fat palms on the chair arms, rocked back and forth, and with a mighty forward lunge rose to her feet.

One day she had already lifted her groceries to her hip and started down the steps, when the sight of Becky and me, once again absorbed in our game of jacks, brought a new subject to mind. She wanted to know if we had entered Rusk School and what grades we were in. We stopped playing long enough to answer her, and she set her groceries on the concrete bannister and nodded her head approvingly. We were indeed lucky, she said, because the Rusk principal, Miss Taylor, was a Baptist.

Mama had come to the top step to bid Mrs. McCabe goodbye and was loathe to detain her but couldn't resist asking why it made any difference that the principal was a Baptist.

"Catholics, that's why," Mrs. McCabe answered, as though that one word explained everything. Mama looked dubious, and Mrs. McCabe was pleased to fill her in. If Becky and I had been unlucky enough to enter the El Paso schools a couple of years earlier, we probably would have had a Catholic principal. You wouldn't believe how many Catholics there were in the school, principals and teachers, just all through the system. Fortunately the Ku Klux Klan—this in a rather confidential whisper—had taken over, elected the right sort of school board, and cleaned out the whole business.

Mama, obviously upset, said she wouldn't have cared at all if Rusk had a Catholic principal. Mrs. McCabe responded that she wasn't naming names or anything like that, but in her opinion you just couldn't be too careful. It made her feel good to know that the Rusk principal, Nell Taylor, was a good Baptist. In fact, Miss Taylor had a sister named Ida who was a missionary to China, and that, according to Mrs. McCabe, was as good a credential as you could get. Finally, she picked up her groceries and puffed on up the hill, leaving us to handle this unexpected information as best we could.

One thing Mrs. McCabe had right: Mountain Avenue was a steep climb. I wasn't fat like she was, but I felt the pull myself when I carried a sack of groceries or an armload of books uphill. But living on a hill had a good side: what a downhill slope for skating! Every Christmas Becky and I got new Union Hardware ball bearing skates. The mileage we put on them, it's a wonder they lasted a year.

I remember sitting on the concrete steps, putting on my skates which were nothing like the modern invention of wheels attached to high-top shoes. I slipped my oxfords between the toe-clamps— school shoes were always bought with an eye to the extended soles to be sure they were thick enough to hold skates—tightened the clamps with the key worn on a string around my neck, fastened the leather straps around my ankles, stood up and tested the hold by stomping each toe against the sidewalk. Satisfied with that, I pumped to the uphill corner where Justus Street crossed Mountain Avenue, stood there a moment, looking downhill and anticipating the long descent, and shoved off.

Sometimes just Becky and I skated together, but more often friends came with us. Beverly Bishop, in my class at school and my good friend, lived up in the next block and loved to skate. Well, Beverly loved to do almost anything. Just tell her something was going on, and she would be right there ready to join in. In all the years I knew her, Beverly never lost that enthusiasm. She contemplated life through sparkling dark eyes, and for Beverly life did sparkle.

Becky's best friend, Gwen Heaslip, also skated with us a lot. She lived beyond the end of the pavement, up near the foothills where there was no place to skate, so she just kept her skates at our house to have them handy. She was careful about it, always putting them under the window seat where nobody would stumble over them.

We started at the Justus corner, and without pumping at all we went clear down to the Enlisted Men's Club on Dyer Street at the bottom of the hill. As we passed our house, Mama was sure to be on the porch and call out a last warning for us to watch for cross traffic, but once we passed the Copia Street corner where Kerry might be backing out the delivery truck there was nothing to worry about except the tracks of the trolley about half way down the hill.

We called it the Toonerville Trolley after a comic strip in the *El Paso Post,* and if it had another name, I never heard it. By the time we reached the trolley tracks, we had gathered a lot of speed and had to be careful to jump our skates over the tracks. There wasn't much danger of the trolley hitting us. It connected the Fort Bliss streetcar with the William Beaumont Army Hospital. Most of the patients out there were veterans and didn't have a lot of visitors, so the Toonerville didn't have many passengers and only ran on the hour. Anyway, the motorman, Mr. Gibbs, looked out for us. When he saw us coming down hill he clanged his bell bloody murder, but he knew we'd have trouble stopping, and at the last minute after all the clanging he would bring the little trolley to a stop right at the pavement's edge, giving us a friendly wave and the right-of-way.

When we were skating downhill, once we jumped our skates over the Toonerville track, it was clear coasting on to Dyer Street at the bottom of the hill. We came to a halt in front of the Enlisted Men's Club. The club was for the soldiers at Fort Bliss, but kids could go to the movies on Friday nights for a nickel. Most of the movies were old Tom Mix films, but sometimes that had something new like Clara Bow in *Wings* or *Dancing Mothers.* Besides the regular movies, they had a lot of funny things like Betty Boop cartoons and scary serials that cut off just when the heroine was either being kidnapped by a stagecoach bandit or was dashing down river in a leaky canoe just above Niagara Falls while her lover swam manfully towards her rescue.

Part of the fun of skating downhill was the chance to read the bulletin board listing all the coming attractions at the Enlisted Men's Club. We fooled around a while, talked about the shows we wanted to see, tightened our toe-clamps with our skate keys, and reluctantly began pumping up the long steep hill.

El Paso, famous for its high, dry climate, grew rapidly during the 1920s; much of the influx due to health seekers, especially people diagnosed with tuberculosis. The discovery of streptomycin was still decades away, and the only known remedy for tuberculosis was rest, nourishing food, and dry air; so desperate people, some already fatally ill, left the industrial east and the humid south to move west, placing their last hopes on the dry climate of El Paso: Where Sunshine Spends the Winter.

Some of the afflicted came alone to various sanitariums, where loneliness and homesickness often hastened the onset of the disease; but many families came with their sick loved ones and made new homes in the little bungalows on Mountain Avenue. The invalids with family support seemed to have a better chance of survival, and, at the same time, the newly arriving families lent a rather cosmopolitan atmosphere to an otherwise working-class neighborhood.

When we left Redlands Mama had mentioned that El Paso was a health resort, and the old man up on the Scenic Drive belvedere had pointed out to us at least one sanitarium, but I didn't give the matter much thought until we had moved into our house on Mountain Avenue and a neighbor visited us and introduced me quite suddenly to this tragic side of life.

On the second morning in our new house Becky and I were on our front porch admiring the lush Virginia creeper, how it went up the pillars at the side of the porch, crossed over the lentil, and dropped slim sprays down over our front steps so low you could hardly walk under them. Becky, reaching up to grasp a tender vine, said our porch had bangs and Mama was going to have to keep them trimmed so we could walk under the fringe without bumping our heads.

We were both laughing at Becky's joke, when we looked up and there was Mrs. Lundstrum, a tall, slim woman coming up our walk. She introduced herself, said she lived on the uphill corner of the block, and asked to meet Mama.

We called Mama from the kitchen, and she invited Mrs.

Lundstrum into the living room, explaining that our furniture had not yet arrived and they would have to share a window seat. Becky and I, never permitted to hang around when Mama had guests, started to go back outside, but Mrs. Lundstrum motioned to us to stay. In fact, she said, we were the object of her visit. Happy to be included, we sat cross-legged on the floor, pulled our short skirts over our knees, and waited expectantly.

Mrs. Lundstrum asked first if our family was well. "I can see you look well, Mrs. King, and the girls are certainly the picture of health. What about Mr. King? Is he well?"

Mama, taken aback at the question, replied that Papa was quite well and that we had come to El Paso because he had a job at the Lone Star Cotton Mill.

Mrs. Lundstrum flushed slightly. "Oh, I do apologize, Mrs. King, for such a personal question. So many families come here because of sickness, it just gets to be a routine question. Well, indeed, you are fortunate."

Mama hastened to put Mrs. Lundstrum at ease, assuring her she was not offended by the question and asking, in her turn: "Is someone in your family ill?"

"Yes, my daughter, Annie Laurie, eleven years old, has tuberculosis but is now convalescent."

I didn't know the meaning of that word, but Mrs. Lundstrum launched into her story, and I began to understand. After a year in El Paso Annie Laurie was a little better, able to come out on the porch in the afternoons and lie in her steamer chair. She was lonesome for friends her own age, which explained Mrs. Lundstrum's visit to us. The minute she saw Becky and me, she couldn't wait to ask us to come up and talk to Annie Laurie. "Out on the porch, of course," she added. "The doctor assures me with reasonable care there is no chance at all of contagion."

Instead of meeting Mrs. Lundstrum's eyes, I found myself staring at her hands. It was hard to believe what she was saying. Her daughter, a girl just like me, was sick with tuberculosis. I had never known anybody who was really sick, and it hadn't occurred to me that a girl just eleven years old and our neighbor could actually be bedridden with tuberculosis. I swallowed hard and thought I should say I was sorry or something, but the words just stuck in my throat. If I had to go to see Annie Laurie, and I supposed I would, what would I talk about to a girl my age and sick in bed?

While I was pondering these rather selfish questions, Mrs. Lundstrum started at the beginning, and often having to control the quaver in her voice, told us the whole story. Annie Laurie, the Lundstrum's only child was born in Chicago and had always seemed perfectly healthy, aside from a few colds, the usual childhood diseases, but nothing to worry about. It was last fall, actually October, that she was out roller skating with friends in the park. It was a chilly day, but she was wearing a sweater. When she came in her face was so flushed Mrs. Lundstrum had taken her temperature.

Mrs. Lundstrum hesitated here and seemed to skip a few details too painful to mention; then she went on in a matter-of-fact tone: "Well, we soon knew the worst. Annie Laurie had tuberculosis."

"The doctors suggested bringing her here?" Mama prompted.

"Well, yes," Mrs. Lundstrum answered. "I wouldn't say they suggested. They ordered us to get Annie Laurie to a dry climate immediately; and in less than a week we were on the train headed for El Paso. In a way we were lucky, if you can talk about luck when your only child is so sick. Mr. Lundstrum works for the railroad and was able to get a transfer, at less salary of course, but we certainly weren't thinking about money at that time."

"At least that gave you some direction—I mean having a job to come to." Mama, with daughters of her own, was clearly moved by Mrs. Lundstrum's recitation.

"Yes, it was certainly better than having to come with no job at all as lots of families do. The company reserved a stateroom on the train so Annie Laurie could lie on the couch all day, and someone in the office here rented the house on Mountain Avenue for us. All we wanted was a quiet neighborhood with plenty of fresh air and sunshine, and Mountain Avenue has that."

As to Mountain Avenue, we all agreed; and now that I understood Annie Laurie was getting better, I found her sickness less terrifying. When Mrs. Lundstrum repeated her request again, Becky and I just nodded assent, and Mama promised Mrs. Lundstrum she could expect us at two o'clock that very afternoon.

At the appointed time, Becky and I walked slowly up the hill, taking the first good look at our neighborhood. Bermuda lawns covered most of the yards, but in some the gray-green grass had given way to bare spots, ant hills, and devilhorns—a creeping weed aptly named by children who often had to stop in their play to pull the two-pronged stickers from their bare feet.

I learned later a weedy yard meant a rental house. In that arid climate even Bermuda grass needed more sprinkling than most renters could afford, and a lawn left to itself didn't survive long. Flower beds followed the same pattern. Tidy plots of zinnias, cosmos, and calendulas bordered porches or sidewalks where the lawns were well kept; but no flower beds survived in the rental yards, although occasional patches of scraggly brown-orange marigolds, and yellowish-green cockscomb had migrated out into some neglected lawns, mute testimony that the house had once seen better days.

At first I detested those ugly little vagrants, but as the years went by I developed a reluctant respect for them, seeing them as degenerate descendants of cultivated varieties. With all the odds against them, they managed to hang on and survive, like stubborn poor relations, ugly and useless, except as a constant reminder of the power of the will to live, which is the very essence of life on the desert.

Becky and I, feeling timid and in no hurry to arrive at our destination, finally turned in at the Lundstrum's house. Annie Laurie was already on the porch, lying in her steamer chair. Mrs. Lundstrum introduced us, and even though Annie Laurie was lying down I could see she was rather tall for her age. She had black hair bobbed straight, fair skin but with a red flush on her high cheekbones, a telltale sign of tuberculosis which I didn't recognize at the time. She was wearing a lovely, red, silk Chinese robe with slippers to match. I had never seen such pretty clothes except in magazine pictures. She gave us a quick smile, revealing slight chips on her two front teeth, which gave her a sort of elfin quality.

Becky and I sat in wicker rockers, and Mrs. Lundstrum sat at the far end of the porch. She was knitting a sweater or something of blue yarn, and she appeared to concentrate on her work, counting stitches and looking back at the pattern, giving the definite impression that she was not eavesdropping on our conversation.

The Mexican maid—Annie Laurie called her Estella—brought a tray with lemonade and cookies for Becky and me and milk for Annie Laurie. Annie Laurie introduced us, "*Mis amigas,* Estella." Estella smiled, "*Me gusta,*" and left us.

"She's teaching me Spanish," Annie Laurie explained. "Since I can't go to school Mama thought it would be a good idea for me to learn Spanish."

Becky asked what they had said in Spanish. Annie Laurie explained, and after that the conversation went flat. Whenever I met new people, I always asked them about school, but since Annie Laurie couldn't go to school, I thought that wasn't tactful. We said a few things about our trip from California and asked about her trip from Chicago, and I couldn't think of anything else. Becky said she liked the cookies, and I was feeling self-conscious at the long silence, when suddenly there was a big commotion inside—in the kitchen, I supposed. We heard a crash like a chair falling, and Estella exclaimed, "*¡Zápe! Zápe! Vámos!*" Immediately, a little black kitten began meowing inside the screen door, trying to get out on the porch. Mrs. Lundstrum and Annie Laurie started laughing at some shared joke. Mrs. Lundstrum laid down her knitting and came to open the door and let the kitten out. Once outside, the kitten seemed to have lost its desire to flee. It approached Becky quite calmly and rubbed its side against her bare leg. Becky picked it up and cradled it in her arms—a solid black green-eyed kitten. Annie Laurie continued to laugh.

"Careful, Laurie," Mrs. Lundstrum cautioned. "Don't laugh too much. It makes you cough."

"I know, but that cat—" The warning was too late. Annie Laurie was already coughing. Becky and I watched uneasily, but it was over in a moment. She spit into a fold of toilet paper which she then dropped into the paper sack tied to the back of her chair. Apparently she was used to doing that, and I tried not to stare.

As Annie Laurie settled back in her steamer chair, her mother glanced at her watch and said, "It's about time to shift your exercise bag, dear."

For the first time I noticed a little bag about the size of a bean-bag lying on Annie Laurie's chest. Nonchalantly she shifted it to the other side, explaining as she did so, "That's just a weight to exercise my lungs. Fifteen minutes on each side to make me breath deeply."

We turned our attention back to the cat. "Estella hates that cat," Annie Laurie said, still amused. "She and that poor little cat are in constant battle. Estella couldn't seem to think of any Spanish words to teach me until we got that cat, but now you should hear her. We don't even want the cat. It just took up here, meowing at the back door, and we started feeding it. We didn't know Estella would mind, but she just hates it. Now she yells at it, and I'm learning some choice words."

The ice was broken, and we were all talking. Mrs. Lundstrum moved closer. "I'm afraid the Spanish Annie Laurie is learning won't be good for polite conversation. I don't know Spanish myself, but I'm pretty sure *caramba* isn't necessary."

"Before *el gato* came, I didn't know anything but *Muy bien, Adiós* and *Grácias,*" Annie Laurie agreed. "Now, I've learned *Vámos* and *Ese es un diablo.* I don't know why Estella hates the cat. Maybe she is superstitious because it's black. We really should get rid of it. When I get better and we buy our own house, I want to get a dog. I had a dog named Buster back in Chicago, but when we left I had to give him to a friend."

While we were talking, Becky was making friends with the cat. She stroked it, and it started purring. Mrs. Lundstrum watched her and had a sudden idea. "Do you like cats, Becky?"

"Yes, and it likes me, too. I can hear it purr."

"Maybe you would like to have it? Do you think your mother would mind? Go ask her."

Becky was on her feet in a minute, saying she would take the cat with her so Mama could see how really cute it was. In a few moments she returned, still hugging the cat. Mama had said she could keep it, and she wanted to know if it had a name.

"Only *el gato,*" said Annie Laurie. "And I think it really deserves better."

"I'll call it Witty, I think," Becky said. I don't know where she got that, but Witty it was.

Before we left, Estella came out on the porch to pick up the tray and glasses. Annie Laurie indicated by gesture that Becky was going to become the owner of el gato. Estella beamed. *"Muy bien, me gusta mucho."*

"How do I say thank you?" Becky asked.

"Muchas grácias," Annie Laurie explained.

"Muchas grácias," Becky repeated as she stroked Witty. The half hour had passed so quickly it was already time to leave. As we were walking down the hill, Becky held Witty to her shoulder and stroked him lovingly. "You know, Mafra," she said, "since I got Witty I just feel like I've already lived here a long time."

3

Mr. Printz owned the last lot on the lower end of the block, the barbershop corner. Behind the barbershop and facing Copia was a little summerhouse, and beyond that, also facing Copia, was the duplex where Mr. Printz lived. A large sign suspended by a chain over the center steps identified the duplex as "Printz Apts."

The houses on our block, all red brick with wide front porches and gabled roofs, had been built for overflow military personnel during World War I and were as identical as beads on a string. But the barbershop and duplex, built a few years later, were white stucco and flat-roofed in the Mexican style, a forerunner of the culture clash which materialized after World War II.

Mr. Printz's backyard was separated from the Williamsons' side yard by a rock wall about five feet high, its flat concrete top embedded with bits of broken glass and amber-colored bottle shards, more suitable for a prison compound than our friendly neighborhood. Other backyards on the block were marked by low red picket fences, the kind used out on the plains to keep snowdrifts off the roads. Wobbly and sagging, the fences were easy to climb over, and in our games of Run, Sheep, Run or Kick the Can we dashed from yard to yard and felt free to hide on top of garages or under back porches. But we never went in Mr. Printz's yard. His summerhouse, however, was too inviting to resist. We knew he would chase us if he caught us, but that just added to the excitement of the game.

Mr. Printz's narrow front yard was terraced from the street up to the porch, the various levels being separated by straight rows of white rocks. The lowest terrace, next to the sidewalk, was filled with pincushion cacti, little dark green half-balls, covered with spiral rows of spines; the middle level was crowded with lace-barrel cacti, more tubular than the pincushions and bearing ribs of white spines which overlapped and gave the plant its lacy appearance; the top level was reserved for prickly pears, its yellow-green, spiny pads crowned by little, burgundy-red, pear-shaped fruit sticking out at awkward angles. Clumps of beargrass yucca, actually belonging to the lily family although commonly mistaken for cactus, stood guard on either side of the porch steps.

Most of the cacti were past blooming when we came to Mountain Avenue in August, but the yucca, a late summer bloomer, still had a few clusters of lily-white cups with the suggestion of green on the petal edges. They were especially lovely in the early evening when yucca moths burrowed deep into the fragrant blooms, laid their eggs, and returned the yucca's hospitality by spreading pollen. I didn't notice the yucca moths at first—not until Dianne came and we got to be friends and talked about them, but that was a year or two later.

Mr. Printz's faced east, and when I walked by early in the morning I noticed the letters spelling out "Printz Apts." They were actually made of blue marbles stuck into holes drilled in the white board. The morning sun shone right through the marble letters and cast bright blue lights on the concrete porch floor and the white stucco wall. When the sign swung in the breeze, blue lights skipped around into various patterns. Years later, whenever I went dancing in a ballroom where multicolored lights flashed from an overhead mirror—that used to be a common ballroom feature—I would always remember Mr. Printz's blue marble lights shifting around on the floor and wall. That would make me think of Dianne, and no matter how happy I was at the moment I would feel icy fingers at my heart and that sense of guilt I could never erase—though God knows it wasn't my fault. It's just that it never should have happened. Maybe that's why I feel compelled to write about it. It never should have happened.

The unpleasant feeling I had about Mr. Printz from the very first seemed justified when our neighbors, Mr. and Mrs. Williamson and their little boy Edward, came up one evening and talked about him. We were sitting on the porch, and I think it was the day after our furniture came from California because I remember I was glad we finally had chairs for all the grown-ups. Little Edward sat next to Becky and me on the steps. Becky was holding Witty, and she let Edward stroke Witty's back.

Mama and Mrs. Williamson talked about housekeeping problems. Mrs. Williamson said Quinn's ran charge accounts, and she knew for a fact certain families in the neighborhood were so far behind on their accounts they'd never catch up. Of course, they couldn't quit, and the Quinns could just charge whatever prices they liked. Mama shook her head reproachfully, and I knew that with Mama at the helm we'd never fall into that trap. In fact, we were already lugging some groceries home from Safeway.

Papa talked about his job at the Lone Star Cotton Mill. Mr. Williamson said he was a fireman working out of the station over on Piedras. I was sort of watching Becky and Edward play with Witty—she was telling him about Annie Laurie and how their maid hated Witty—but I wasn't missing any of the grown-up conversation.

After the casual subjects had been exhausted, Mr. Williamson cleared his throat, giving notice he was about to make a serious pronouncement. He was a blond, heavyset fellow, very slow and deliberate, and he hesitated so long between words you wondered if he'd ever get on with it. He finally got around to the point of the visit. He wanted to warn us that Mr. Printz was making trouble in the neighborhood about property lines. When Copia had been paved a few years earlier, it seemed his lot came out a foot short, forty-nine feet instead of fifty, and he now proposed to get the foot back by moving his stone wall—that eyesore topped with broken bottles—a foot up hill. If he took a foot from the Williamsons' yard, of course they would have to recover it by moving their other fence, and so on up the hill. Mr. Williamson wanted Papa to be aware of the threat so that the neighbors could unite and not let Printz get away with it. Mrs. Williamson, though silent, underlined her husband's remarks by vigorous, affirmative head-nodding.

Papa thanked Mr. Williamson for the warning, and Mrs. Williamson said she wanted to caution Becky and me that Mr. Printz didn't like kids to come on his property. By that time I was tired of being quiet and added the information about the summerhouse I had already picked up. That very afternoon when we were playing Kick the Can, Robert Earle Martin, the boy who lived next door, and his friend Raymond from down in the next block had told us it was all right to hide in the summerhouse if we were careful not to let Mr. Printz see us. The four of us, along with Raymond's dog, Cinco, had been hiding there and the boys were making jokes about the "Dogs Keep Out" sign, saying Cinco was a Mexican dog and couldn't read an English sign. We were laughing so much the other kids caught us and we had to run for base.

Becky broke in to say when she ran out of the summer house she got stuck on a spiny bush growing by the door, and she was sure Mr. Printz put it there to keep kids out. She couldn't remember the name of the bush, and I told her the real name was catclaw because of the black thorns that curl in like a cat's claws. Then she remembered that Robert Earle said most people call it wait-a-minute, because that's what people always yell to their friends when they get caught on the thorns.

Becky, having suddenly remembered her scratches, put Witty down so she could show Mama her arm; and Mama was wondering if she should put peroxide on the scratches, when Witty let out a loud hiss in the dark corner of the porch, and the acrid odor of vinegar filled the air.

Papa turned on the porch light, and there stood Witty, his back arched and his fur bristling as he challenged a large black bug, shaped like a cockroach but about six times as big and with a three-inch long, needle-like tail.

Mrs. Williamson grabbed little Edward and held him close, and Mr. Williamson excitedly pushed the rest of us back, explaining the bug was a vinegaroon and had a very poisonous sting. Papa snatched Witty up, threw him to safety in the front yard, and then got a big rock from the edge of the flower bed to smash the vinegaroon. The odor of vinegar permeated the porch until it stunk like the inside of a pickle barrel. I was glad when the Williamsons went home, and we could go inside.

I remember that scene vividly because it was my first encounter with a vinegaroon, and the experience was underscored when other kids assured me that one stab of the vinegaroon's needle-like tail and I would be mortally wounded. Years later I found out the vinegaroon is a common whip scorpion, found throughout Mexico and the Southwest, and so named by Mexicans because of its defensive mechanism, the highly irritating gaseous secretion. It has highly developed jaws which can inflict a painful but not fatal sting.

Mrs. Wells, our fifth grade teacher, was as optimistic as a seed catalogue. We were the best class she had ever had, and only good things would happen to us. She was sure of it.

In spite of Mrs. Wells' abundant faith, we kept disappointing her in one important area. School policy allowed the class a quarter holiday if we had no tardies for a whole month. The months went by, and we didn't get the quarter holiday. Something always happened.

One month we missed because of the fight Herbie Riddel and Francis Manheimer had about the Panama Canal. We were studying about the canal in geography class—all the trouble they had building it, including yellow fever—and Francis raised his hand and said his father was a sergeant in the army and had worked on the Panama Canal.

Before Francis had a chance to tell us more about it, Herbie, who was always bragging that his father was a captain, guffawed real loud and said, "Francis, you gotta be crazy from eating loco weed. Your father's only a sergeant. He couldn't have anything to do with the Panama Canal."

Well, the class was real quiet, and I thought Francis was going to haul off and sock Herbie right there, but instead he just looked Herbie in the eye and said, "I don't care if your father is a captain, you don't pull rank on me. See you in the arroyo at noon."

The arroyo, across Justus Street from the playground, was a perfect place for a fight. Miss Taylor watched the playground from her office window, but the sides of the arroyo had been cut so deep by cloudburst floods rushing down from McKelligon's Canyon that the bottom of the arroyo was hidden from view. At noon recess, we collected down there to watch Herbie and Francis fight.

Most of us wanted Francis to win because we were sick of Herbie's bragging about his father. Worse than that, once he caught a tarantula and put it in a Mason jar and brought it to school. It was a horrible looking big black spider with hairy legs, and Herbie was chasing the kids, saying he was going to throw it on them. Everybody was yelling and running from Herbie, because we all knew a tarantula can jump about ten feet and the bite would kill you. Finally somebody told Miss Taylor, and she whipped Herbie with the rubber hose. The janitor threw a net over the jar and broke it with a baseball bat and smashed the tarantula. After that, nobody liked Herbie.

Down in the arroyo the day of the fight, with all the excitement and yelling back and forth, the hour went by real fast, and we didn't hear the warning bell. After the other kids went inside and the playground quieted down, we heard the last bell. The fight stopped without anybody actually winning, but it was too late. Miss Taylor saw us running across the school ground. In no time at all she found out about the fight and called Francis and Herbie to the office. We all knew that meant the rubber hose, even though it hadn't been much of a fight.

I knew about the hose firsthand. Once Beverly and I kept talking in art class, and Miss Fuller, the art teacher, sent us to Miss Taylor's office with a note. Beverly opened the note in the hall, and it said we had disrupted the class and needed to be disciplined. I was pretty scared when we were standing in front of Miss Taylor's desk, watching her read the note. She wore her long hair in a bun on top of her head, and it made her angular face look severe. While she looked straight at us, she just reached down with her right hand and opened the bottom desk drawer. That red rubber hose—thin like the rubber hose on an enema bag—was coiled there. She didn't actually mention the hose but just looked at it and said, "I guess you know what happens to people who break the rules."

My mouth was dry, and I had trouble finding my voice, but I finally answered, "Yes, ma'am." That was a mistake.

"And another thing, Mary Frances, don't ever 'ma'am' me. My name is Miss Taylor, and that's the way I expect to be addressed."

"Yes, Miss Taylor," I answered, and Beverly and I quickly escaped.

When I got home from school that afternoon Mama was ironing in the kitchen, and I told her about being sent to the office. Becky and Gwen were sitting at the kitchen table, talking about an advertisement in a magazine that promised they could earn all the pocket money they would ever need by selling packets of garden seeds. They were trying to decide how many packets to order, but they stopped to listen to me, and we all wondered why Miss Taylor didn't want me to say "Yes, ma'am," when I was just trying to be polite.

Becky said that the kids were always saying "ma'am" in those southern books our Aunt Louise and Mama's other sisters sent us for Christmas—*Little Missy* and all that stuff about life on the old plantations. We both liked to read the books, and Mama thought it was funny that her family had never become reconciled to her move out west. They did what they could to instill a bit of southern culture into Becky and me. Sometimes Mama read their letters aloud. Her family expected us to be bitten by rattlesnakes or scalped by Indians any minute.

Mama listened to our discussion and interrupted to explain that Miss Taylor was a Yankee. When we talked to her we would be well advised to forget our southern background. I thought I was lucky that the conversation had turned to southern culture, and Mama didn't scold me about being sent to the office in the first place. Anyway, I remembered never to use the word "ma'am" again.

Another month we lost the holiday because of our burro, Pronto. Living on the edge of the desert, we were imbued with the notion that herds of wild horses roamed the western plains and that some day with a little bit of luck we would be able to capture a wild horse and spend the rest of our lives charging about on horseback like Tom Mix. We never caught a wild horse, or even saw one, but we did get Pronto, a silver-haired burro. Never did a genuine cowboy love his bronco more than we loved Pronto.

Pronto belonged to the fifth-grade girls. We had a good title, having purchased him for twenty-five cents from some Mexican boys who lived in an adobe hut up near Mount Franklin. The boys told us they had caught Pronto, a wild burro, in McKelligon's Canyon. They named him Pronto because when someone was riding him he liked to make a quick start.

We tied a lead-rope around Pronto's neck and used both carrot and stick to motivate him. Emmaline, who had the distinction of being the only Mormon in our class, was my good friend and very dependable. She brought a carrot in her lunch every day. When we rode Pronto, both during our lunch hour and after school, Emmaline led the way, holding the carrot about a foot ahead of Pronto. We took turns sitting on his bare back, usually two at a time, while one girl brought up the rear, hitting Pronto with a stick, but not too hard. In this fashion, with many cries of encouragement, we prodded Pronto out of the back yard into the alley, where, unfortunately, he took more interest in open garbage cans than in Emmaline's extended carrot.

We kept Pronto tied in my backyard. One night, when we believed we were starting to get him trained, he disappeared. We thought maybe he had responded to the call of the wild. Rope in hand, we spent hours combing the desert and searching McKelligon's Canyon. Not a trace. A week or two later, on a Friday when the girls were eating lunch in our sleeping porch—once a week they liked to bring sack lunches and meet at our house at noon—someone glanced toward the alley and there was Pronto, ambling through the open gate into the backyard, as serene as though he'd never been away. By the time we found our rope and tied him up, the warning bell and tardy bell had rung at school. We were at least ten minutes late when panting and red-faced we rushed into our classroom. We missed the holiday, but it was worth it.

The school year was almost gone, and we had never earned the quarter holiday. I finally quit thinking about it, but Mrs. Wells never gave up. Finally, in the last week of school—in fact, the next to last day—she saw her chance. "Class," she said, happily, "I have just been looking over the attendance this month. With just one more day to go, I think you've made it with no tardies. That means you can get out at two o'clock tomorrow, Friday, the last day of school. I knew you could do it. Why not plan a celebration?"

The idea caught on like wildfire, and we all started talking at once. Memorial Park swimming pool had opened that week. A swimming party! That was it! Usually the class voted on important things, but this was so exciting it was just decided by acclamation, everybody saying, "Yeah, yeah, let's do it. Let's go swimming." What a great way to end the school year!

Plans for the swimming party fell right into place. The pool cost a nickel. We would bring our bathing suits and nickels to school on Friday and leave the building promptly at two o'clock. Emmaline gloated that we would be the first class out for vacation. We all felt smug, thinking how surprised the other classes would be when they saw us leaving early. We realized some of the kids might not have carfare, three cents each way, so we agreed to walk to Memorial Park instead of taking the streetcar. It was only a mile, and all we had to do was follow the streetcar track. We could easily make it in a half-hour.

All Friday morning, we couldn't think about anything but the swimming party. We weren't used to having money at school, and kids kept dropping their nickels and crawling around under the desks, picking them up. My blue, wool bathing suit, rolled up tight and jammed into my desk, was a constant reminder of the big treat ahead. I could practically feel my first plunge into the pool and that cool green water splashing over me.

After lunch most of us were in our seats before the warning bell rang. Mrs. Wells had said we could use the one hour to check in our state-issued books, and by two o'clock we would be ready to go. We were busy piling our books on our desks when Charleston McAfee suddenly exclaimed, "Hey, where is Sadie Lou?"

Sadie Lou's desk, right in front of Charleston's, was empty.

"Where is she? Where is Sadie Lou?" everybody was asking at once, and some of the boys started saying, "Where is Old Sears?"

Sadie Lou's last name was Sears, and the boys liked to make her angry by calling her "Old Sears."

"Old Sears ain't here! Damfino where Old Sears is at!" That was from Elmer Bronson, the class wit, and "Damfino" was the name of a new candy bar. There were lots of funny names for candy bars that year, names like Cherry Flapper and Black Cow, but Damfino was the one that really caught on. It gave the boys a chance to say "damn if I know" without being accused of swearing, and they never missed a chance. Now the other boys took up the cue from Elmer, "Damfino what happened to Old Sears."

But it really wasn't funny. It hit us all at once. If Sadie Lou was late, what about the holiday? We ran to the windows, all twenty-seven of us, and poked our heads out. We had a second-floor room on the front side of the building, facing Copia. A narrow strip of lawn separated the building from the street, and next to the curbing two stunted locust trees cast small spots of shade on the thin grass. Standing under one of the trees and looking defiantly towards our classroom windows was Sadie Lou. She held an apple in her right hand. As we watched, she lifted the apple to her mouth and bit into the shiny red skin. Even from the second story window I could see the crisp white pulp. With the back of her hand she wiped the juice from her lips. Her motions were studied and deliberately slow.

Somebody yelled, "Sadie Lou, you're going to be late. The tardy bell hasn't rung yet. Run for it, Sadie Lou, run! You can make it!"

For an answer, Sadie Lou raised the apple to eye level and took another bite.

As I looked almost directly down on her, I thought how slight her figure was. As usual she was wearing a black silk skirt—too big in the waist and lapped over with a safety pin—and a long-sleeved blouse with purple flowers. She always wore clothes like that: mismatched hand-me-downs, the sort of stuff that turns up in the church charity bazaar. And the way she wore her hair: a long ugly part from her forehead right across the top of her head down to the nape of her neck, with two long pigtails, screwed into a tight rolls over each ear. She had told me once that her father said short hair on a woman was sinful, against the Bible. About a year ago, her older sister, Eloise, had sneaked off and cut her hair. She got a beating and ran away from home.

In a flash I remembered all that, but the cries of the kids standing beside me brought me back to the horror of the moment. "Our holiday, Sadie Lou, remember we're going swimming! Come in, Sadie Lou." They were all yelling at once, but she gave no sign of hearing, just a defiant tilt of her chin, and a sassy smirk on her pert little face. She continued to eat her apple.

We couldn't believe she was just standing there. We kept yelling at her, and some of the boys leaned out the window as though they could grab her and pull her inside. "Come on in, Sadie Lou, come on . . ."

The tardy bell clanged. The hideous, metallic shriek echoed and died away. We stood frozen by the windows. Nobody spoke. Down below Sadie Lou examined her apple core, turned it around, decided she was through, and tossed it into the street.

She did it on purpose!

I gasped, put my hand over my open mouth, and stared ahead with wide-opened eyes as I stumbled back to my desk. How could she have done it? How could she? *On purpose!*

A few moments later Sadie Lou walked in the door, looked at no one, tossed her head high and took her seat. The classroom was still—just stony silence. I stole a glance at Sadie Lou. How could she come in and just sit there? She didn't even care.

For once, even Mrs. Wells had no cheerful words. She filled out the attendance slip: Tardy, Sadie Lou Sears, and put it in the little box next to our door in the hall. She came back into the room, rubbing her palms together. "Well, no holiday," she said to the stunned class.

The afternoon dragged on. There was nothing to do. No one spoke to Sadie Lou.

Just before the three-thirty dismissal bell, Emmaline had an idea. Since we all had our nickels, why not go over to Quinn's after school and buy Popsicles. We could eat them on the carryall. Half-heartedly, some of us agreed.

School was finally over. We told Mrs. Wells good-bye for the summer. Since it was the last day, we didn't have to march out but walked down the front hall in groups. Sadie Lou was next to me. Bad as I felt, I thought she must feel worse. The long silence made me uneasy, and I finally spoke to her. "Do you want to get a Popsicle and come with us on the carryall?" I asked.

"I have to go home. I have company," she answered.

I knew that wasn't true. I had been to her house once, and as we walked along in silence I recalled that embarrassing visit. It had happened during the winter when my Sunday school class at Altura Presbyterian put on a drive for new members, and I invited Sadie Lou to join. She was excited about it but said I'd have to ask her father first. So one afternoon when we left school I went with her to the three-room shack on Nations Avenue, the street in back of our house. Her mother did housework for some rich people out in Austin Terrace and wasn't home. Her father who had tuberculosis and didn't work, was sitting in a straight chair beside a coal stove in the kitchen. His pale face was drawn, and he hunched over the fire, coughing and spitting into the ash bin of glowing coals. Nobody offered me a chair. I stood straight, leaning against the kitchen table covered with green oilcloth.

"Papa, Mafra wants to ask you something," Sadie Lou explained.

Mr. Sears accepted this information without changing expressions. I cleared my throat and wished I had prepared my speech better. I reminded him Altura Presbyterian Church was just three blocks away, and I said we had a good class and I wanted Sadie Lou to come. His dark eyes looked straight through me. He spit into the coals. I couldn't tell how my spiel was going and decided to omit no details. I told him about our teacher, our Christmas party, our weekly paper, Queen's Garden, and offered to stop by on Sunday morning so Sadie Lou could walk with me. I finally finished the hard sell, could think of nothing more, and stopped.

There was a long pause. "She ain't going," he said. It was a final answer, even before he supplied an exclamation point by shooting a fresh sizzle of spit on the glowing coals.

Now, as Sadie Lou and I walked down the hall, that scene flashed through my mind and I felt uncomfortable. Sadie Lou probably realized I knew she was lying. The silence between us was painful.

Elmer, walking behind us, had heard Sadie Lou's remark. "Old

Sears hasn't got a nickel," he chortled. "Hasn't got a nickel! Damfino why she did it, but she's in a pickle—in a pickle—hasn't got a nickel. That's why she did it."

Sadie Lou pretended not to hear. But others heard it and once again took up the chant from Elmer: "Damfino! Old Sears!" We had reached the sidewalk. Sadie Lou running ahead, crossed the street and hurried out of earshot. The rest of us went into Quinn's and bought Popsicles.

Because I had promised Emmaline, I got on the carryall with my Popsicle, but I hated the dizzy spin. I felt sick at my stomach and was afraid I was going to cry. I jumped off and tried not to watch the others whirling around. Sadie Lou didn't have a nickel! If only I had known. I had sixty-five cents in my bank at home. I would have given her a nickel. Mrs. Wells would have given her a nickel— if we had only known. Nobody was having fun. The carryall slowed down and finally stopped.

Emmaline was in the habit of going by my house on her way home from school, so she quite naturally joined me. She was still angry and wouldn't stop talking, which annoyed me when I had so much to think about. Of course I should have realized that Sadie Lou didn't have a nickel—probably didn't have a bathing suit either. She never had anything, and nobody, not one of us, thought about it. All that time we were talking and planning the party, she knew she couldn't go. She just had to listen to all the fun we were going to have, knowing she would be left out. That still didn't give her the right to be late and spoil it for the rest of us, but when you really thought about it—

Emmaline and I crossed the street at the corner. We stepped up on the curb and started up the sidewalk towards my house. "Wasn't it the meanest thing you ever saw?" Emmaline persisted. "I mean, really, Mafra, don't you just hate her?"

I felt my dry bathing suit, held in a tight roll under my arm. The disappointment was still fresh. I started to agree with Emmaline, but the anger in her face dispelled me. I wasn't angry. I was sad. "I don't know, Emmaline. Maybe in a way I feel sort of sorry for her."

"Sorry? Well, sure, everybody hates her. But she deserves it. Don't you think so, Mafra?"

"Damfino," I said angrily. Emmaline was shocked. She had never heard me use that word. I glanced at her and enjoyed the confusion in her face. I couldn't explain how I felt. I didn't have the words.

4

A wonderful thing happened that summer. I joined the elite: I "took" piano. Taking piano wasn't quite as good as taking dancing. I didn't have white satin toe-slippers to carry to school and dangle from my wrist like my classmate Mary Barnett. While she talked about exercising her great toe, I sprinkled my conversations with casual remarks about how busy I would be all summer taking piano from Mrs. Heaslip. No need to explain that Mrs. Heaslip, Gwen's mother and Mama's good friend, was giving me free lessons or that we didn't even have a piano and I would have to practice on the Heaslips' golden-oak upright which half filled their tiny dining room. I planned to be the most diligent student, the youngest-ever church pianist, the charmer of future audiences. My dreams were unbounded.

Mrs. Heaslip scheduled my lessons twice a week at nine in the morning, after she got back from taking Mr. Heaslip to the Juarez Distillery where he was head bookkeeper. "Oh, no, he can't drive through Juarez by himself," she told me once in answer to my innocent question why he couldn't take the car himself and save her the long trip twice a day. "Of course, he did drive himself when it was the El Paso Brewery on this side of the river. When Prohibition came and they had to move across the river, we agreed that I'd do the driving. You see, coming home through Juarez he'd have to pass the Tivoli Casino. Born gambler that he is, he'd stop for one hand of poker or blackjack, and before you know it he'd have lost everything: me, Gwen, the house, the car, right on down to Henrietta and Narcissus." She concluded with a hearty laugh, the last reference being to the two odoriferous milk goats she kept in her backyard. She had a way of mixing the serious and the ridiculous like that. I wasn't quite sure if I should laugh or not.

The Heaslips' Spanish-type house was up near the foothills. After we had established the half-hour lesson and half-hour practice routine, Mrs. Heaslip let me come early and ride over to Juarez with her and Mr. Heaslip. I had to be at her house by seven o'clock, and I loved my early morning walks up the long hill. A couple of blocks above our house the asphalt pavement stopped, and the sandy road, just parallel ruts separated by a center strip of devil-horn stickers, meandered carelessly around boulders and clumps of creosote in its steady climb towards the mountain. My sun-back dress, made of a pink chambray mill-end that Papa got at the cotton mill for ten cents a yard, was cool; and the sun felt good on my bare arms and back.

As I looked up towards Mount Franklin I could see the Mexican goatherd come out of his adobe hut and free his flock from the little pen made of tall cacti, straight as rails, some still holding a few, crimson, springtime blooms. The goats filed out through the open gate and nibbled the sparse vegetation as they began their trek around the foothills. They moved so slowly that if I hadn't known better, I would have taken the flock for an outcropping of white rocks against the brown mountain.

Sometimes Gwen came along to the brewery just for the ride; but usually she stayed home, and I had the back seat of the Model T to myself. I loved the wind in my hair and the sights and sounds of the city waking up. Down in the Mexican section of South El

Paso, the two-room adobe huts abutted the sidewalk, and the doors, painted blue to keep out the evil spirits, were open to pick up a chance breeze. I tried to peer through the openings and catch a glimpse of family life in the crowded rooms. Mrs. Heaslip drove slowly, often honking at mangy dogs scavenging in the gutters, the half-clad Mexican children starting their street games, and the tamale vendors pushing their white carts.

The Mexican customs officials at the International Bridge recognized the Heaslips and waved us on. We left Juarez on the Calle de Diablo—I loved that name—and went on south towards the brewery. Out of town the road became narrow and rough as it passed through fields of alfalfa, knee-high with purple blossoms. Meadow larks, darting from spray to spray, flashed their yellow breasts and sang their three sweet notes, giddily greeting the morning. My eye followed a lark across the alfalfa. On the far side of the field, easily visible above the purple blooms, was a long line of whitewashed adobe rooms, each with its own door but sharing common side walls so that they formed a single building. A red lantern, still aglow in spite of the broad daylight, swung above a sign: "Red Light Apartments." The apartment doors were closed, and except for the brightly burning lantern there was no sign of life.

Alone in the back of the car, I sat upright on the edge of the seat and strained my eyes to be sure I was reading the words right. Red Light Apartments! That meant white slavery! I felt my heart pound as I squinted at the closed doors. I wasn't quite sure what was going on in there, but I knew it was something dreadful. I had read all about it in an old copy of *True Story* that I found in the cupboard when we moved into our house. The story told about a beautiful girl who was forced by a group of beastly men into a Red Light Apartment where she became a White Slave and cried all the time because her life was ruined. Oh, how I wished a door would open and a beautiful girl would come out—maybe just to watch the meadowlarks—and we could rescue her from her terrible fate, whatever it was.

We drove by, but nothing happened, not a sign of life. Beyond the alfalfa field we let Mr. Heaslip out at the brewery. I got in the front seat beside Mrs. Heaslip. As we passed the red-light sign on our way back, I asked her what the sign meant.

"What sign?" she asked, as though it wasn't perfectly obvious.

"Red Light Apartments. I mean, it's funny. That's in English, and all the other signs over here are in Spanish."

Mrs. Heaslip agreed that the sign was indeed in English and began talking about the meadowlarks. After that, we drove along in silence. I was wondering what it was that grown people didn't like to talk about. Mama had taken *True Story* away from me, saying it was trash. She wouldn't even talk about the story. Now, Mrs. Heaslip, who talked freely about Mr. Heaslips's gambling and almost anything else, wouldn't talk about the Red Light Apartments.

Oh well, back to the piano lessons. I had advanced to sheet music: "Now my fingers, say your lesson. . . ."

After my lesson and a half-hour or more of practice, I had the long walk home. It was hot now, the sun burning my face, and the heat of the sandy road or black asphalt penetrating the thin soles of my brown sandals. It was good to reach the shade of our front porch, where I usually found Mama and Mrs. Martin, our next door neighbor, sitting in the rockers, enjoying a break from their household chores.

After I reported to Mama how well my piano lessons were going, she would tell me to get three nickels out of her purse, four if Becky happened to be around, and run down to Quinn's for cold Cokes. Back on the porch, I served the Cokes and sat on the top step, my back against the brick pillar, and an open book, *Under the Lilacs* or *An Old Fashioned Girl*, on my lap. I sipped my drink and pretended to read, but actually I was listening. Alcott was no match for the reminiscences and neighborhood gossip that Mama and Mrs. Martin exchanged.

I liked to hear about the old times before I was even born. Mama told about her own wedding back in Georgia. Her father, a Presbyterian minister, had performed the ceremony, and she and Papa had left for Oakland—four nights and five days on the train. Mrs. Martin told Mama she had married right out of high school; but her first husband, father of her son, Robert Earle, had been killed in an accident. Later she trained to be a nurse and was working out at William Beaumont Hospital where she took care of Mr. Martin, a veteran who had been gassed in the Great War. He fell in love with her, and, although he knew he didn't have long to live, he wanted to get out of the hospital and have a home of his own. He had inherited a little money so they married, he adopted Robert Earle, and they bought the house next to ours. I already knew the story, but sometimes when she was telling it, we could hear Mr. Martin over there in his bed coughing, and I had a hard time holding back the tears.

Except when she was talking about Mr. Martin, Mrs. Martin was a naturally cheerful person, and she liked to sing. She was a member of the choir at the little Baptist church over on Fort Boulevard, and she sang Baptist hymns while she worked around her house:

> Lord, lift me up and let me stand,
> By faith on heaven's table land,
> A higher plain than I have found,
> Lord, plant my feet on higher ground.

Her voice was strong and sweet and easily carried through the open windows. Sometimes I stopped whatever I was doing just to listen to her. I sort of wished we would sing like that at the Presbyterian church, but we were more dignified—always starting off with "Holy, Holy, Holy," which doesn't have much swing to it.

That spring we had taken Mrs. Martin and Robert Earle in our car to the Easter sunrise service up at the high-school stadium. It was a bitter cold morning, still dark when we backed out of our driveway. Mrs. Martin, Robert Earle, Becky, and I crowded in the back seat of the open car, pulled the army blanket over our faces to protect ourselves from the cutting wind. We parked below the stadium, walked up to the gate, and climbed the concrete tiers to find our seats. My ankles were so cold I thought my bones were cracking, but once we took our seats and tucked the blanket around our legs, we began to warm up. The stadium was a semicircle facing east, and as the sky lightened, we watched the morning star high above the eastern plains fade and melt away.

Down on the field, a white cross dominated the big, wooden platform. In front of the cross, white-robed choir members drifted around finding their places. Behind the cross, the rows of chairs provided for members of the clergy were filling up. The dark suits and overcoats of the ministers contrasted with the white cross and white robes of the choir. Even at that distance I was able to pick out our minister, Dr. McSpadden; and Mrs. Martin pointed out her preacher, Reverend Bigelow. She had been invited to sing in the choir, but couldn't do it because of the evening practice and not being able to leave Mr. Martin alone at night.

The choir led us in several songs—"The Old Rugged Cross" and things like that—but the really beautiful music was timed exactly right. As the sun broke over the Hueco Mountains, the sky turned from lavender to red, to bright orange and gold, and in a climax of emotion the crowd rose and joined the choir in that glorious Easter hymn:

> *Vainly they sealed the tomb, Jesus my savior,*
> *Vainly they watched the dead, Jesus my Lord,*
> *Up from the grave he arose,*
> *With a might triumph o'er his foes,*
> *He arose forever from the dark domain,*
> *To live forever with the saints who reign.*
> *HE AROSE, HE AROSE, HALLELUJAH, CHRIST AROSE!*

The cross, silhouetted against the rising sun, glistened, silvery white. I was standing next to Mrs. Martin, and when she let go on the *Hallelujah*, it was magnificent. I felt myself drawn up in to the glorious drama, believing every word and wishing it would last forever.

Sitting on the top porch step in the shade of the Virginia creeper, Becky and I concentrated on our game of jacks, unaware of the gathering storm. The sharp ting of the metal jacks striking together as we tossed them out, followed by the harsher scratching on concrete as we scooped them up again. The rhythmic game was broken only by our announcements of progress up the game ladder: Free Throw, Eggs in a Basket, Pigs in a Pen, Double Trouble, and so on. The list was interminable, and the game could go on for hours. The fingernails on my right hand were worn to a lopsided point from scooping the jacks off the concrete floor—the badge of a dedicated player, and I wore it proudly.

The neighborhood was strangely quiet. Our interest in our game lagged as our attention was drawn to the huge raindrops making a dark polka-dot pattern on the gray concrete walk. Overhead, the drops splashed against dusty leaves of the Virginia creeper, and the acrid odor of settling dust filled the air.

By common consent we stopped playing, gathered up our jacks and ball and put them away in their draw-string bag. Witty woke from his nap in the rocking chair, meowed and rubbed against Becky's leg. She held him on her shoulder, stroked him, and invited me to feel his bristling hair. Mama came out on the porch, glanced at the dark sky over McKelligon Canyon, and asked us to help pull the porch furniture inside.

Robert Earle and his friend Raymond, returning from a bike ride, paused for breath in front of our house. Robert Earle pointed to the black clouds over McKelligon Canyon. "Oh, boy, it's a cloudburst!" he shouted gleefully.

Above the canyon clouds roiled off the mountains, surged inward against the canyon walls like a flock of angry black buzzards caged in by the rocky cliffs. A flash of lightning zigzagged from the black heavens down to the bottom of the canyon, a single instant of light followed by the deep roar of thunder that bounced from peak to peak, tumbled out across the desert, and faded into the distant valley.

The scant rain on our street ceased entirely, and the sun cast an iridescent glow over the landscape like unseen footlights lighting up a stage. Neighbors, standing in their front yards watching the gathering storm, seemed strangely unfamiliar, two-dimensional characters making awkward, jerky gestures as they pointed towards the distant canyon. Voices carried, lending weight to insignificant remarks.

Gladys Quinn in her front yard held little Clarabow by the hand, and Becky and I ran up to talk to her. Gladys, one of the few people we knew who had actually grown up in El Paso, was an authority on the weather. If we had thought the spring sandstorms were bad, she warned us, just wait until we saw a cloudburst. "A gully washer, that's what it is. Believe me, we'll have a real flood."

While she was talking the black clouds up the canyon gave way to a solid sheet of rain, a gray velvet curtain blocking the mountain peaks and McKelligon Canyon from view.

Down at the corner, Kerry Quinn, still wearing his white butcher's apron, came out of the store and started running up the hill. It was strange to see him out on the street in his butcher's apron. He wore it in the store when he was helping Mr. Quinn, but when he made deliveries he was always neatly dressed: khaki shirt, black tie, and carefully creased trousers. He had dark wavy hair, brown eyes, and a boyish look that made him seem even younger than his twenty-two years. When he reached us, he was grinning with excitement, anticipating the gathering storm.

Gladys greeted him apprehensively. "Now, Kerry, don't act crazy like you did in the last cloudburst. Running around in knee-deep water. You scared me to death!"

Kerry picked up Clarabow, did a little tap dance and laughed at Gladys and her fears.

"I mean it, Kerry," she pursued. "You know a cloudburst washes down all sorts of garbage: centipedes, tarantulas, and even rattlesnakes. Why, last summer the day after a cloudburst flood they killed a rattlesnake in the Williamsons' yard. Six-feet long and eight rattlers, and that close to little Edward."

Kerry wasn't listening. He gave Clarabow a smacking kiss and set her down. With Gladys still protesting, he ran across the street and through the school grounds up to the corner where the arroyo emptied onto Justus Street. I wished I could go with him, but Gladys said we'd see plenty of flooding just where we were, so I stayed with her. She had to raise her voice above the loud roar coming off the desert, which she explained was caused by rocks and small boulders, unearthed by the flood, tumbling down the arroyo under the foaming brown water.

The rain up at McKelligon Canyon had ceased, and the mountains were visible again. Leaning out over the curbing and watching the uphill corner as Gladys directed, we saw the water, brown as a chocolate cake batter, ooze from Justus onto the middle of Mountain Avenue, hesitate briefly, and pivot downhill. By the time it reached the curb where we were standing, it had collected its force and was rising rapidly. Uprooted cacti, old tires, rusty garbage pails—all the trash that had been dumped on the desert since the last cloudburst—bobbed along in the churning flood.

Kerry, having watched the flood gush out of the desert onto the paved street, was trying to rejoin us. He had taken off his shoes, knotted the laces, and hung them around his neck. Barefoot and wet up to his thighs, he made his way across the flooded school grounds. When he reached the curbing opposite us, Gladys urged him to wait until the water had crested, but he ignored her, teetered uncertainly against the current, and managed to force his way through the floating debris. He reached the curbing and picked up Clarabow who shrieked with delight, "Daddy's wet! Daddy's all wet!"

The water continued to rise. In a few minutes it began to lap over the knee-high curb, and our little crowd broke up as we went back to our own porches. Mama joined Becky and me there, and we watched the water spread over our lawn and around the house, flooding the basement excavation. After about a half-hour the flood reached its crest, and in another half-hour it was reduced to a trickle. The street was littered with small boulders, cacti, old tires, all sorts of debris, and even small sandbars.

Papa usually got home at six, but he was late. When he finally came, he said Piedras had been flooded as bad as Mountain Avenue, and traffic at Five Points had been stalled for hours.

The next morning the city trucks were out, cleaning the street. Some of the workers told us they would pump out the basements in a day or two. Considering the big area that had been flooded, we thought the service was good, but it wasn't fast enough for Mr. Printz. The basement of the little barbershop that he owned had been flooded. Although it contained nothing more important than some old shelves that had been stacked down there when the little white grocery store had been converted into the present barbershop, Mr. Printz wanted the city to pump the water out immediately.

Dressed in a brown suit with matching striped tie—an unusual attire on our street where suits were generally reserved for church wear—he went from door to door, trying to persuade the neighbors to sign a petition protesting "the inefficiency of our city government," as he termed it.

When he knocked on our door, Mama was polite. She invited him into the living room, and I was glad to get a close look at him. He spoke precisely and was quite formal, which seemed as inappropriate to the occasion as his business suit was for a morning call. After hearing him out, Mama said we really hadn't suffered any damage and she had no reason to sign the petition.

When Mr. Printz realized Mama was not going to sign, he excused himself and left. We watched him go down the hill, and for a moment Mama seemed at a loss for words. Suddenly she remembered that somebody—probably Mrs. McCabe—had told her something about Mr. Printz getting married, and she wondered if it was true.

I told her I knew it but hadn't thought to mention it. Just before the close of school a new girl, Dianne Mel, had entered our class at school. I talked to her once and she told me that she was from Nebraska. Her own father was dead, and she and her mother were living in a little town in Nebraska where her mother was a seamstress. Mr. Printz was from the same town, and her mother had always known him. Last spring, when he went back to Nebraska to sell some property, he had married her mother, and now they all lived in his duplex.

Mama said I should have been more friendly to a new girl in my class; but I explained it all happened right at the end of school, and Dianne was sort of hard to talk to. Mama let that pass, but she kept thinking about Mr. Printz. "I don't know what it is, but there is something about that man." She shrugged. "Well, I just don't like him."

5

On any random day that summer—except, of course, my piano lesson days—Mama was likely to hustle Becky and me from the breakfast table to round up our friends to go swimming at Washington Park. "Hurry," she would say, "get a move on before it's too hot to walk to the car line. Looks like a scorcher." A safe enough prophecy—every day was a scorcher.

Even today, that magic name, Washington Park, evokes wonderful images: the crowd of excited kids gathering on our front porch, the walk with Mama to the car line, my dash into the corner bakery for a sack of cinnamon buns to eat on the streetcar, the jolting car ride, the path through the park, parasols on the sandy beach, that first plunge into the block-long pool, the picnic lunch spread on the grass in the shade of a giant cottonwood tree. Since Mama suggested the trips herself, it didn't occur to me until many years later that she probably didn't have quite as much fun as we did. I should have thanked her more.

Telephone calls were enough to alert Gwen and Beverly that this was a Washington Park day. Next, Becky took off to scout the uphill neighbors, while I went down the block, stopping first at the Williamsons' house right next to the barber shop. Little Edward always went with us, but each time Mrs. Williamson required my personal assurance that we would take good care of him.

After leaving Edward's, I went to recruit Florence and Tommy Greer down in the next block. The black and white sign, "Colonel Thomason Greer," on their doorstep always impressed me. Being a colonel he could have lived in one of those two-story brick houses out at the Post, but he had four kids and chose to live in town where he could keep milk goats. The goats, penned in the backyard, were concealed from view by a salt-cedar hedge but betrayed their presence by frequent bleating. A Mexican maid answered my knock and invited me to sit in the living room while she called Florence and Tommy. The house was the nicest one on our street, and I enjoyed my few moments with a chance to look around. Shades were drawn against the morning heat, and there was a cabinet full of souvenirs, German beer mugs and other stuff that the Greers had collected when Colonel Greer had foreign duty. I marveled at how rich he must be: such a nice house, expensive things, and keeping a maid when nobody in the family was even sick. Florence and Tommy came in and were immediately recruited for the park trip. They would be up at our house as soon as the maid fixed their lunch and they got their things together.

As I passed Quinn's on my way home, Dianne Mel happened to come out of the store with a sack of groceries in her arms. I remembered Mama's saying I should have been more friendly to Diane, and on an impulse I invited her to go to the park with us. She smiled and tossed her head a bit so that her blonde hair, cut in a rather long page-boy style, fell back from her face. She was obviously pleased at the invitation, but her answer was hesitant. She wanted to go, but she would have to ask her mother and Mr. Printz.

I gave her some instructions: Bring her bathing suit, a towel, and a rubber bathing cap. It cost a dime to get in the pool, and three cents each way for carfare. We were all collecting at our house, but we had to walk right by Mr. Printz's duplex and we'd stop for her.

The kids had begun to collect on our porch. Becky was there with Beth and Buddy Christianson from over on Nations Avenue. Sometimes they didn't have the carfare and swimming-pool money, and I was glad they could make it today.

I asked Becky if she had invited Judy and Jammie Sue Jackson, the two girls from St. Louis who had moved into the corner house left vacant that spring when the Lundstrums, hoping Annie Laurie would soon be well enough to attend El Paso School for Girls, at least part-time, had moved out to Austin Terrace. Mrs. Jackson had tuberculosis; and the front porch was now closed in with canvas so she could have her bed out there and get lots of fresh air.

Judy and Jammie Sue often came down to play Parcheesi or jacks on our front porch. I took it for granted Becky would have invited them. To my surprise she gave me an indignant look. Yes, she had asked Judy and Jammie Sue, but it was the last time she would ever ask them to do anything. They didn't want to go to Washington Park because it was in South El Paso and the swimming pool would be full of Mexicans. Becky mimicked the condescending tone of voice in which this pronouncement had been made.

"So what's wrong with Mexicans?" I demanded angrily. "They take showers before they go in the pool, same as we do. Judy and Jammie Sue don't even know any Mexicans. They just never like anything in El Paso—always talking about how great everything was back in St. Louis. If you ask me, they're missing a lot of fun."

"They never have any fun," Becky agreed. "They can't skate down the hill, because Kerry might back the truck out on Copia and run over them. They can't hike in the desert, because a rattlesnake might bite them. They can't even go outside without a sun hat, because they don't want to get a suntan."

"They're just prissy," I concluded, "and I'm glad they're not coming."

Mama had come out on the porch and cut this conversation short. She had visited Mrs. Jackson several times, and she said it was no wonder they were all homesick for St. Louis. We were all familiar with the Jackson's story; but Mama, disturbed at our callousness, saw fit to repeat it. Mr. Jackson had died of tuberculosis in St. Louis, and when it was discovered Mrs. Jackson had it too, her brother Horace had sent her and the girls to El Paso. Fortunately,

Mrs. Jackson's sister, Auntie Ruth, had been willing to come along to run the household. Every time Mama went to visit, she had found Mrs. Jackson propped up in bed, sewing for the girls. Auntie Ruth did the machine stitching, but Mrs. Jackson chose the patterns and basted all the seams. Horace owned a department store, and in addition to paying all the household expenses he sent boxes of dress material and trimmings, whatever the girls needed. They were pretty girls and certainly had lovely clothes.

I felt a little ashamed of my outburst, but I still didn't like Judy and Jammie Sue and the way they didn't like Mexicans or anything else in El Paso. Beverly and Gwen had arrived, and I changed the subject by telling them I had invited Dianne. Beverly said it was a good idea since Dianne was new in our class, and we started talking about how good Dianne was in art. Once we had to draw our favorite flower, and she drew a picture of the clump of yucca in Mr. Printz's front yard. Everybody liked it, and Miss Fuller put it up on the board.

At last the crowd had collected, and we were ready to go. Everybody gave their carfare and pool money to Mama for safe-keeping, and we started down the sidewalk. We rounded the barbershop corner, and Mr. Wilson, sitting on his green bench as he waited for his first customer, took his pipe out of his mouth long enough to wish us a good swim.

I was expecting to see Dianne waiting under the PRINTZ APTS. sign, but she was not in sight. I ran up and rang the bell. The screen door was latched and the wooden door closed. After a long wait Dianne opened the door and, talking through the screen, said, "I'm sorry, Mafra, I can't go." Her eyes were red, and I knew she had been crying. I could tell she didn't want to talk about it, so I just said I was sorry and left.

The kids, impatient at the slight delay had run ahead, but Mama was quite upset. She kept repeating she wished she'd known earlier so she could have called and talked to Dianne's mother. It wasn't right to disappoint a girl like that.

The car not in sight, Mama tried to line us up in some order, but there was another distraction. The spicy aroma of cinnamon buns from the ovens of the little bakery on the corner filled the air, and most of us were looking hopefully in that direction. Edward, unable to contain his exuberance, stuck his blond head out over the car track and peered up the hill towards Fort Bliss—still no car in sight. He sidled up to Mama. "The car ain't coming yet, Mrs. King, I was just wondering—could we maybe get some of them bums?" He pointed towards the bakery, sniffing audibly, his little nostrils quivering in anticipation.

"Why, Edward, what a grand idea!" Mama acted surprised, but she had two dimes ready and had just waited to hear him ask for "them bums." He did it every time, and every time she found it amusing. She handed me the money, and when I entered the bakery the sales lady was already breaking off a sheet of luscious buns, full of cinnamon and raisins and topped with sticky, white frosting. She remembered me from other trips, and as she handed me the big white sack she wished us a happy day at the park.

I ran back to the car stop just as the streetcar was arriving. Mama was already helping the kids climb up onto the car's folding step. Edward, terrified that I might not make it back in time with my sack of buns, stood at the back of the line, yelling, "Run, Mafra, run." I boosted him up onto the high folding step, and got on myself. In back of me Mama pulled her narrow skirt up a bit with one hand so she could manage the high step, grabbed the pole by the door with her other hand, and swung herself aboard. The kids ran noisily through the almost empty car, choosing seats.

The motorman, familiar with our swimming trips, called out, "All aboard for the Ole Swimming Hole," gave the bell an extra clang, and swung the lever in a half circle to close the door behind Mama. The car started, and Mama steadied herself and dropped the money in the fare box. As the coins tinkled down the little chute, the motorman counted out the transfers, looked at Mama approvingly, and said, "Best pair of legs I've seen this morning!"

Mama didn't say a word. She blushed fiery red, sat down next to me, and made a great fuss about counting the transfers to be sure she had the right number. I pretended I hadn't heard, handed the sack of buns to Becky to divide, sat next to Mama, and stole a furtive glance at her legs. She was wearing the chiffon, full-fashioned, French-nude hose that Papa had given her for a birthday present. You could tell they were very expensive because they had little dots along the back seam, letting in extra fullness to fit the calf of her leg. Her Enna Jettick shoes were blonde with straps and Cuban heels.

With all the getting on, finding seats, watching for the right stop, pulling the bell cord, getting off, Mama counting the transfers and calling out, "Be careful, don't leave your bathing suits on the car," the trip lasted at least an hour. After two transfers, we arrived at the park, ready for swimming.

Inside the separate stalls in the big, wooden bathhouse, we wriggled our sweaty bodies into our wool bathing suits—always wool, as it was common knowledge the wool would keep us from getting chilled and catching cold when we emerged, dripping wet, from the pool. Mama had made my suit from one of her old coats. It was navy blue, one piece with short skirt attached. She had gone to the trouble of trimming the neck, arm holes, and skirt edge with red, rickrack braid. I made a quick dash through the required shower, barely getting wet, and raced to be first into the water.

Mama didn't go swimming. She sat on the sandy beach under a parasol and watched the younger kids in the shallow water. Those of us who could swim went out to the pier. We did a few dives off the five-foot board, ventured up on the ten-foot board, backed down, went up again, and finally jumped in feet-first. Then we decided to see how far we could swim. We figured the pool was a block long. If we could swim it sixteen times, eight round trips, we would have made a mile. We were all self-taught, and our advanced dog-paddle stroke didn't net much distance. We usually gave up after five or six laps. Finally, utterly exhausted, we got out of the pool.

After we were dressed, we stood in line at the hand-wringer outside the bathhouse and turned the crank with one hand as we guided our suits through the double rubber rollers with the other hand, pressing out as much moisture as possible so they would be easier to carry. Then Mama counted us all again, to be sure she hadn't lost anybody, and we sat on the grass under a big cottonwood tree and ate lunch. Some of it we shared. Beverly divided dill pickles—big juicy ones that Kerry had fished out of the Quinn's pickle barrel for her. Edward passed his Tootsie Rolls around and looked longingly at Tommy Greer's box of Oreo cookies.

"I sure do like them orioles," he said, hopefully.

"Oriole!" Gwen said disdainfully. "Hope they don't fly away!"

Edward ignored Gwen, and Tommy passed the cookies around. Edward examined his carefully, separated the halves, licked the white frosting from one side and then the other, and finally ate the chocolate cookies, savoring each crumb.

We were too tired to talk on the streetcar going home. Edward wanted to sit next to me. With his head against my shoulder he asked, "Mafra, you ain't going to get off and leave me on the car? You'll tell me when to transfer?"

"Sure, Edward, I won't go off and leave you." Sometimes he was asleep before I finished the promise.

Those swimming-pool trips were a summertime ritual.

That summer I had my first adventure on a bike. Robert Earle and his friend Raymond had gotten bikes for Christmas. That was no surprise. All the boys I knew had bikes by the time they reached junior high. They either got them for Christmas or earned the money throwing papers. One way or another, boys got bikes. Girls—never. I didn't know a single girl who owned a bike. I wasn't even aware that bikes without center bars were made for girls.

On Saturday mornings I stood behind the Virginia creeper on our front porch and listened to Robert Earle and Raymond in the Martins' front yard, checking out their bikes and discussing their plans for the day. Would they go out to Beaumont Hospital and ride around the grounds, over to Memorial Park and do the hills, or maybe try something new? Oh, the freedom of it! They could go wherever they wanted.

As I watched, they mounted their bikes: a downward step on one pedal, the other leg thrown carelessly over the center bar, and they were off. Sometimes they pumped around the school block and came coasting down the hill in front of our house, arms folded over their chests, not even touching the handlebars. They disappeared down the street, and I went in to call Beverly to see if she wanted to go skating. That's the way it was. Boys rode bikes; girls skated.

Through the winter and spring the Saturday-morning ritual

seldom varied. Then it was summer; school was out, and a little of the new had worn off the bikes. At noontime on a hot June day I was on the porch when Robert Earle returned from his morning ride. Whistling as usual, he parked his bike by his front steps and started to go in for lunch. Suddenly, I realized this was the opportunity I had dreamed of. Did I dare? Why not? Impulsively, I ran across the yard and blurted out the question: "Robert Earle, sometime when you're not using your bike, could I try it out? See if I could ride it, just once?"

He stood on the top step and looked down at me in surprise. Now that he was in junior high and going out for football, he didn't play around the neighborhood any more. I guess he had forgotten that I existed. Nevertheless, I remembered he had always been good natured, and my heart stood still while he mopped the sweat from his face, shrugged, and said he supposed I could have a turn sometime when he wasn't using it.

"Right now!" I said. "Right now, while you're eating lunch, I'll just take it up to Justus Street where it's level and have a turn."

He was headed for the front door and called over his shoulder, "Okay, for a little while. But be doggoned sure to have it back when I want it."

Hardly able to believe my good fortune, I rolled the bike out to the parkway, bumped it over the curbing, and started pushing it up the hill. The neighborhood was quiet and deserted—not a soul around to observe my ecstasy. Oblivious to shimmering heat waves, salty sweat blinding my eyes, and melting asphalt burning through the soles of my thin sandals, I gripped the handlebars and turned the bike around the corner onto Justus Street.

The curbing, built knee-high in the hope it would contain cloudburst floods, was just the right height for boarding the bike. With my right foot on the curb, I held tight to the handlebars, threw my left foot over the seat, reached the left pedal on its downward spiral and caught the other pedal with my right foot, just as I had seen the boys do—or at least I thought it was. I didn't realize I was getting on from the wrong side. I fell, but it didn't matter. Ignoring my scratched knees and the throbbing pain in my head, I tried again and again.

Suddenly I caught on: it was the forward motion that mattered. Elated at the discovery, I willed myself forward. "Go, go, go!" I whispered aloud in the deserted street. I had the secret now. All I needed was practice.

I forgot all about time. Maybe as much as an hour passed before I realized I was dying of thirst and must get the bike back to Robert Earle. Holding the handlebars, I rolled the bike down the hill, stopped in front of the Martins' house and called Robert Earle. After a cursory glance at the bike to be sure I hadn't broken anything, he accepted my thanks and agreed to let me try it again. "But only at noon when it's hot and I'm eating lunch. Otherwise, I'll be needing it."

Days of ecstasy! I woke each morning, wondering when I could get my hands on the bike and how far I would be able to ride without falling. In less than a week I could get on from the curbing and make it up to the far corner of Justus Street. I had fresh trouble there because of the sand that cloudburst floods had washed out of the arroyo and spread over the pavement. After a few falls I mastered the loose sand, made a wobbly circle, and headed back in the other direction, coasting to a halt before I reached Mountain Avenue.

Soon I felt so confident I thought I deserved some praise, and I wanted to show Mama what I could do. All I needed was a practice run down Mountain Avenue, and then I would call her to come out on the porch to watch me. I made my usual circle on Justus Street, but this time when I got to Mountain Avenue I did not coast to a halt but rounded the corner and headed downhill.

Suddenly the wheels were turning faster, picking up speed. All my practicing had been on level ground, and I had no idea how fast I would roll downhill. There had to be some brakes, but where? The wheels turned faster and faster. I passed the Jacksons' house, Mrs. Pope's house and, clinging tightly to the handlebars, whizzed along. The Martins' house was coming up and I wanted to call for Robert Earle, but the words stuck in my throat. Then our house, two more houses, and, all too soon, the barbershop corner. What if Kerry was backing the truck out onto Copia? No time to think about it. Maybe I could turn on Copia and level off. I maneuvered the handlebars, but not enough. I dashed up Quinn's driveway and crashed smack into the side of the store.

I fell in a heap, the bike on top of me. The wheels stopped turning, and I was conscious of a shooting pain in one shoulder and a stinging sensation in my right leg where the jagged edge of the pedal had cut a deep gash. I lay quite still, looking at the blue sky while everything spun around me.

It was probably just seconds until Kerry, who had seen it all through the store's picture window, ran out to help me. He moved the bike and had me wiggle my toes and lift my arm to make sure nothing was broken. Mrs. Quinn brought a wet towel to try to stop my bleeding, and I thought how strange it was to see her away from her usual station behind the store counter. She said I looked pale, and her dark eyes, looking closely at me, seemed very far away.

After a few minutes, when time seemed to be standing perfectly still, she helped me sit up. Kerry brought me a glass of water, and when I said I was able to go home he helped me to my feet and pronounced the bike was in good condition—not hurt at all. Slowly, still shaking and trying not to cry, I wheeled the bike out into the street and up the hill.

Robert Earle and Raymond, waiting in the Martins' front yard, couldn't believe I had actually crashed into the store. The bike had perfectly good brakes—why didn't I use them?

Furious at their lack of sympathy, I turned on both boys but held Robert Earle, the owner of the bike, responsible. "Well, Robert Earle, you could have told me how to brake. Somebody taught you. Just because you're a boy, you weren't born knowing how to brake and neither was Raymond. Somebody showed you, and you could have had the decency to show me."

They both looked taken aback at my outburst, but Raymond let Robert Earle handle it. "Gee, Mafra, I thought you knew how to brake," he said. "I saw you riding up there on Justus Street, and you looked okay to me. Look, here's what you do." He took the bike, and showed me how to push backwards on the top pedal. "Here, you can do it!"

He thrust the bike towards me, but I was feeling too sorry for myself to accept his help. "I can't now. I have to ask Mama to put iodine on this cut, so it doesn't get infected." With this face-saving show of physical courage, I limped towards my own yard.

Halfway up the steps, I felt the boys, more amused than sympathetic, were still watching me. I turned and faced them. "But I'm going to ride your bike again, Robert Earle. Tomorrow, probably. And don't you forget it. Leave it by the steps for me at noon. That's the least you can do."

The screen door slammed behind me.

6

"Pigeons mate for life." Mr. Mae made that clear to Papa when he first mentioned giving us the flock. "A hundred pigeons in the flock, and they're monogamous. You know that, don't you, Mr. King?"

Of course Papa didn't know that or anything else about pigeons. Mr. Mae was general manager of The Lone Star Cotton Mill and was responsible for Papa's getting the job as head dyer, so Papa wasn't about to disagree with him. Papa just smiled agreeably and accepted pigeon fidelity as part of the conventional wisdom, nothing to be concerned about.

Mr. Mae also told Papa that the big restaurants would take as many squabs as Papa could raise. A sellers' market, he had called it. That was the phrase that caught Mama's ear, and she agreed with Papa right off that we should take the pigeons. To her it was a chance to make some much needed extra cash, but Papa's ideas were more grandiose. He had always wanted to go in business for himself, and this could be just the break he needed. Anyway, they both wanted the flock, and once it was settled we were all so excited we couldn't talk about anything else.

The decision made, Mr. and Mrs. Mae invited us to their house over on Piedras on a Saturday. They had owned the flock for a year and really hated to part with it, but they were building a house out in Austin Terrace where the zoning prohibited pigeons or any kind of livestock, so they had no choice. They greeted Becky and me warmly, saying that pigeon-raising should really be a family project and it would be a wonderful experience for both of us.

Mr. Mae and Papa went out to look at the flying coop, and Mrs. Mae took Mama, Becky, and me to the nesting shed. After the bright sunshine it took a few minutes to adjust to the dim light of the shed. A few tiny feathers wafted about in the dust filled air, and two or three pigeons on a high perch cooed softly. At first I thought all the nests were empty, but Becky called my attention to one containing two tiny squabs, bald and naked of feathers. Their sharp beaks, open in a perpetual squawk, revealed greedy, pink gullets. I leaned forward to examine the noisy creatures more closely but recoiled with an involuntary shudder, repulsed by their ugliness. At that moment a large, brown pigeon flew in and settled on the narrow ledge in front of the nest. As Becky and I watched, it placed its beak inside a squab's open beak, and regurgitated partly digested food. Becky and I turned to Mrs. Mae in astonishment.

"Yes, that's the way they feed the squabs," she explained. "Pigeon milk, I think it's called. Both male and female feed their young. Fascinating, isn't it? Pigeons are monogamous. You know that, don't you?"

Mama did know—Papa had repeated it often enough—but she just nodded and let the question pass without comment.

Becky, however, picked up the new word. "What's monogamous?"

"Oh, it means the father, the male, stays around and helps the mother, the female, raise the young," Mama explained, naively unaware that the flock of pigeons was about to deliver a crash course in sex education to both Becky and me.

Mrs. Mae picked up one of the cooing pigeons, showed Mama its numbered leg band, and advised her to be very careful about banding each nesting pair. She admitted, a little guiltily, that she had been so busy planning the new house she had neglected the banding, but it was an important part of pigeon raising. Mama should band pairs in their nest or out in the flying coop when she caught them—er—treading, this with a cautious glance at Becky and me. Band the workers and cull the non-workers, she emphasized, as she led us out into the sunshine to have lemonade in the wicker chairs under the cottonwood tree.

I was satisfied to rest in the shade, but Becky, interested in any living thing from her cat Witty to pigeons in a pen, insisted I come with her to check out the flock in the flying coop. The pigeons, some cooing on swinging perches and some busy at the feeders, were different colors: slate gray, teal, brown, and even two or three solid whites with feathered legs. Becky asked Mr. Mae about the different colors.

"Oh, yes, we have several breeds," he explained. "The big brown ones are Giant Homers. They have the biggest squabs, but they don't nest as often. The greenish-blue are Carneaus, I guess, or maybe Mondains, and the white ones are White Kings." Having run out of information, he gave Becky a friendly pat on the shoulder, congratulating her for being a born pigeon-fancier.

While the Maes waited for their new house, we had a few weeks to get ready for the pigeons. Papa started work on the nesting shed and flying coop, and Mama began collecting as much information as she could on raising pigeons.

A loom-fixer at the cotton mill named Stone—Papa called him Rocky—came out on Saturday afternoons to help Papa with the building. Mr. Stone had grown up on a farm back in Georgia and knew something about carpentry. He looked at the old chicken coop on the back of our lot, never used except as a hiding place when we played Run, Sheep, Run or Kick the Can, and pronounced it worth renovating. Every Saturday afternoon he and Papa worked on it, bracing the supports and even putting on a new roof.

Mama started her research by sending me to the library with instructions to get everything they had on raising pigeons. She frowned in disbelief when I returned with a single volume, but it was all the librarian could find. Mama opened the book and read aloud from the first page: "'The ideal spot for breeding pigeons is the loft over the horse stable.'" She was furious. "Horse stable!" she cried. "When was the last time I saw a horse stable?" She turned to the flyleaf. "This book was published in 1890, the year I was born. This is not useful at all, Mafra. You can just return it to the library, and I'll look elsewhere."

She quickly found other sources. She telephoned the county agent, wrote to the Department of Agriculture in Washington, to the University of Texas in Austin, to Texas Agriculture and Mechanical College at College Station, to the New Mexico Farm Extension Center at Mesilla Park forty miles up the valley, to a magazine called *Pigeon Stock Selection and Mating Strategies,* and maybe to a few others.

Mr. Stone and Papa finished renovating the nesting shed and began digging holes to support wire for the flying coop. Mama's pamphlets were arriving daily. She arranged them in a neat stack on the kitchen counter. Some were addressed "Dear Pigeon Fancier," and she rejected them out-of-hand. She did not consider herself a fancier. She was a breeder for profit, and she took special note of pamphlets that addressed her in that manner.

One such pamphlet stated that tobacco stems when used for nesting material prevented pigeons from having mites. The hint of mites horrified Mama. After a series of telephone calls she announced she had located a little cigar factory down on San Antonio Street where she thought we could get tobacco stems. On the next Saturday afternoon—for some reason Mr. Stone wasn't available for building—she put a couple of cardboard boxes in the back seat of the car and sent Papa and me to find the cigar factory and bring home tobacco stems. The address she gave us was beyond the end of the pavement on San Antonio, and Papa had to drive around several unmarked streets and blind alleys before we finally located the factory.

The proprietor, a serious little Mexican, spoke no English. He was puzzled at our cardboard boxes, obviously wondering what we intended to put in them. "Tobacco stems for pigeon nests," Papa explained. The little man smiled agreeably but shook his head from side to side, not understanding. Papa kept repeating, "Tobacco stems for pigeon nests," saying it louder and louder each time, as though sheer volume would break the language barrier. The Mexican smiled but kept shaking his head.

We resorted to gestures. Papa set his box on the counter, put his thumbs under his armpits, and with elbows extended flapped his arms up and down. This flying motion was accompanied by a pigeon-like cooing. I took the hint, put my box on the floor, cupped one hand to indicate a nest, and made weaving gestures with my fingers.

Suddenly the little man's face brightened. "*Sí, sí, paja de tabaco!*"

"*Sí, paja,*" we echoed, hoping it was the right word.

From the back door, the man pointed to a spot down the alley where he customarily dumped his tobacco stems.

"*Grácias, muchas grácias,*" Papa repeated a few times as we picked our way through a litter of old oil cans, broken bottles, and abandoned wash tubs, down to the pile of smelly stems. We filled both of our boxes and carried them back to the car.

Driving home, I tried to wipe my hands clean on my skirt and complained bitterly about the whole expedition. I looked at the offending boxes on the back seat and hoped we had enough tobacco stems so that we never had to come back to that filthy alley. Papa, surprised at my outburst, offered some platitude about doing things the right way; and when we got home Mama was so delighted with the haul that she brushed aside my complaints. She grasped a handful of straw, held it to her nose, and sniffed appreciatively. Just what she wanted: wonderful nesting material, no mites, and absolutely free!

One of Mama's pamphlets suggested that if the pigeon pen was unsightly it should be concealed behind a row of sunflowers. That idea intrigued Mama, but when she saw how hard it was for Papa and Mr. Stone to dig post holes in the rocky soil, she had doubts about raising sunflowers. She scooped up a trowel full of sun-bleached sand and let it trickle through her fingers. "No use in planting sunflowers in this sand," she admitted, "but maybe something else."

"Oh, sure, Mama, let's go up the hill and ask Mrs. Pope." The idea hit me all at once. "You know how good she is to me: saving sewing scraps and stuff. She likes to help people, and you should see the flowers in her backyard—and all native. She's always telling me that. Let's go ask her what to plant."

We found Mrs. Pope working in her rock garden. She pushed her straw hat back on her forehead and greeted us warmly. She already knew Mama as a neighbor, but when I explained we wanted information about native plants, she was radiant. She held up the clump of white flowers she was ready to plant. "Blackfoot daisies," she said. "A descriptive name. See the little, black foot-shaped bracts on their stems." As she eased the brown roots into a crevice between the white rocks and covered them gently with sand, she explained the dainty, little flowers were tough survivors, managing to bloom in severe droughts where nothing else survived.

She finished her task, dusted her hands on her garden apron, and led us through the gate into the backyard where flower beds ran around the sides of the yard and across the back. While Mama admired the masses of color, Mrs. Pope launched into her favorite subject, the tenacity of desert plants. "Once I get them started," she explained, "I usually just leave them on their own. Their survival instincts are amazing. Some that require water, like mariposas and rain lilies, absolutely refuse to bloom during droughts. Their roots lie dormant, maybe for years, and you can walk right over them and not suspect a thing. Even a single cloudburst will not trigger them. They wait for a wet season, and then burst into bloom."

Mama stooped to admire a wild, purple verbena. "See, it looks fragile," Mrs. Pope explained, happily. "Desert flowers always look fragile, but they have their clever tricks and they *endure;* and once you appreciate that, you begin to really love the desert."

Mama was absorbing the information, and I knew right then it was only a matter of time until our own yard went native; but for the moment we came back to the purpose of our visit. There were no secrets on Mountain Avenue, so naturally Mrs. Pope had heard the hammering in our back yard and already knew about our venture into the squab market. She agreed a hedge of flowers to conceal the pen was a lovely idea and without hesitation pointed to a clump of bright yellow flowers, a little higher than my head, next to the back fence. The blooms looked like small sunflowers, but instead of a single stalk the stem branched out forming sprays or clusters of flowers. "This is golden-eye. Grows anywhere and you'll love it," she said, as she pinched off one of the blooms, bruised it between her fingers, and held it out for us to breathe the rich, musky aroma.

Mama was delighted with the golden-eye and wanted to plant some immediately, but Mrs. Pope cautioned we'd have to wait for fall to get seeds. She could give us some or, better yet, I could go up to the foot of Sugar Loaf where there was a whole field of golden-eyes and gather the seeds myself. I remembered the spot and promised to do it.

When Papa and Mr. Stone finished work on the nesting shed and flying coop, Mama showed Mr. Stone where she wanted him to dig a trench for the golden-eye. He had some misgivings about anything growing in that hard baked soil, but Mama insisted. Digging the trench, he unearthed some good-sized boulders, that Mama set aside for a future rock garden.

After Mr. Stone finished the trench, he pointed to a clump of creosote bushes in the far corner of the yard opposite the pigeon pen. With his ax over his shoulder he said to Mama: "I can get rid of that there creosote for you, Mrs. King, so it won't bother you no more."

"Oh, no, I don't think so, just leave it." Mama had walked over to examine the corner bush more carefully.

"Sure, I can do it easy," Mr. Stone insisted. "Just chop it off and the next time I change the oil in my car I'll just pour the old oil on the stumps and on the roots. You won't have no more trouble."

Mama was touching the sticky green leaves with her fingers. "Why would I want to kill it?" she asked.

"Creosote, that's why. Don't nothing grow under creosote." Mr. Stone, aiming his ax menacingly, approached the bush. "Drops some kind of poison on the ground, killing its own young. Wherever you got creosote, you ain't got nothing else." He made ready to swing his ax at the nearest limb.

Mama held up her hand. He stopped awkwardly in the midst of his swing. "No, don't chop it down. I sort of like it."

"Smells like creosote."

"Indeed, it does, especially after a rain, a nice clean smell. I rather like it."

Mr. Stone stared at Mama, wondering if he had heard right. She leaned over the bush, examining the tiny yellow blossoms carefully. "It's a native plant and gives the yard a natural look. These little yellow blooms last all summer, and then it has those little woolly seeds. It's evergreen too, and when the leaves are covered with snow, I just love it. Not that we have much snow here."

"It'll kill everything around it."

"Well, when you think of it, it's just a survival instinct, isn't it? I mean, the soil won't support a lot of bushes close together, so it stakes out its territory, taking exactly what it needs." She was sounding like Mrs. Pope already.

Mr. Stone let his ax fall to the ground and folded his arms across his chest, looking at Mama in disbelief. She stepped back, rubbed her palms on her skirt, trying to get rid of the sticky feeling from the resinous leaves, and returned his gaze steadily. "No, don't cut the creosote," she repeated. "I like it."

Mr. Stone turned on his heel and shrugged his shoulders. The gesture seemed to indicate that out of his vast well of experience he had never before encountered a woman who liked creosote bushes. Nevertheless, Mama was the wife of the head dyer, and he, Rocky Stone, was only a loom-fixer. He sauntered back to the flying coop, muttering to himself but wanting to be heard. "I sure as hell got rid of it in my place. Took two doses of old motor oil, but it worked. I got rid of every damn bush."

By late August the nesting shed and flying coop were finished, and Mr. Mae made arrangements for Manuel, one of the Mexican mill hands, to deliver the pigeons in the mill truck. For the short drive from Piedras Street to our house Manuel stuffed the pigeons into various sized boxes and crates. In late afternoon he backed the truck into our driveway and started unloading the flock.

Edward, Becky and I stood outside the flying coop and watched the unloading of the pigeons. When the last pigeon was in, and Papa had closed and latched the gate, Edward slipped away, unnoticed. In a few minutes he was back with Prince, his black-and-white spotted puppy, on a leash. Papa, carrying water out to the pigeons, stopped Edward in the yard. "Not too near the pigeons with the dog," he warned. "Not too near. Don't scare the pigeons."

Edward held tightly to the leash, but Prince had already spotted the pigeons. He lurched with all his strength toward the pen and pointed with his right paw. "He's pointing! He's pointing!" Edward shouted with delight. "I knew it all the time. Prince is a genu-*wine* bird dog. Good old Prince!" Edward knelt beside the dog and threw his arms around its neck. "Boy, am I going to train you! A genu-*wine* bird dog."

While Manuel was unloading the pigeons, Mama stood by, pencil and notebook in hand, making a desperate effort to tally the birds as they arrived. She wanted a proper inventory, but there was too much confusion. In the end she had to give up and accept Mr. Mae's figures. On the first page of her account book, spread out on the corner of the kitchen counter, she noted: "September 5, 1925, 4:00 A.M. one hundred pigeons, fifty pairs, received." That went on the asset side of her ledger.

During the next couple of weeks two pairs of pigeons built tobacco-stem nests and laid eggs. Mama found that the nesting pairs were already banded and made the proper notations in her ledger. The days passed, and except for those two nests there was no activity in the pigeon pen. Mama took it in stride. Her *Pigeons for Profit* pamphlet assured her that pigeons often rested during the fall and winter but were "raring to go" in the spring. She quoted that phrase several times and said she was prepared to wait.

After school started, except for gathering golden-eye seeds and helping Mama plant them around the pen, I didn't pay much attention to the pigeons. Four squabs hatched in early October. Papa said instead of trying to sell just four squabs we could have them for Thanksgiving dinner ourselves and be ready to hit the market in the spring. Mama entered the selling price of the four squabs, two dollars each according to Mr. Mae, in her ledger. She had to admit that was the most expensive Thanksgiving dinner we had ever had, but even so the entry in her ledger didn't do much to balance the list of expenses, growing longer by the day.

When we sat down to Thanksgiving dinner, Becky took a look at the baked squabs and grimaced. "I just don't want to think about where they came from," she said. I was thinking the same thing, and I guess my face showed it.

Papa glowered at us from across the table. Instead of the one-sentence blessing which he usually mumbled under his breath, he cleared his throat and proclaimed:

> *Some hae meat and canna eat,*
> *And some wat eat that want it,*
> *But we hae meat, and we can eat,*
> *And sae the Lord be thankit.*

"I made a nice celery dressing," Mama said, by way of changing the subject. The cookbook said you should always make a celery dressing with squabs. But we're not going to be eating squabs often. When spring comes, we'll be selling them. We'll soon recoup our expenses and be making a nice profit. I'm looking forward to that."

7

Birthday parties were big on Mountain Avenue, almost as big as Christmas. Becky's party was scheduled for the seventh of June, her eighth birthday, and she and Gwen sat at the dining-room table, addressing the invitations. They did it geographically. Every kid on the street, unless too young or too old, was invited. The invitations came a dozen to the box, and after carefully checking the list Becky found she had one extra. She didn't want to waste it. What to do?

Mama, busy in the kitchen, overheard the discussion, stepped to the dining-room door, and suggested Becky invite Dianne Mel, "such a sweet, little thing." Mama saw Dianne down at Quinn's once in a while, and she always described her that way.

Becky balked. She sure as heck wasn't crazy enough to go down there by herself and run the risk of having to talk to that awful Mr. Printz. I was in the living room reading *Little Men*—I was still working on Alcott—but I stopped long enough to call out to Becky that I'd go with her to take the invitation, or even do it myself, because I really wanted Dianne to come. Thus reassured, Becky started working on the invitation; and I added the further information that in art class Dianne painted beautiful watercolors, especially flowers.

When Becky was ready to deliver the invitations—starting with Beverly and her two little brothers, Jack and Sonny, up in the next block—I volunteered to go along. The street seemed unusually quiet that morning, and as we approached the Bishops' house I wondered what had happened to all the action. The Bishops' front yard, a fifty-foot strip of scruffy grass, served as a football field for the boys in the neighborhood. Whenever I went to see Beverly I had to weave my way through a melee of yelling boys and yapping dogs. But this morning the yard was deserted. We silently mounted the steps and crossed the front porch. The door was closed and the window shades tightly drawn. I thought of Mrs. Bishop. She had tuberculosis, an arrested case. Could she be worse? My heart stood still at the thought. Beverly didn't like to talk about her mother's tuberculosis; but during the winter when Mrs. Bishop had a hemorrhage and had to spend several weeks in bed, I could tell that Beverly was terrified. Now, on this bright, summer morning, as I faced the closed door, I tried to stifle my fears and knocked lightly, respectful of the silence.

In a moment the door opened just a crack, and Jack and Sonny both peeked out. Jack held his finger to his lips, cautioning us not to speak. He took a quick glance up and down the deserted street before permitting us to slip stealthily into the room. He closed the door securely behind us and explained in a stage whisper: "It's the dogcatcher. I seen him over on Nations, and he's headed this way."

The room was almost dark, stifling hot, and smelled like a kennel. A number of mongrel dogs—I couldn't count how many but recognized several as neighborhood strays—were barking and milling about. As my eyes became accustomed to the dim light, I saw Mrs. Bishop sitting on the couch in her usual spot. *So she's okay,* I thought with relief. I stepped closer and saw she was very much occupied, holding Jack's little dog Boozer in her lap, and from time to time leaning forward to pet Don, Sonny's big collie, curled at her feet.

Jack divided his attention between keeping vigil at the window and trying to comfort the restless dogs. "Quiet, now, Poochy. That old dogcatcher ain't gonna get you. No he ain't." He stroked a brown Airedale soothingly, while he peeked under the shade and looked down the deserted street. Sonny, a year or two younger than Jack and proud to be assisting in this worthwhile project, peeked out the other window and kept repeating in a horrified tone that the dogcatcher would actually kill the dogs if he got half a chance.

Beverly had not heard us enter. Now, she brought a pan of water for the dogs and tried to find a clear space in the crowded room to set it down. As she pushed a chair aside, she greeted us cheerfully but made no apology for the turmoil. Somewhat surprised at her nonchalance, I realized she accepted the situation as nothing unusual. It was, after all, just an ordinary day at the Bishops'.

A shaggy, white dog had escaped into the kitchen. Maria, the Mexican woman who worked for the Bishops, stopped ironing long enough to bring him back into the living room. Stroking him gently in an effort to soothe him, she noticed several burrs matted in his long hair. She knelt down and with nimble fingers untangled one and held it up for us to see. "Ah, ha, *mala mujer*," she exclaimed triumphantly. Beverly asked her what she meant by *mala mujer*. After a lot of repetition and body language, we made it out: Mexicans called the burrs mala mujer because like a bad woman they cling too tightly. Maria smiled approval when we understood, and continued working on the ensnarled burrs.

Jack, from his station at the window, signaled for quiet. The dogcatcher was on the street. I stood on tiptoe to look through the little windows at the top of the door and saw a truck marked "Animal Control" parked at the curb. A small man in a green uniform got out and walked up and down the sidewalk. He carried a long pole with a net on one end, as he searched between the houses and even underneath in the crawl spaces. Up one side of the street and down the other, he found nothing. He got back in the truck but stuck his head out and continued to gaze up and down the empty street, apparently unable to believe his eyes: not a single dog on Mountain Avenue. Finally, he gave up and drove slowly up the street. Jack saw the empty wire cages on the back of the truck and was jubilant. "Ha, ha, he didn't catch a one—not one dog," he chuckled. "How do you like that, Old Lady McCabe? She's the one that done it. I know she done it. Every time she sees Boozer or Don on her stupid old grass, she calls the dogcatcher. Ha, ha for you, Old Lady McCabe. I guess we fooled you, all right."

I wasn't sure that Mrs. McCabe had called the dogcatcher, but, knowing her, I thought it was likely. Even though she knew Beverly and I were best friends, when she stopped by our house to chat with Mama, she always managed a few scornful remarks about the Bishops. "Mrs. Bishop lets those kids do absolutely anything they want," she liked to repeat. "Of course, she's got TB, and I'm sorry about that, but sometimes I think she just uses it for an excuse. Never a cross word to those kids. She told me so herself. She's afraid she won't live to raise them, and if she dies, she wants them to have only happy memories of her. So, she never corrects them. Never. Can you imagine that?"

Mama said she couldn't think of a sadder thing than a mother being afraid she wouldn't live to raise her children. This response caused Mrs. McCabe to purse her lips, rock a little more violently, and repeat the admonition. "Mark my words: no good will come of it. 'Spare the rod and spoil the child.' That's in the Bible, and it's good enough for me."

In the Bishops' crowded living room, I thought it was lucky Mrs. McCabe didn't know what really went on at the Bishops'. Jack and Sonny continued to berate Mrs. McCabe, and Mrs. Bishop, still sitting on the couch, was not at all upset with the morning's events. In fact, she seemed unusually cheerful as she murmured something about being kind to animals and smiled indulgently at her boys.

When the dogcatcher's truck was well out of sight, Jack opened the door and released the dogs, admonishing them to stick around and not chase the truck. Things having quieted down, Becky delivered the party invitation to Beverly, who of course already knew about the party and said she and her brothers would love to come.

Becky and Gwen spent most of the day delivering the other invitations. Gwen had gone home and the sun was already behind Mount Franklin when Becky and I got around to delivering Dianne's invitation. Dianne herself answered the door, so we were spared a conversation with Mr. Printz. Dianne seemed a little taken aback at our friendliness but after consulting with Mr. Printz and her mother, she said she'd love to come.

The party was the best one ever given on Mountain Avenue. Everybody said so. Mama had put all the extra leaves in the dining-room table, but, even so, her linen tablecloth hung well down over the sides. I loved that snowy white tablecloth with its embossed chrysanthemum design and perfect hemstitching. Every time she used it Mama reminded us that it was a wedding present from one of Papa's rich relatives back in Georgia. Even here in El Paso, in real life, the pure linen cloth sort of set us apart. Nobody else in the neighborhood had anything so festive.

Another elegant touch for the party was the sterling spoons, part of Mama's set of Chantilly silver, also a wedding present. Mama was proud of that silver. When I helped her polish it, using an old tooth-brush to rub the polish into the delicate curves, she never failed to remind me that it was real silver, sterling and not plated like the Rogers silver Mrs. Williamson and some of the other neighbors bragged about owning. It was always a source of great annoyance to Mama that some people didn't understand the difference between *sterling* and *plate*—or at least pretended they didn't.

Mama strung streamers of pink crepe paper from the chande-lier to the sides of the birthday table, like a garden-party canopy; and the big, white, coconut cake with pink candles served as a cen-terpiece. Mama made the cake herself. In fact, her birthday cakes were so famous that she often made them for other kids in the neighborhood; and I couldn't count all the cakes she donated to the Wednesday night suppers and ice-cream socials the church was always putting on to raise money for the stained-glass window fund.

Mama's secret about cake making—and she did keep it secret—was the way she creamed the Snowdrift and sugar. She would mea-sure it into her crockery bowl, a big yellow bowl with a double blue stripe around the rim, and take it out to her favorite rocking chair on the front porch. Comfortably rocking, the bowl cradled in her arm and resting on her apron-covered lap, she creamed the mixture with a big spoon according to her cookbook instructions: for fifteen minutes or until exhausted, whichever came first. For Mama, the exhaustion never came first. It was always fifteen minutes, or, if a neighbor dropped by to visit a while, the minutes flew by uncounted, and the mixture got so creamy it was light enough to float right out of the bowl. The resulting cake was so tender it would melt in your mouth. I never knew anyone else who could make such a cake. When the electric mixer was invented, and later even cake mixes, the hand skill was lost, but the cakes were never quite the same.

Along with the cake we had ice cream—all you wanted. This was a rare treat since standard birthday party fare was the birthday cake along with a bowl of red Jello and a dab of whipped cream, or, in the winter, a cup of hot chocolate fancied up with a floating marshmallow.

The first thing at the party was opening the presents. One of the best was from Mama and Papa, a framed poem by Ella Wheeler Wilcox:

> Laugh, and the world laughs with you;
> Weep, and you weep alone.
> This old earth has need of your mirth;
> It has sorrows enough of its own.

Funny pictures of laughing children were scattered around the margins of the written words, and just looking at it made you laugh. Becky said she would hang it in our bedroom over the bed so she and I could wake up with a laugh. In addition to presents from the guests, Becky got five dollars from Uncle Baxter, Mama's brother who was a lawyer in Atlanta. He always sent money on our birthdays, and we used it for school clothes. There were also packages from Aunt Mary Frances and Aunt Louise, Mama's sisters back in Georgia. I didn't know them, but I was especially interested in anything from Aunt Mary Frances, because I was her namesake. This time she had sent a Japanese parasol made of a sort of crinkly red waxy paper with a bamboo handle. All the kids were getting Japanese parasols that summer, and Becky was delighted. The present from Aunt Louise was a crocheted purse with a long strap for carrying. Becky put it over her wrist and walked around the room, trying it out.

At Mama's suggestion I gave Becky a harmonica, a gift I was to regret before the summer was over. She mastered "Dixie"—at least she claimed it was "Dixie"—and insisted anybody with proper respect for the South should stand when she played it. That brought on a lot of argument, and in the end little Edward was her only convert.

After the presents came the games: prizes for carrying black-eyed peas on a knife from the kitchen door around the birthday table and for spinning around blindfolded and pinning a flower in the basket. Becky had wanted to have pinning the tail on the donkey, but after many efforts we couldn't draw a recognizable donkey so she settled for pinning flowers in a basket, which we drew easily. Then, of course, we did musical chairs. I operated the Victrola, using the record, "It Ain't Gonna Rain No More."

After the party was over and the other guests had gone—everybody remembering to say thank you—Gwen stayed a while so that she and Becky could review the presents. They focused on the quarter the Greer children had brought. Mrs. Greer didn't have time to go shopping so she had wrapped the quarter in a series of boxes which Becky had to open until she finally reached the quarter wrapped in red tissue paper. Holding the quarter in her hand, Becky had a wonderful idea. "Hey, Gwen, just what we need to go shopping by ourselves," she exclaimed. "We can buy a Kewpie doll to sew for."

Gwen agreed. It was uncanny how they always seemed to be thinking along the same lines. "We'll take the streetcar by ourselves and go to Kress and buy a doll to sew for. That's the two main things we meant to do this summer: ride the streetcar to town by ourselves and learn to sew."

The expedition was planned for the next day.

For Becky and Gwen, as for all the children of Mountain Avenue, that first trip to town on the streetcar, unaccompanied by an adult, marked a significant change of status, in classic literature described as *rite de passage*.

Confidently they boarded the streetcar, chose one of the

maroon-colored wooden benches, together grappled with the window latch, and—although the car was already breezy enough—managed to push the window to its maximum height. By the time they were settled on the slick bench, the almost-empty car had left Fort Boulevard and was swinging downhill on Copia.

The motorman, enjoying the lull in the midday traffic, picked up speed as he rounded the curves. He clanged the bell at every cross street just for the fun of it, whether a car was in sight or not. Overhead, leather straps—a welcome anchor for straphangers during rush hour but useless for seated passengers—swung crazily from side to side in rhythm with the swaying car. Becky and Gwen, their feet dangling in midair inches from the floor, often grabbed the back of the bench ahead to keep from sliding sideways into the aisle. On one especially sharp curve, just before Five Points, the iron wheels screeched harshly against the steel rails and the overhead trolley jumped the electric cable, sending sparks far and wide. The motorman, accustomed to the nuisance, got out, walked to the back of the car and manipulated the pulley back onto the cable.

After Five Points the traffic was heavier, and the streetcar continued at a more sedate pace until it finally slowed to a stop at San Jacinto Plaza, the very center of town.

The journey itself consumed less than thirty minutes. From the time the girls boarded the almost empty streetcar at the familiar Fort Boulevard corner until the moment they made their way with a score of other passengers out the exit door at the final stop, they had traveled more than geographic miles. They had escaped, albeit temporarily, both parental authority and the friendly confines of Mountain Avenue. They paused a moment on the shady sidewalk to relish their independence, their first plunge into the grownup world of unlimited horizons.

The departure from home earlier that day had been difficult. We weren't a hugging and kissing family, but separations were always painful for Mama. Gwen had come for an early lunch, a nourishing repast that Mama had prepared especially to sustain the young shoppers through their adventure. While they were eating Mama hovered nervously over Becky, smoothed her short, blond hair, and checked the crocheted bag to be sure she had the right money.

Even when they finished lunch and were trying to get away,

Mama and I followed them out on the porch, and she repeated all her warnings about being careful on the streetcar and getting off at the right corner. Then there was a discussion about how to make the best use of the Japanese parasol. It was decided that Gwen, being taller, should carry it. Becky, at least a couple of inches shorter, would stand close enough to partake of the small spot of shade the parasol afforded. This arranged, they set out.

Mama and I stood on our sidewalk to watch them as far as the corner. Gwen held the parasol over her shoulder at a jaunty angle, so that I could just see the two of them from the waist down, and the sight stuck in my memory. Gwen's dress made of blue gingham was, as usual, too long, hitting her mid-calf. Mrs. Heaslip, sewing Gwen's dresses, always allowed "two inches to grow," a challenge Gwen never quite caught up with. On the other hand, Becky's blue chambray sundress left over from last summer was, in spite of the let-out hem, far too short. It hit her well above her knees, and at each step the crochet bag which she carried on her outside arm flopped against her bare legs.

Once they were out of sight Mama and I went back inside, and with an eye on the mantel clock Mama began counting time. Five minutes to the car line, she figured, and thirty minutes to town, the walk to Kress, and so on. They should be back at two-thirty at the latest. I reminded her to add some time for the Dr. Peppers. Becky was furnishing carfare, and Gwen had brought a dime for a treat: Dr. Peppers at Warner's Drug Store.

Mama conceded an extra twenty minutes for the drinks but regretted that Gwen had added that unnecessary complication. Getting the doll was enough, she felt, and they should have been satisfied with that. She busied herself washing the lunch dishes but couldn't seem to find anything else to do. The more she fretted, the more the time dragged. It was going to be a long afternoon.

About two o'clock I was so exhausted by Mama's nervousness that I volunteered to go down to the corner and sit on the barbershop bench and look toward the Fort Boulevard car stop. When I saw the girls get off the car, I would dash up the hill and tell Mama.

Sitting on the green bench—rather on the back of the bench with my feet on the seat so I could get a better view of the car stop—I had a long wait. Streetcars passed without stopping, and minutes seemed like hours. I tried to amuse myself watching customers going in and out of Quinn's. Mr. Wilson came out of the barbershop and sat on the other end of the bench. He knocked his pipe against the bench, dumped out the ashes, and allowed that everything would turn out all right. The afternoon was still young, only three-fifteen, he remarked calmly.

I had begun to grow nervous myself, and I resented his nonchalance and didn't answer. Finally, it was almost four o'clock, and a streetcar stopped. I stood up on the bench for a better view. Even at that distance there was no mistaking the red parasol, the long and short skirts, and the dangling white handbag. I raced up the hill to tell Mama, and in a few minutes the girls themselves walked in.

They were exhausted. Gwen closed the parasol and without speaking tossed it on the couch. Becky, also silent, threw the bag and several packages down next to it. Together, they headed for the kitchen and long drinks of water.

Now that Mama's fears were stilled, she tried to appear casual, but the girls' monosyllabic answers were certainly provoking. No, they had not gotten lost. Yes, they had bought the Kewpie. In fact they had two Kewpies. As proof, Becky unwrapped two packages and displayed the dolls in all their pink nakedness. The trouble had started—she paused deliberately to catch her breath, or maybe just for effect—the trouble started when they went to Warner's soda fountain for their Dr. Peppers. They were sitting on the stools, waiting to order, when they noticed a big Dr. Pepper ad at the back of the counter with the words: Drink Dr. Pepper at Ten, Two, and Four o'clock, the same ad we had all seen in magazines. Well, they had just read the ad when Gwen looked at a clock right next to the ad and noticed it was only half-past one. She whispered to Becky that people would think they were crazy, coming in there thirty minutes early to get Dr. Peppers, so they just slipped away from the counter and went over to the plaza to wait until two o'clock.

They spent some time looking at the alligators in the pond, and they read the plaque about some explorer named Juan or something like that planting a garden in San Jacinto Plaza, probably the oldest garden in America. Then Gwen figured it was almost two o'clock and time to go get the Dr. Peppers.

"Surely it didn't take two hours to drink a Dr. Pepper," Mama suggested rather crossly, trying to get Becky beyond the soda fountain scene.

"Oh, that was okay," Becky said, wearily. "After we left Warner's we went back to the plaza and sat on the bench to wait for our streetcar. Sitting on the bench, I put my hand in this stupid bag, and guess what? No carfare!" Now, telling about it, she held up the bag and poked a finger through one of the crochet loops. "A purse full of holes!" she exclaimed indignantly. "What could be dumber?"

"No carfare? You lost your carfare?" Mama echoed faintly.

Becky, too exhausted to go on, leaned back on the sofa, and let Gwen summarize: "Well," she said, "a Fort Bliss streetcar stopped, but without money we couldn't get on. When the car pulled away, we both started crying. We thought about walking home, but it was at least five miles and we didn't know the way, so we just sat there and cried. After a while a lady passed in a hurry. She was about to get on a car herself, when she took a second look at us and stopped to ask what was the matter. We told her we'd lost our carfare, she gave us a dime and rushed to her car before we could even thank her."

"Oh, so then you came on home," Mama sighed with relief.

"Well, not right away," Gwen continued. "While we were drying our eyes a man came by and asked what happened. I started to tell him that we had lost our carfare, and before I could finish about the lady giving us the dime, he just handed Becky a silver dollar. I think he said, 'I wish my troubles were so simple,' or something like that, and went on."

"So then you came on home?" Mama prompted.

"Gosh, no, Mama!" Becky was now revived and irritated at Mama's persistence. "I hope you don't think we're that stupid. There we were downtown with all this money plus carfare, so naturally we went back to Kress and shopped."

Mama just looked at her, and she explained by reaching for the other sack and opening it. "Well, we had the one Kewpie, so we bought another." She held the second Kewpie aloft. "Now we each have one to sew for. We'll play like they're twins."

"Oh," Mama said, "and what's that?" She pointed to another

package.

"Well, we even had enough money to buy us each a pencil box." Becky pulled two bright red pencil boxes out of the sack and displayed them. "See, with drawers for pencils, erasers and rulers, and even a collapsible drinking cup."

Mama, remembering her anxiety during the long afternoon, tried to show some disapproval but couldn't seem to find the words. She did explain about the Dr.Pepper ad: "You can buy Dr. Pepper anytime. All you need is a nickel."

"Any time? Not just when the ad says?" Becky and Gwen looked at Mama and, realizing their mistake, broke into gales of laughter.

Gwen gathered up her things to leave, and Mama followed her to the door. "Your mother often says she worries about you having more sense than you need, Gwen. I see what she means. Dr. Pepper at Ten, Two and Four. Who else would have thought of it?"

8

It was the third morning of "learning to sew." Becky and Gwen sat side by side on the top porch step, casting occasional baleful glances at the Kewpies, naked as the day they came from the factory. The clutter on the floor resembled debris scattered by a desert sandstorm: scraps of pink chambray, bits of lace, several spools of thread, scissors, a red strawberry-shaped pin cushion only slightly ripped, and even two small thimbles—discarded as utterly useless, over Mama's bitter protest.

Becky paused in her attempt to thread her needle. "You'd never guess just by looking at a Kewpie how fat it really is," she complained.

Slouched in a rocker behind the Virginia creeper, I sighed aloud, echoing her frustration. I was supposed to be embroidering a table scarf—Mama's idea of a useful summer project for me—but it was hard to concentrate on the tedious task. The pattern Mama had selected was a basket of flowers on a white linen cloth. The wicker basket made of brown cross-stitch had come out all right, and I was moderately pleased with my daisy petals, but even by the most lax of standards I had to admit my flower centers, clusters of tiny French knots, were just awful. I held my work at arm's length and wondered if I could pull out the French knots one more time without ruining the whole thing.

Except for the buzzing of bees around the tiny white blossoms on the Virginia creeper, silence fell over our little group. Witty, lost in cat dreams, snoozed in the chair beside me. I let my work fall idly to my lap and wished something, just anything, would happen to break the monotony of the morning.

A few doors down the street, Edward emerged from his front porch. The motion attracted my eye, and out of sheer boredom I watched him start up the hill. The concrete walk, glaring white under the morning sun, was already hot as a stove top, and Edward's bare feet, so lately confined to school shoes, were still tender. Every few steps he jumped off the pavement and stood on the Bermuda grass parkway long enough to cool the soles of his feet. So handicapped, his progress was erratic, but he finally made it to our house and turned in our walk.

For the first time I noticed that he carried a closed shoe box under one arm and a deck of cards in his other hand. Below our steps he balanced first on one foot and then the other and greeted us. But the pavement was burning his feet, and, without waiting for a response, he bolted up the steps, jumped over the dolls and sewing scraps, and seated himself cross-legged on the concrete floor. Becky and Gwen looked up from their sewing and acknowledged his presence grudgingly. Undaunted, he deposited his covered shoe box next to the Kewpies, opened his deck of cards and started shuffling.

After a moment he took a closer look at the naked dolls, and the situation suddenly dawned on him. "My gosh!" he exclaimed. "What are you doing with them there dolls? You're too big to play dolls."

Becky, her needle poised for another stab at the pink chambray skirt she was trying to gather, leveled her gray eyes at Edward. "Well, for your information, Edward Williamson, we are not playing dolls. It just happens we are learning to sew."

"How come you got them dolls, if you ain't playing dolls?"

Gwen echoed Becky's disdain, "We are not playing with 'them dolls.' They are celluloid dolls, otherwise known as Kewpies, and we are using them for models. Did you ever hear of a model? Well, we are sewing for models. Learning to sew is part of our summer agenda." Gwen loved new words and found many uses for "agenda," her latest discovery.

Edward leaned down to get a closer look at the naked dolls. He squinted owlishly through his round glasses and concluded: "They sure are fat."

Neither Becky nor Gwen chose to argue the obvious. Edward continued to shuffle his cards. "I brung my Old Maid cards. We could play."

When this suggestion brought no response, Edward noticed Witty sleeping in the rocker and tried another approach. "Witty sure has gotten big," he said. "He's pretty, too. Black as coal. Becky, I bet that girl that gave him to you sure would be surprised to see him now."

Becky was always willing to talk about Witty. "Yeah, Witty has grown a lot. That girl was named Annie Laurie. She moved out to Austin Terrace and goes to El Paso School for Girls, and we don't see her anymore. She didn't get well of TB, but her case is arrested."

"Arrested! Is she in jail?" Edward thought he had finally hit on something interesting.

"Oh, not that way. Of course she's not in jail." Gwen hastened to set him straight.

"Well, she sure must have done something real bad to get herself arrested."

"Arrested means—well, she still has TB but she isn't sick any more, at least not right now." Gwen started to explain but interrupted herself when she noticed the holes punched in the top of Edward's shoe box. "What's in that box?"

"Just Horny, my pet horned toad." Edward opened the lid and shoved the box in Gwen's face. She glanced at the mottled brown creature covered with sharp horns and pulled back in disgust. "Get that ugly thing out of my face," she exclaimed. "I've already seen him plenty of times, and I don't like him. You had him so long, I thought maybe he died."

"No, Horny ain't dead. He's doing fine." Edward reassured himself by peeking into the box.

"What do you feed him?" Becky asked, only mildly interested.

"Well, that's the trouble. He don't eat nothing but live ants—big live ants—that's what he likes. But I'm not going to get stung to death trying to catch live ants. I give him dead ants sometimes, but he don't much like them."

"Seems like he might starve to death," Gwen suggested. "Why don't you just take him back to the desert where you found him?"

"I ain't letting Horny go," Edward said. "I guess I already saved his life. You just don't know what could've happened to him. The day I caught him, Daddy and I were hiking up in McKelligon Canyon, and we saw a roadrunner—you know them long-necked birds that run so fast, their tails sticking straight up?" Edward held up his hand, fingers extended, in imitation of a roadrunner's tail. "Well, what happened, we saw a roadrunner catch a horny toad. The roadrunner just held the horny toad in its long beak, ran over to a rock and knocked the horny toad—"

"Don't tell us that again, Edward. We already heard it a hundred times, I guess." Gwen bit her sewing thread angrily.

"And it knocked the horny toad's head against a rock. Killed it right there." Edward finished stubbornly and with a last affectionate glance closed Horny's box.

A dead silence followed; but in a moment Edward noticed the old automobile tire at the bottom of the steps. "Becky," he said hopefully, "we could roll tires. We ain't rolled tires in a long time." He let his eyes wander wistfully to the big school ground across the street. During the spring he and Becky had spent many hours rolling their tires around the block. Sometimes when they reached the uphill corner on Mountain Avenue they curled up inside the tires and somersaulted down hill as long as they could keep their balance.

Becky glanced at the tire but brushed off the suggestion. It was too hot, and, besides, Gwen didn't like to roll tires.

Edward sighed. "Sure is going to be a boring summer."

Becky was tired of the subject. "My gosh, Edward, you don't have to just sit around like a dummy all summer and complain. Do you want to sew? Mama will get you a needle."

"Boys don't sew."

"Men do. They call them tailors."

"Yeah, but not for a big, fat salad oil doll."

Gwen bristled. "Oh, Edward, I didn't say 'salad oil.' I said cel-lu-loid. You are the dumbest—salad oil doll!"

"Well, I ain't sewing for no fat doll—whatever you call it."

Gwen, after several dismal failures, had finally finished gathering the doll's skirt. She knotted her thread and held the finished product up to one of the Kewpies. Although she tried hard to stretch the gathers over the Kewpie's ample waist, she could not make it fit. Disgusted, she put the Kewpie down and held the gathered chambray in her hand.

At that moment Witty, bored with the morning's activities, slipped off the rocker, stretched himself, and wandered over to examine the pink Kewpies. Impulsively, Gwen plopped the pink chambray skirt on Witty's black head. "Look, Becky, look!" she cried. "Witty has a boudoir cap."

Fortunately, we had a new interruption. Edward heard it first: from down the hill the unmistakable sound of horse hooves and the grinding of heavy wagon wheels on asphalt. "Hey, maneuvers," he exclaimed. "The army's on maneuvers! Let's go!"

We all knew that sound and needed no urging. In a flash we abandoned our sewing and ran out to the curbing. The dusty cloud, approaching slowly, was just a couple of blocks away. "It sure is good living here," Edward said. "Almost every month we get to watch a parade right on our own street. I sure do love maneuvers."

The neighbors shared Edward's enthusiasm. Several neighborhood kids and even some grown-ups had come out to watch. We stood on the curbing, just the right height to give us a good view. First, flags flying, came officers on horseback, the big black and gold First Cavalry Division insignia on their shoulders; the the horse-drawn two-wheeled caissons followed, and finally the heavy wagons loaded with hay, four mules pulling each wagon, two soldiers on the front seat and two more standing on the little step behind.

Robert Earle and Raymond were watching from the Martins' yard. Raymond called out to the soldiers: "Hey, if you'd leave the hay at home, you wouldn't need to take all those mules."

Robert Earle completed the other half of the joke: "Or leave the mules at home, and you wouldn't need to haul all that hay."

There was a delay up ahead, and the line halted. A wagon in front of us, marked "Fort Bliss Cavalry," stopped. "I think I'll sing for them," Edward announced, and without further warning broke into "Onward Christian Soldiers."

"Oh, Edward, don't do that," Gwen ordered. "This is just Fort Bliss on maneuvers. They aren't Christian soldiers."

"They are, too," Edward insisted. "It says so on the wagon. C-A-V-A-L-R-Y. We had that same word at Sunday school. I read it in the song book—Cross of Cavalry."

"That's not what it says," Gwen insisted.

"I guess I go to Sunday School just as much as you; and you don't know everything." Edward had suffered enough corrections for one day, and this time he realized Gwen wasn't quite sure of her ground. "I can sing if I want to." He began the objectionable song again.

"For heck sake, Edward, will you please shut up?" Gwen asked angrily. "Just stop that crazy singing. That's not the right word."

Edward's childish treble rang out clearly:

> Onward, Christian soldiers,
> Marching as to war,
> With the cross of Jesus
> Going on before.

The soldiers on the wagon laughed and even clapped. Gwen said to Becky, "I think its simply embarrassing. I feel like a fool just standing by him."

Becky agreed, and the two girls went to join Robert Earle and Raymond on the Martins' curbing, leaving me alone with Edward.

Edward was now into the second verse. I was not embarrassed because I thought it was funny. I only wished Mama could hear him. She used to laugh so when she took us to the park and he asked for "them bums," but there was no time to call her. There was a shout ahead, the soldiers honored Edward with a farewell salute and moved on.

We watched until the last wagon reached the top of the hill, turned left, and circled around the foot of the mountain. Even when we couldn't actually see the wagons any more, a cloud of dust marked their progress up Scenic Drive.

"We sure are lucky," Edward said, for the second time that morning. "Just think: a parade right on our own street."

I thought so, too. For the moment, at least, we had all forgotten about naked Kewpies and even French knots.

9

If anyone on Mountain Avenue had owned a flag, it would have been lowered to half mast that day.

Becky and I slept in the front bedroom, and I was awakened that morning as usual by Witty crying at the screen door to get out. Becky, in the bed beside me, stirred a little, and I heard Papa open the door for Witty and go back to the kitchen where Mama was wrapping his lunch. I yawned, took a final stretch, and was just about to get up, when the single shot rang out, shattering the morning stillness. I sat bolt upright, frozen with the horrible premonition that something awful had happened to Witty.

At the sound of the shot, Mama and Papa ran out to the front porch. Becky and I, both wide awake now, bounded out of bed and rushed after them. We demanded to know what happened, but Mama, her open hands pressed against her heart, ignored us and gazed apprehensively towards the corner, the direction of the shot.

Papa, in spite of Mama's plea to be cautious, had already started down the hill to investigate.

Once he disappeared around the corner, Becky and I, barefoot and shivering in our thin summer nightgowns, searched Mama's face for reassurance—surely she didn't think something had happened to Witty? She did her best to appear calm. Probably somebody cleaning a gun, she suggested, or maybe shooting at a rattlesnake. Her voice lacked conviction, but it didn't matter. Already, Papa was coming back up the hill, almost running, and even at that distance something about him telegraphed disaster. By the time he reached our yard, I could see he was furious. Red in the face and clenching his fists, he gasped: "That bastard Printz shot Witty! Killed him!"

I cried out in horror, and Becky's face went dead white. Her eyes filled with tears, and she placed both hands over her face, sobbing that it couldn't be true. She would go see for herself. Maybe Witty wasn't really dead. She could take him to a doctor. She tried to free herself from Mama's embrace; but Mama held her close and started asking more rational questions: How did Papa know for sure it was Mr. Printz?

Simple enough, Papa said grimly. A trail of blood led from the summerhouse where Witty had been shot out to the gutter where Mr. Printz had dragged him. In fact, when Papa got down there, Mr. Printz was still standing on his front steps, holding his pistol, and he didn't try to deny it. Papa had called him a crazy bastard, and he just said it was his property and he wouldn't allow trespassing.

As Papa finished this brief account, he looked at Becky's pathetic little face and her big gray eyes imploring him to say it wasn't true, and his rage at Mr. Printz gave way to sympathy for Becky. He asked Mama to find a box so he could go get poor Witty out of the gutter and bring him home. When she brought the box, he wouldn't let Becky and me go with him, so we just stood there next to Mama, watching the corner and not talking much, until he came back up the hill. He was walking slowly this time, holding the box tenderly in his arms. After a low-voiced discussion about a suitable spot for the grave, Mama suggested the aster bed around at the side of the house where it wasn't too hard to dig. While Papa worked on the little grave, he said he didn't even care if he was late for work. He would just tell Mr. Mae the ox was in the ditch—and that was a fact.

The neighborhood grapevine, efficient as the modern day hotline, crackled into action; and the response was immediate. Mrs. Williamson had heard the shot, and she was the first on the scene, bringing the still sleepy-eyed Edward with her. She hugged Becky, urged her to stop crying, and immediately launched into a diatribe against Mr. Printz. She guessed this proved once and for all that the things she had been saying about him were true. Now everybody could see that he was worse than mean. He was cruel, that's what, just plain cruel. God help that poor woman who had married him and her daughter too, whatever her name was.

Mama managed to break into the monologue to defend Dianne and her mother. Certainly they had nothing to do with it and should not be blamed, she said. At the mention of Dianne's name, I felt a new surge of grief. It was going to be hard on her, just when she had come to Becky's party and was trying to be friendly.

After Mrs. Williamson had finished her tirade—most of it quite justified in my eyes—she went home, leaving the tousle-haired Edward sitting on the porch with Becky and me. Edward was thoroughly awake now, and once he grasped the situation his first impulse was to think of a punishment suitable for Mr. Printz. Being a Tom Mix fan, he had plenty of ideas. We should tie a rope around Mr. Printz's waist and let a wild horse drag him across the desert. Edward rocked his chair silently a moment, relishing this gruesome scene, but then his eye fell on sewing scraps on the floor, left over from yesterday's project, and he abandoned his efforts to be manly. Openly wiping his tears on the short sleeves of his khaki coveralls, he lamented: "Just think, only yesterday we were sitting on this very porch with Witty, and now he's gone."

It wasn't long until Gwen arrived. I don't know who told her, but she had made the run down the hill in record time and, without waiting to catch her breath, demanded to know the details. We were more than willing to tell her. Talking at the same time and interrupting each other, we poured out the story, starting with the single shot we had heard from our bedroom and ending with the grave under the blue asters.

Naturally she wanted to see the grave, so we all went around to the side yard and stood silently by while she stared at the mound of fresh dirt and tried to comprehend the dreadful reality. Mama came out, glanced at our woebegone faces, and suggested we decorate the grave with flowers from the yard. We could pick anything we wanted.

The physical activity was welcome. We started by laying flat sprays of pungent-smelling creosote leaves over the fresh-dug soil. We let the little yellow flowers show, but covered the sticky leaves with tiny, white daisies and sprigs of wild purple verbena from Mama's rock garden. The verbena had a spicy aroma, and the purple and white colors, spotted here and there with the tiny yellow creosote blossoms, made a beautiful canopy. Edward thought of framing it all with little, white rocks which were easy to find in the backyard. We picked up enough rocks to encircle the flowers, and when we were finished, the whole thing looked like a valentine edged in white lace.

We all felt better just looking at the beautiful memorial we had made for poor Witty. Best of all, the work had diverted us, and the long morning was finally over.

It was early afternoon when Mrs. Riddel came. The Riddels—he was an army captain—lived up the hill in the house above Kerry Quinn's. Their only son, Oscar, was a senior in high school and didn't play in the neighborhood very much. Mrs. Riddel was the member of the family everybody knew. A large, florid-faced woman with a booming voice, she always dressed in long, billowing, black skirts, designed to hide a club foot. Although her club foot was thus concealed, she made sure that everyone was aware of the deformity. If she happened to meet a stranger—a new postman, for instance—on the sidewalk, her greeting was: "Don't stare at deformity. Just say to yourself, 'there but for the grace of God, go I.'"

The startled stranger, having stepped off the walk to make room for Mrs. Riddel's ample bulk, would then step back on the pavement and glance over his shoulder to peek at the deformity that he had originally missed.

Mrs. Riddel had two passions: gambling at The Tivoli in Juarez and raising canaries. Every Saturday night she and Captain Riddel took Oscar with them and went to The Tivoli. Rumor had it that

Mrs. Riddel had money of her own, and we all hoped it was true. Certainly a captain's salary could not have paid for the losses, and all of us who attended Sunday School regularly were convinced gamblers have tremendous losses—they never win.

The magnitude of the Riddels' gambling losses was pure speculation, but we knew firsthand about the canaries. Mrs. Riddel had six or eight canaries in cages in her sunny sleeping porch. She liked for Becky and me to come in to see them and hear them sing. Sometimes the canaries' eggs hatched, and she sold the young birds.

Becky and I, sitting on the porch after lunch, were first aware of Mrs. Ridell's approach when we heard her call out the usual admonishment about staring at deformity to Robert Earle and Raymond who were working on their bikes in the Martins' yard. The boys were accustomed to Mrs. Riddel's warnings and merely muttered a polite "Yes, ma'am," hardly glancing at her. At that point she came limping up our walk. Her black skirt was blowing in the wind, and with both hands she clutched a bamboo bird cage containing a frightened canary. So encumbered, she had some difficulty negotiating our steps, but before we could get up to help her—and she really didn't like to be helped—she managed to gain the front porch. Puffing audibly from her exertions, she greeted Becky and thrust the bird cage at her: "I heard all about it. This is Peepsie. Take care of him."

Becky gasped, trying to find words to express her delight. Joyfully, actually smiling for the first time that day, she took Mrs. Riddel out to the sleeping porch to select a suitable place to hang Peepsie's cage. Mrs. Riddel ordered Becky to get a pencil and paper and write down Peepsie's diet: "seeds, grit, lettuce leaf." Becky wrote diligently. When she had finished she looked up. "Should I put a blanket over his cage at night?" she asked.

"Would you want someone to throw a blanket over you?" Mrs. Riddel retorted.

Becky apologized. "I think I heard that somewhere."

"Don't believe all you hear, my dear. I suppose you'll have Mr. Printz in court?" This last question was directed at Mama.

"I don't know," Mama ventured. "After all, Witty was in Mr. Printz's summerhouse."

"Hurumph!" answered Mrs.Riddel. "Well, take care of Peepsie," and she was gone.

Later in the day Becky received another gift, or at least the promise of one. Mrs. Wood lived across the alley directly behind our house, and her big yellow cat had given birth to six kittens. She invited Becky over to choose one for herself. For the second time that afternoon, Becky's spirits soared. She asked me to go with her to make the choice. The kittens were all so cute that Becky had a hard time deciding, but she finally picked out a yellow and white striped one. Mrs. Wood said it was too little to leave its mother, but Becky could come over every day and get acquainted with it and in a week or two take it home.

Going home across the alley Becky told me she had decided to name the kitten Pity. "Sort of short for Pretty," she said. "Of course no cat will ever take the place of dear Witty, but Pity will be nice in his own way."

All winter, while the pigeons enjoyed their rest, Mama studied her pamphlets, particularly the one entitled *Pigeon-Breeder for Profit.* Spring came, and she was in no mood for excuses. She often stood at the kitchen door, the pamphlet open in her hand, and stared at the flying coop, hoping to spot raring-to-go activity.

The leg bands Mrs. Mae had given Mama were spread on the kitchen counter. Mama checked them again and was troubled because the lowest number was eleven. "Was it possible," she asked aloud, "that Mrs. Mae had owned the flock for a whole year and banded only ten pairs?" Becky and I, having breakfast at the kitchen table, heard the question, but had no answer.

Mama addressed us directly: "Now, girls, both of you, watch for treaders. You are doing that, aren't you? You are watching for treaders?" The situation was becoming desperate, and she was no longer coy about using that word.

Becky and I stirred the crisp bacon and black-eyed peas into our buttered grits, savored the steamy aroma, and stuffed our mouths appreciatively before assuring Mama with silent nods that yes, indeed, we were watching for treaders.

Daily, Mama went out to the flying pen, pushed tobacco stems into tempting piles, and *willed* the pigeons to start nesting. All through the spring when I was absorbed with my schoolwork Becky surprised me with her continued interest in the flock. Every day, the first thing after coming home from school she ran out to the nesting shed to check for eggs. In late March she actually discovered one. Mama professionally noted the date and number of the nesting pair in her ledger and read aloud from one of her pamphlets: "'When the first egg appears, watch the nest carefully. In forty-eight hours there will be a second egg. Then the pair will take turns sitting on the nest—the female in the morning and the male in the afternoon.'"

The second egg appeared two days later exactly on schedule. Mama and Becky were now convinced that the pamphlet could be trusted, and Mama read with confidence: "'The first egg will hatch in eighteen days.'" She circled the expected hatching date on the calendar. A few more nests were built and eggs laid, all duly noted by Mama in her ledger.

After eighteen days, Mama and Becky peeked under the first nesting pigeon. Both eggs were still intact. They waited another day. Maybe they had miscounted. Nineteen days, still nothing. Mama read again from her pamphlet: "'If egg does not hatch, hold it up to a flashlight and see if there is a dark spot. If not, it is infertile, no embryo.'"

Our only flashlight was in Papa's car. As soon as he came home from work, Mama took the flashlight, muttered something about getting to the bottom of all this foolishness, and strode towards the nesting shed. Papa had gone in the house to clean up, but Becky and I followed Mama's purposeful steps to the nesting shed. She pushed the sitting pigeon rudely aside, and held one egg up to the light. Nothing. She tried the second. Not a speck, nothing.

Back in the kitchen, she broke the news to Papa. "Not a speck in those eggs," she said, "not a speck."

"What do you mean, 'not a speck'?"

"Infertile."

"You mean they're not—"

"Right. I mean they are not fertile. There has been no springtime raring-to-go activity, no treading." While she talked she had been putting dinner on the dining-room table, and we all sat down. When Papa finished the blessing I looked at Mama, expecting her to go on with the discussion; but she just sat there, elbows on the table, looking completely dejected and saying nothing—quite unlike her usual self.

Papa served our plates and finally broke the silence: "I don't understand. Not fertile—what is it, immaculate conception?"

"Not even that," Mama said wearily. "There won't be any squabs."

"We've been feeding the bastards all winter. Why don't they mate? I bet it's that damn monogamy." Papa was growing angrier as he spoke. "If they haven't got a mate, what's wrong with taking a new one? A hundred pigeons out there—plenty to choose from."

Mama bristled a little. She assured Papa the last thing she needed was a lecture on pigeon morality, but she did have a suggestion. She had read about a certain kind of pellet that made pigeons more inclined to breed.

"Oh, an aphrodisiac?" Papa asked sarcastically. "A pigeon aphrodisiac! Now I've heard everything!"

"What's an aphrodisiac?" Becky and I chorused.

"Something to make the damn birds mate—you know, have squabs." Papa glared angrily around the table as though his wife and daughters were personally responsible for the frigidity prevailing in the mating pen. Then, directly at Mama: "Well, Mabel, why didn't you give the damn birds those pellets—aphrodisiacs—whatever you call them?"

The pellets, Mama explained, were very expensive, and she was a little doubtful about their effectiveness. Through the rest of the dinner she and Papa debated this interesting question, the pros and cons of aphrodisiacs. I didn't interrupt, but, listening to the discussion, I realized there was more to this mating business than I had suspected. I made a mental note to talk it over with Beverly. She seemed to know more about such things than I did—maybe because she had brothers. Anyway, by the time we had reached the bread-pudding desert, Mama and Papa had decided to make the aphrodisiac investment.

.The next day Mama ordered the pellets, and three days later Papa asked for a progress report.

"Diarrhea," Mama answered simply.

Papa suddenly remembered Mr. Mae's advice about identifying the non-maters and culling them out. That must be the problem: Mama had not culled the flock properly. Papa would take it over himself and do it right. They were talking in the kitchen, and, to my surprise, Mama made no objection. She simply handed Papa a pamphlet and pointed to the proper passage. He read aloud: "'The breeding habits of pigeons are unique. There is no fool-proof way of sexing pigeons.'" He turned a page and went on. "Then it explains here in parentheses what they mean by sexing pigeons. It means telling which is male and which is female." He looked up from the pamphlet and glared at Becky and me to be sure we got the point. We nodded that we understood.

Papa cleared his throat and turned a page. "It goes on to say the only sure way to know you have a pair is when they produce squabs. All right, if they produce squabs I don't care which is male and which is female. Just have squabs. That's all I'm asking."

We remained silent while Papa scanned the next page and read aloud: "'When a male has selected the female he desires for his mate, he struts around. The strutting male is easily recognized by his bedraggled tail feathers—a sure giveaway that he has been courting.'" Papa pounced on that statement triumphantly, as though he had at last found the clue, and directed an accusing gaze at Mama: "Did you think of that, Mabel? It's right here in the book. Did you notice any bedraggled tail feathers?"

"The whole flock looks bedraggled to me," she replied.

Papa continued reading aloud: "'Of course, the best way is to catch the male treading. Always have your banding gear at the ready, and as soon as the treading is completed, grab the male first and band him. The female will remain on the perch, and you can band her second.'"

"I know. I've read all that," Mama said in an even voice, indicating she was not inclined to go on with the argument. An awkward silence followed, but Papa seemed to realize he was beaten. Rather apologetically he returned the pamphlets to their proper place on the counter and conceded there just wasn't anything else to do. Summer was coming on, and we'd just wait to see what happened.

Before leaving the kitchen, Becky and I exchanged relieved glances. Tension between Papa and Mama—mild enough by today's standards—made us nervous, and we were glad it was over.

Nature—or maybe it was the pellets—came to the rescue, temporarily at least. During the next week or so Mama was actually able to band a few pairs. Becky and I stayed on constant alert to watch for treaders, and even Edward, who had no monetary interest in the mating habits of pigeons, caught on to the problem. He liked to bring Prince on his leash up the alley to stalk the pigeons. While Prince pointed, Edward sometimes spotted a treader and shouted to Mama as loud as he could, "Come here, Mrs. King! They're doing it! They're doing it again! Come quick, Mrs. King."

When Mama heard Edward, she grabbed some bands and dashed out, but by the time she got to the pen the male had already disappeared into the flock.

"Which one?" she would ask, looking at the placid pigeons accusingly, even holding out the numbered band as though they could understand. She warned the non-performers they were going to have to go, but the only answer was soft coos and innocent not-my-baby expressions. Disgusted, Mama walked about the pen, wondering which female deserved the leg band. It was impossible to tell. She asked Edward to call sooner next time, returned to the kitchen and tossed the unused bands back into the box.

There was never raring-to-go activity, but a few pairs actually produced fertile eggs and raised squabs. In late June Papa had twelve squabs big enough to sell and called the chef at the Harvey House down at Union Depot. Just like Mr. Mae had promised, it was a sellers' market. The Harvey House would pay two dollars apiece for all the squabs we could furnish. The chef said to kill them by slashing their throats, leave the heads on, don't draw them, and pick the feathers dry without scalding. Just pack the plucked squabs in ice and bring them in immediately. Saturday afternoon would be fine.

After an early lunch, Mama cleaned the kitchen and spread white butcher paper on the table to make ready for squab plucking. Becky and I stayed inside while Papa butchered the squabs. It was bad enough just thinking about it, especially for Becky who knew each squab individually and probably would have given them names if we'd kept them much longer. I wasn't so crazy about pigeons, myself; except that I hoped to make some money selling squabs.

It didn't take Papa long. He brought the butchered squabs into the kitchen and laid them, still warm, on the table. Mama, who had busied herself in the yard without watching the actual killing, sat at the table, picked up a squab, and went to work. Her fingers flew, and she explained she'd had plenty of experience plucking feathers when she was a girl back in Georgia and the family always had a flock of chickens.

Papa started plucking, too; but Mama finished her squab first, except for the pinfeathers. She handed it to me: "Here, Mafra, your smaller fingers will make easy work of the pinfeathers."

I held the limp warm body in my hand and picked at a pin-feather gingerly. "Pull it out, Mafra," Mama ordered in a strictly businesslike voice. She was already well into her second squab and reminded us all to work fast so Papa could get the squabs down to the Harvey House before night. Lint and feathers flew about the kitchen, and I hated the smell of the freshly killed birds piled on the kitchen table. Papa had handed Becky his squab to finish up the pin feathers. She held it in her open hand. The head hung down grotesquely and she seemed unable to dislodge a single pin feather. Finally, Mama took pity and found a pair of tweezers to pull the toughest little feathers. Realizing there was no escape from this loathsome task except to finish it, Becky and I quit complaining and worked as fast as we could.

Mama had bought extra ice that morning, and Papa lined two boxes with white butcher paper and cracked ice, wrapped each squab separately, and placed them on the layer of ice in the box. While he and I took a little time to clean up and change our clothes, Mama laid the boxes carefully on the back seat of the Overland and spread an army blanket over them to hold in the cold. Papa and I climbed in the front and were off to make our first sale.

I had driven by the red brick Union Depot with it square belfry tower many times, but I had never been inside. Papa parked around at the side of the building. We each carried a box, not too heavy but awkward to hold. I balanced mine carefully so the squabs and ice wouldn't slide around.

We went through the brick portico into the cavernous waiting room. Someone I couldn't see was calling trains: "Southern Pacific leaving for Del Rio, San Antonio, Houston, New Orleans, on Track 2." And even louder: "Missouri Pacific leaving for Belem, Santa Fe, Salt Lake City and points west on Track 11—all aboard." As the trains were called, waiting passengers got up from the oak benches, picked up suitcases and packages, and filed out the big open doors. I could smell coal smoke, and beyond the doors I glimpsed railroad tracks where a huge black engine noisily emitted spurts of white steam. It was so exciting, for a moment I forgot about the squabs and just wished I was going somewhere.

Papa finally located the Harvey House sign over an arcade beyond the ticket counter, and we walked towards it. People slid their luggage around on the red and green tile floor, making room for us to pass. I acknowledged the courtesy with a cool smile, thinking everyone must be wondering what important business a girl like me had in such a busy place.

The arcade led into a huge dining room. It was not yet dinnertime, and waiters were hustling about, setting silverware and sparkling glasses on the starchy white tablecloths. We passed through the dining room and pushed open the swinging door leading into the kitchen, where we were greeted by the aroma of spices and cooking food, and the deafening racket of clattering pots and pans. We stood awkwardly by the door until a white-clad man noticed us and pointed to a counter at the back where the chef joined us. It was hard to hear him above all the noise, but he spread the squabs on the counter, felt their breasts, admired the light color of the skin, and congratulated Papa on a fine batch.

He invited us into a small office where he wrote out the check. We could hear better in the office, and he urged Papa to bring more squabs. "Squabs on the menu always mean a sellout," he said. "You know the Harvey House is run by the Santa Fe Railroad and it's a famous restaurant. We've got about twenty-five trains coming through here every day—even international traffic because some go to Mexico—and passengers like to arrange their trips with a stopover in El Paso just so they can eat with us—we're that famous. Bring us more squabs—keep our customers happy."

Back in the car with our empty boxes, Papa and I were so pleased with our success that he said we ought to celebrate. Instead of going straight home, he parked the car near Warner's Drug Store, and we went in to the soda fountain. I said I would order an ice-cream cone. Papa laughed. "No, daughter, get a soda or a banana split, whatever you want. Twenty-four dollars in one day—I'm in business for myself now. Let's go first class. What will you have?"

I decided on a chocolate soda, but I felt a little guilty and reminded Papa that our funds were somewhat limited. Mama was waiting for the money to buy pigeon feed, and maybe even more pellets. Papa's spirits were soaring and he just laughed at my caution. "Don't worry," he said. "We're over the hump now. We've got a sellers' market."

He easily won me over, especially when he tipped the waitress a whole dime—a suitable climax to a truly memorable evening. I sipped my chocolate soda blissfully and asked when we would have more squabs to take to the Harvey House.

Papa said he had a batch coming up in a couple of weeks, but not for the Harvey House. He would sell them to the Paso del Norte Hotel. I was puzzled, because the Harvey House had asked for more, but Papa explained to me the advantage of being in a sellers' market. "Play the market," he said. "When you're in business for yourself, you don't put all your eggs in one basket. You always want to keep them wanting more."

I understood and promised to go with him when he delivered squabs to the Paso del Norte. I didn't have to wait long. In early July we had fourteen squabs for the hotel. The chef had directed Papa to park in the alley at the back of the hotel and come in through the delivery door. The kitchen was exciting like the Harvey House, but I was a little disappointed that we had to come in the back way and not have a chance to see the lobby and dining room. Maybe my disappointment showed, because after the chef had paid Papa, and we were about to leave by the back door, he called: "Hey, I guess the young lady might like to look around. We're not too busy right now in midafternoon. Come, I'll show you. We've got a Tiffany dome, did you know that?"

I shook my head, not even knowing what Tiffany meant. He led us through the empty dining room. "The Paso del Norte was built in 1905. It's the finest hotel west of the Mississippi," he said proudly. He patted the white plaster dining-room wall as we passed. "All fireproof, made out of the white gypsum from White Sands up in New Mexico."

He led us on into the lobby, and I gasped with delight when I looked up at the Tiffany dome. He smiled at my awestruck expression and pointed out the European chandelier, black serpentine marble trim, and furniture from Europe. The winding stairways leading up from the lobby had banisters of dark cherry. We started back towards the kitchen, and the chef was still explaining: "Not only an elegant lobby, but the finest cuisine this side of the Mississippi. If anybody asks you, say Louis Papas, the chef, told you so himself. Thirteen years I'm here at the Paso del Norte, and here I stay."

After the tour, we took our empty boxes back to the car and stopped again at Warner's for sodas. Papa patted the check in his breast pocket and talked about being in business for himself. "Louis Papas wants more squabs, too," he chortled. I've got them bidding against each other—a real sellers' market."

But the good times were short-lived. After the springtime flurry, most of the pigeons ate, cooed, and ignored each other. The days were hot and long. The border of golden-eyes around the fence was waist high, but the lack of squabs was depressing. Mama kept hoping, but Papa's temper was short. "Bunch of celibates," he scolded the idle flock. "What are you, anyway? Bereaved widowers? Cut out the grieving and find a new mate. Even the Bible allows that. What do you think this is—Habersham King's monastery?"

Sometimes Mama tried threats. "My literature says you can live for fourteen years," she addressed the flock at large. "Let me tell you something—not on my grain. I've got books on you, and the day of reckoning is not far off."

"Well, pigeons mate for life. Mr. Mae told me that in the beginning," Papa admitted. "He was sure as hell right about that."

As the summer wore on, Mama was at last ready to call it quits. "I think we could have made it with chickens," she mused. "One promiscuous rooster chases a dozen or more wanton hens, and the first thing you know the market is glutted with fried chicken. But pigeons? It's actually an ethics problem. As long as pigeons are monogamous—and who am I to say evolution made a mistake—but as long as they're monogamous, squabs are going to be scarce. If spring was our high production season, I hate to think what lies ahead."

Production didn't improve, but just when we were most discouraged rescue came from an unexpected source. Since working on the nesting shed and flying pen, Mr. Stone had developed an interest in the pigeons. When Papa said we were tired of the whole business, he asked for the flock. He said that he used to raise pigeons back in Georgia when he was a kid, and he never heard of anything so silly as feeding pigeons. Now that he was living in a little adobe house up in the desert near the goatherd's, it would be easy to handle the flock. He would just build a shed for nests and let the pigeons fly free. They could find plenty of seeds and insects on the desert, and they'd come home to nest—always do.

"A good home for the pigeons whether they deserve it or not," Mama said with relief. In one swoop she tossed out all the pigeon pamphlets and account books and touched the empty counter thoughtfully. "I'll keep my books on native plants here" she said, cheerfully. "Mrs. Pope said the native plants are famous for *tenacity*. That's something I can work with. And by the way, I noticed some buds on the golden-eye today. That's a nice start."

*Becky (holding Witty), Mafra and Mama in front of the house at
3320 Mountain Avenue, 1925.*

Becky, Papa and Mafra (left to right).

Playmates on the monkey bars at Rusk School.

In the back row: Becky, Mafra and Edward.

Edward.

Becky (left) and Gwen.

Mafra's high school graduation 1931.

Beverly in front of the used car.

College of Mines campus, summer 1931.

College of Mines. Courtesy of the El Paso Public Library.

10

We were a godly people on Mountain Avenue. We went to church—not just once a week, but to scores of meetings, many considered compulsory. Sunday began with nine o'clock Bible classes for the grown-ups and Sunday School for the young people; at eleven, the formal sermon for everybody including squirming children; in the early evening, about six o'clock, Christian Endeavor for Presbyterian young people and Epworth League for Methodists; then the Sunday evening service, less formal than the morning service.

During the week: Wednesday night prayer meeting preceded by Wednesday night supper in the church basement; the Ladies Missionary Society at least once a month, and various money raising endeavors such as cake sales and ice-cream socials. So secure were we in our religious practices and beliefs that the heretical headlines generated by the Scopes trial way back in Tennessee during the summer of 1925 were generally ignored. Not to say that we missed that spectacle entirely. We read about it later, when it hit the funny papers. The hilarious notion that man was descended from monkeys was a boon to many a cartoonist and gave rise to a rash of schoolyard jokes. If one of our companions behaved in a stupid or clumsy manner, we wittily dubbed him the missing link between man and monkey and warned him to lie low: Barnum and Bailey was looking for him.

Our science class in the sixth grade was not biology but hygiene. The few illustrations in our text were gender-neutral: the human form in spread-eagle stance, possessing a brain, heart, lungs, nerves and blood vessels but devoid of reproductive organs. The emphasis was on good health and cleanliness, a theme driven home by the axiom written on the blackboard: Cleanliness is next to Godliness.

Mrs. Wells was also a believer in axioms. In her soft, round letters she wrote on our homeroom blackboard: Education is a <u>Godly</u> nation's greatest need. She underlined the word "Godly" to make sure we didn't confuse the priorities.

In spite of our feverish Sunday activities, we didn't concern ourselves much with doctrine. We believed what our parents believed—the natural thing to do. Three small churches: Baptist, Methodist, and Presbyterian, served the neighborhood needs.

The Baptists attended a little white church, actually a renovated house, on Idalia Avenue. It wasn't much of a building, but they were conscientious about attending or at least sending their children to Sunday school. Some adults went to the First Baptist Church downtown, which was worth the trip because their preacher, Dr. Neal, was renowned for the jokes he told right from the pulpit. Some of his wisecracks about local politicians were even quoted in the *El Paso Post*. Beverly and I visited First Baptist once just for fun. His joke that day was that the Sunday before the church treasurer had found a five dollar bill in the collection plate. Would whoever made the mistake please drop by the treasurer's office and pick up his four dollars change? Beverly and I were still laughing on the streetcar going home as, sucking peppermint Life Savers, we repeated the joke to each other. We almost wished we were Baptists. They seemed to really enjoy their church. Besides, they had great revivals.

The Methodists had just built a little brick church over on Fort

Boulevard. They seemed to be rather easygoing. Once in a while I went with a friend to Epworth League, but it was boring, just like Christian Endeavor at Altura Presbyterian, my own church.

Altura Presbyterian Church on Morehead Avenue, three blocks from our house, had an impressive building, a two-story magenta-colored brick, complete with belfry and a big iron bell. Not that there were enough Presbyterians in the neighborhood to afford such a structure. We owed our good fortune to the fact we were classified as a "Home Mission" and received a stipend from Presbyterian USA, a philanthropy that I took for granted at the time and didn't properly appreciate. Another good fortune was our beloved minister, Dr. McSpadden, who could have made more money elsewhere but was willing to work for a pittance because his wife had tuberculosis and needed the dry climate. My Sunday school teacher was Ruth Jackson, whose only qualification for teaching our class was that she was available. We all called her Auntie Ruth, which we picked up from Judy and Jammie Sue Jackson, her nieces, who were in the class. We liked her, but she had no idea how to teach a class. We just read the scripture printed in the quarterly and then talked about other things. Sometimes she told us about living in St. Louis.

In addition to the little neighborhood churches, there were lots of big churches downtown, representing every denomination you could think of. Mr and Mrs. Pope went every Sunday to the Church of Christ. Most of the military families in our neighborhood belonged to the Episcopal Church but usually preferred to sleep late on Sunday mornings and sent their kids to the most convenient neighborhood church. That's how the Greer kids, who were really Episcopalians, happened to go to our church. However, Colonel Greer was fair about it. I went by his house once to sell fifteen-cent tickets to the church ice-cream social, and I was really bowled over when he bought tickets for Florence and Tommy and had me wait while he wrote a check for ten dollars—just to help the church. The Finkes, the only Jewish family I knew, went to the synagogue on Mesa Avenue on Saturdays. I didn't know any Catholics until I went to high school, but there was a Catholic school for girls, Loretta College, out in Austin Terrace.

My friend Emmaline Pratt was a Mormon. I knew she went to the Mormon Temple, but she didn't talk about it, and I didn't even know where it was. I liked going home with Emmaline after school once in a while. The Pratts had a big, gray frame house on Fort Boulevard. It wasn't so big at first, but as the family grew—nine children when I knew them—Mr. Pratt had a basement dug out and bedrooms built in, one for every two children. Emmaline and I always went in by the kitchen door and were greeted by Mrs. Pratt wearing a big white apron, her arms usually flour-covered to the elbows as she kneaded bread or rolled out pie crust. The kitchen was immaculate. Shiny pots and pans big enough for a restaurant kitchen hung over the stove, and there were various appliances such as an electric ironing mangle and an electric refrigerator—inventions not yet popular in private homes. In addition to her own family Mrs. Pratt cooked for the three women missionaries who shared the Pratt residence. When I was older I caught on to the knowing winks the neighbors exchanged about the "missionaries," always saying the word as if it was in quotation marks, and I resented it. I was always made to feel welcome at the Pratts'. It was a happy place.

The Holy Rollers, a sect of some twenty-five or thirty members, had no building. On summer nights they met over on Piedras in a vacant lot under the stars, not even a tent to cover their roughhewn benches and battered piano. I didn't know of any of the members except by sight, but I loved it when we stopped by on our way home from buying ice at Five Points and watched the meetings.

The trip to buy ice was a treat in itself. Mama usually proposed the excursion as it was a little cheaper to buy ice at the plant in Five Points than to get it off the truck. Becky and I liked it because we took neighborhood kids along and everybody enjoyed the ride. At the drive-in ice station the attendant would put a circle of rough hemp string on the running board and place the twenty-five pound chunk of ice on the string. For some reason we never figured out the ice did not slip off, even when we turned corners. Sometimes on Saturday nights, if there weren't too many kids jammed in the back seat of the car, Papa would drive into the root-beer stand and buy everybody a root beer. But on other nights, when there was no chance of such a treat, Becky and I led the back-seat chorus begging

Papa to stop and watch the Holy Rollers. Apparently they didn't mind being watched. They simply ignored the circle of cars parked around the benches, driving in and out at will.

We called them Holy Rollers and kept hoping they would start rolling, but actually we never saw them do it. There didn't seem to be a regular pastor, but the members took turns testifying. A woman called Sister Tiffany took the lead. She recounted many colorful and heart-rending experiences she had suffered before she was finally called to Christ and washed in the blood. Her audience was appreciative and joined in with a chorus of amens. Mama made us be quiet in the car, and if anybody giggled she ordered Papa to back the car out at once. Anyway, we couldn't stay long because the ice was melting.

The second year we were in El Paso, Papa was elected a deacon at Altura Presbyterian, and assigned the duty of tolling the bell at the proper hour on Sunday morning, a singular honor in my estimation. In spite of his early rising on week mornings, he never failed his Sunday duty. Sometimes he drove the car the three blocks to the church, but if the weather was good he walked. Exactly at eight o'clock he was in the vestibule energetically pulling the bell rope to alert all the faithful—and that meant everybody east of the mountain—that it was time to be up and dressing. The boom of the bell, not a tuneful tinkle of chimes like you hear from city churches and college campuses today, but a low ding-dong that rolled across the mesa and came to rest against the mountain with a dull thud, always filled me with a sense of proprietorship, and I paused in whatever I was doing and pitied those unfortunate people of lesser faiths who had to attend churches without bells.

After ringing the eight-o'clock bell, Papa took care of a few housekeeping duties. Deacons were in charge of the practical chores; elders handled the spiritual. He made sure the dog-eared blue hymnals were in the racks; in the summer he laid palm-leaf fans on the pews; in the winter he checked the furnace. At eight-thirty he tolled the bell again, just a couple of clangs to remind people time was passing. Promptly at nine he gave the bell rope another vigorous pulling, the last call to announce Sunday school was about to "take in." By that time Mama, Becky and I had arrived at church, and we waited in the vestibule while Papa looped the bell rope over a nail high on the wall to keep it out of the grasp of mischievous boys.

Every Christmas we had a play depicting the Nativity. Once, as one of the wise men, I wore a gunny sack and for a shepherd's crook carried a curtain rod.

At least once each quarter we had a sermon on temperance. Dr. McSpadden praised prohibition and exhorted the congregation to work for the closing of the International Bridge at six o'clock each evening. The idea, pushed by local merchants as well as the churches, was to prevent men from getting drunk in Juarez, and, at the same time, keep the money on our side of the border.

Another quarterly sermon was on foreign missions. Although a mission church and unable to support ourselves, we had a special collection for foreign missions. Mama was one of the few people who objected to sending money abroad; but I liked Foreign Missions Sunday. It gave us something to talk about, even in Auntie Ruth's class.

Looking back from the perspective of the Space Age, I wonder if those decades between the two great wars of this century might not be appropriately described as the Foreign Mission Age. Isolated as we were in El Paso, primarily a city of health seekers struggling for the necessities of life and often indifferent to the mainstream of political thought, we, nevertheless, had implicit faith in the power of our foreign missionaries to hasten the millennium by spreading the gospel around the world: to the savage in the Congo, the benighted Hindu in India, the leper in Brazil, the unsaved and sinful, wherever they were to be found.

On foreign mission Sunday Dr. McSpadden usually took his text from the Gospel according to Mark: "Go you into all the world, and preach the gospel to every creature." And we got off to a good start by singing all the verses of that rollicking Reginald Heber hymn:

> *From Greenland's icy mountains,*
> *From India's coral strand,*

126

Where Africa's sunny fountains
Roll down their golden sand

. . . .

Though every prospect pleases,
And only man is vile.

It's only fair to say that in the 1940s the phrase "only man is vile" was stricken from the hymn; but in the 1920s nobody objected. We meant it and sang it with gusto.

Although not many had the *privilege* of serving in the foreign field, there were ways of helping beyond putting money in the collection plate. A good example was Miss Taylor, the principal at Rusk. The first time Mrs. McCabe visited us, she had explained with some pride that Miss Taylor was a Baptist, and later school friends supplied further details: As a girl Miss Taylor wanted to be a missionary but could not leave home because she had to care for her aged parents. However, as she assumed the burden of caring for her parents, her younger sister, Ida, was free of that obligation and did go as a missionary to China. From the day Miss Taylor started working as a teacher, and later as a principal, each month she sent one-fourth of her salary to Ida to assist her in her work.

Foreign missions being such a high priority on Mountain Avenue, we were pleased to accept when the First Presbyterian Church extended an invitation to the public to hear Dr. Blevins, a missionary on sabbatical from his post in the Congo. He would "occupy the pulpit" on the coming Sunday and even show slides of his little mission in the evening.

That Sunday morning, the first time I had visited First Church, I was awed by the solemnity of the sanctuary. The light, filtering through stained glass windows, created a quiet, holy atmosphere very different from Altura where shafts of sun poured through white, frosted windows and noisy kids scuffled in the aisles. A soft prelude was coming from the organ. A boy in his early teens, wearing a badge embroidered with the words "Comrades of the Cross" like a bandoleer across his chest, solemnly escorted us to our seats.

After a few gracious remarks about the pleasure of being with us here in El Paso, this beautiful desert city, Dr. Blevins gazed over the congregation, and asked all of us who would be in junior high or high school the next year to raise our hands. I was about to be a seventh grader at Austin Junior High, and I sat on the edge of the pew and proudly raised my hand. Would we please come forward and sit in the front pews which had been roped off for us?

I had to slip by Papa's knees to reach the aisle, and I stood there a moment, resting my hand on the back of the pew, my heart pounding, while two boys, also wearing Comrades of the Cross badges, went forward to remove the ribbons from the reserved pews. The pause gave me a moment to reflect: What did it mean— this strange man calling me forward in this unfamiliar place, away from my family, where even Becky couldn't follow? When I took my place on the front pew, surrounded by boys and girls I didn't know, had never even seen before, I ignored them and kept my eyes on Dr. Blevins.

Dr. Blevins had come a long way to talk to us, and to make sure he had our attention, he had to digress a moment, reminding us of the parable of the sower. Of course we were all familiar with the story, and he simply repeated it to emphasize that he was hoping his message would find some fertile soil, that at least one of us would hear him, ponder the message, and some day see fit to answer: "Lord, here am I; send me."

After this introduction, Dr. Blevins talked about his own life's work: his trials, successes, and failures as he devoted every waking moment to spreading God's word among the less fortunate villages of the Congo, and the joy of it all, the indescribable satisfaction of knowing he was doing God's will. It was gratifying, he said, to see we were all intensely interested in the story of his life in the Congo; but no doubt we were having serious thoughts about how is this possible—how do I get from here, this comfortable life in this beautiful city, to the very heart of darkest Africa? To show us it was possible, he had only to tell us the story of his own life.

He asked us to visualize him as a poor boy with no financial help from his own family, working his way through Park College, a Presbyterian school in Missouri. How thrilled he was at the wonderful opportunity for an education. How he loved his studies, the professors, the other students. He was successful: president of the

Debating Society, on the Dean's List, president of his senior class. But something was lacking. At times, surrounded by his friends and classmates, he felt terribly alone. In the spring of his senior year, when his classmates looked forward to graduation and a chance to make money and pay off their college debts, he found he was out of touch. Was that the purpose of his education—a chance to get the right job? It all seemed meaningless, and his life was unfocussed and without purpose. Then, just when his outlook was most hopeless, an understanding professor sensed his loneliness and placed in his hands a wonderful book, *The Personal Life of Livingstone.* Miraculously, a new world opened to him.

David Livingstone! What a life, what a story! Think of the eleven-year old David working in the spinning room of a cotton mill in a little village in Scotland. Dr. Blevins' mention of the spinning room, something I could have described myself, gripped my attention. Papa could run every machine at the Lone Star Cotton Mill, and often when he had to go back to the mill after supper to check some problem I went with him—to the spinning room, the weave room, wherever the trouble was. Now, it was easy for me to visualize the cotton mill in Scotland, and David Livingstone, just my age, traipsing up and down the long rows of spindles. I heard the deafening whir of the machines, I felt the static in the air and the impulse to cough because my lungs were choking with lint and dust. I saw David's nimble fingers piecing together the breaks in the long ropes of yarn as it spun into finer and finer threads.

With a rhetorical question Dr. Blevins brought me back to his lecture. Was the young boy bored with this monotonous job? No! There at the end of the aisle, propped against a bobbin but hidden from the overseer's probing eye, was an open Latin book; and every time young David passed the book he read a word or two. Against impossible odds, David Livingstone was educating himself.

The story went on. Self-educated, David Livingstone was sent by the London Missionary Society to Africa, and Dr. Blevins described his work there, his trials and triumphs as he battled wild animals, disease, and slave traders, all in the service of the Lord. All of this would be more meaningful to us when we came back in the evening to see Dr. Blevins' slides.

It was a long afternoon for me, reflecting on the morning message and waiting impatiently to see the slides. Beverly had missed the morning service, but when I told her about the slides, she joined us for the evening service. The slides were shown in the basement auditorium, and this time there were no reserved seats for the young people. Dr. Blevins admitted that we were going to see some mighty unpleasant sights, and it was fitting that we sit with our parents. As the slides flashed on the screen, he explained each one: a village street, mud huts with thatched roofs, cripples and people covered with horrible sores waiting in line before the little clinic. Dr. Blevins was seen in each picture, usually in the center. When I was close to weeping because of all the misery and suffering, he adroitly changed slides, and my heart was lifted up by scenes of little native children happily singing, "Jesus Loves Me."

After the slides were finished and the lights went on, we had a chance to look at Dr. Blevins' exhibits: a cowhorn cup that the natives used for bleeding the sick, sheets of bark cloth beaten until smooth, fetishes in the shape of kidneys, gourd bottles, cowry shells used for money, ivory beads, and all sorts of things.

While Beverly and I were looking at the exhibits—you could even pick them up and handle them if you wanted to—a dark haired young woman, Miss Clayton, introduced herself to us. When she learned we were Presbyterians, just visiting from Altura, she immediately invited us to the Daily Vacation Bible School, beginning the very next day at First Church. She would be one of the teachers, and there would be study groups, field trips, even a croquet tournament played on the church lawn. Beverly and I, liking Miss Clayton and bored with our long do-nothing summer, accepted her invitation, and promised to be there the next morning.

In the back seat of the car going home, Beverly kept talking about the Vacation Bible School and how glad she was Miss Clayton had invited us. I agreed with her, but I was thinking about the new world Dr. Blevins had opened for me, and I was glad when we let her out at her house and drove on to our own driveway. Mama and Becky went straight in to bed. I was too excited to sleep. When Papa walked out on the front lawn to look at the stars, I followed him.

As though the affairs of the day had already slipped from his mind,

Papa said the stars were brighter than ever and launched into one of his favorite pastimes—trying to tell time by the way the Little Dipper journeyed counterclockwise around the North Star. He always started with the Big Dipper over McKelligon Canyon, the two stars on the outside pointing to the North Star directly over Sugar Loaf. Then he insisted that I imagine a man, the North Star was his bellybutton, and his extended arms, shoulder blades and spread legs established points of the compass. The Little Dipper off to the right was moving counterclockwise. He always lost me at that point, but I pretended to listen because there was no stopping him. At last, lamenting as usual that he really needed a nocturnal to make it more exact, he concluded that it was nine-thirty and he was ready to go to bed.

As we went inside I was glad to hear the mantel clock strike the half-hour, confirming Papa's conclusion. He was always gratified when his calculations came out right, or nearly so. Mama had left the lights on in the living room for us. Papa loosened his tie, yawned, and started winding the mantel clock.

At last, I thought, I could get his attention. "Papa," I asked, "did you like Dr. Blevins' slides?"

"Yes, quite interesting." He put his ear to the clock to make sure it was still ticking and checked the time against his watch.

"Papa, can girls be missionaries? I mean do they have women missionaries—like in Africa?"

"Oh, I suppose." He yawned again. "I can't imagine why anybody would want to go to some godforsaken place nobody ever heard of and live in a mud hut, but I guess they can if they want to. Oh, well, every man to his own poison, I always say."

"Oh, I was just wondering."

"Sure, daughter. Well, it's been a long day. Goodnight."

"Goodnight."

The Vacation Bible School wasn't all games. One Calvinistic doctrine the Presbyterians never forget is the work ethic. Long summer days permitted some frivolity such as croquet and handicrafts, but there must be a counterbalance, something worthwhile. We would study foreign missions.

Miss Clayton tacked the map of foreign lands on the board, stuck red thumbtacks in the spots where Presbyterians had missions, and asked each girl—there were ten or twelve of us—to choose the mission or missionary she wished to write a paper on. We would read our papers to the class, and one girl would be chosen to present hers at the commencement exercises at the close of Vacation Bible School.

Not too enthusiastically, the other girls began to study the map, but I spotted the thumbtack marking the Presbyterian mission in the Congo and told Miss Clayton I was ready to start. I would study David Livingstone. Delighted with my interest, Miss Clayton left the other girls to make their choices and asked me to come with her to the church library upstairs, where she would show me some books on Livingstone. We took the outside steps up to street level and entered the library by way of the Office of Religious Education, which gave Miss Clayton a chance to introduce me to the director, Mrs. Randolph.

Mrs. Randolph greeted me graciously, speaking with the faintest Virginia accent. She wore her silver-gray hair in a pompadour, held in place by silver combs, which seemed to accent her rather tall and graceful figure. Although her manner was outwardly friendly, for the first time since coming to First Church I felt strangely inadequate, not knowing exactly what was expected of me. Miss Clayton, usually quite cool and poised, also seemed thrown off balance for a moment, but she quickly recovered herself and explained to Mrs. Randolph that she was showing me the library.

When we were alone in the library, Miss Clayton assured me that I would like Mrs. Randolph very much. "We're so fortunate to have her," she said. "She's so good with young people." I soon learned that "so good with young people" was a virtue the conventional wisdom always attributed to Mrs. Randolph.

The library was a small room, well lighted and made quite cheerful by the red carpeting which matched the aisles of the sanctuary. Miss Clayton quickly located a small shelf of Livingstone books: *Life of Livingstone*, *Livingstone's African Journal*, *How I Found Livingstone*, and some others. She said I could study any time I wanted to at the big table or I could simply sign a card and check books out to read at home. When she saw how interested I was in the books, she told me just to stay and browse while she went back to her class.

Voices were coming from Mrs. Randolph's office, so Miss Clayton took the other way out through the sanctuary. I heard her footsteps fade away down the long aisle of the sanctuary, and except for the intermittent conversation in Mrs. Randolph's office and the distant sound of traffic on Yandell Boulevard the library was perfectly still. I sat down at the polished table and opened one of the Livingstone volumes. Sitting on the edge of my chair, I turned pages slowly, reading snatches here and there. I felt my heart race. I wondered if this could be like the experience Dr. Blevins had described when his professor gave him his first book on David Livingstone. Straightway I corrected myself. I was being conceited, rushing ahead like that, but still I knew it was an important moment, one I wouldn't forget.

When I returned to class I found that the other girls had chosen their subjects, and Miss Clayton urged us to start work immediately. I took three Livingstone books home with me that afternoon, wanting to read them all at once. The next day we discussed the papers that we would work on, and before I had written a word I was selected to give my paper on Livingstone at the commencement exercises. Secretly, I knew that the act of being selected wasn't exactly a triumph. Truth was: competition didn't exist.

Lest I had any doubts, on the streetcar going home Beverly told me right out that she and the other girls in the class thought studying foreign missions was a heck of a way to ruin a perfectly good summer. As far as she was concerned, the croquet tournament was more interesting. The boys, too shy to ask us voluntarily, had drawn names of the girls for croquet partners, and made a lot of jokes to hide their embarrassment at being paired off. George Cochran, probably the most popular boy there, had drawn Beverly's name— Beverly was always lucky with boys—and his friend Everett Gillis had drawn mine. Everett was all right, just a little hard to talk to. Anyway, we would have fun playing as a foursome. Coach Wyatt-Browne would teach us.

Once I was selected to make the Livingstone speech, Mrs.

Randolph started coaching me. I was happy about it in a way, but I was scared, too. I had heard her address the Bible School assembly, and there was something so *polished* about her manner I wondered if I could possibly please her. Oh, but I did want to do it right.

Mrs. Randolph lost no time. She took the speech I had penciled out in an old notebook, cut it in half, and gave me a day or two to memorize the part she had selected—especially the direct quotes. I was too short to see over the lectern, so I stood in front of it, and she stood halfway down the aisle, insisting that I raise my voice and make the proper gestures. We gave special emphasis to Livingstone's encounter with the lion. I had to hold out my left arm, mangled and bloody, while I shouted I felt no pain because God had kindly numbed my nerves. I told how heartbroken Livingstone had been when he had to leave his family temporarily in England and return to Africa alone, how he had been lost in the wilds for a year or more until H. M. Stanley, a reporter for the *New York Herald,* traced him down and made the famous "Dr. Living-stone, I presume" remark, how he died cursing the African slave traders, and how the natives, though returning his body to England for burial in Westminster Abbey, managed first to remove his heart and bury it in his beloved Africa.

Although the month of Vacation Bible School passed quickly, I was well prepared when commencement night arrived. When I finished my speech the applause was gratifying; but before I could leave the platform Mrs. Randolph came up the steps, took me by the arm, and led me back towards the lectern. "This young lady," she announced, "is Mary Frances King, and she is visiting us from our sister church, Altura. As you can tell from her speech tonight, she is seriously considering devoting her life to missionary work. She has been such an inspiration to our Vacation Bible School this summer, and we hope she will be with us again. In the meantime I ask your prayers that she does not falter as she works towards her lofty goal of serving our Lord in the foreign missions field."

There was more applause, and as Mrs. Randolph led me off the platform I realized that without saying a word myself I had made the commitment: "Here am I. Send me."

11

Mama loved Baptist revivals, not for the religion—she had quite enough of that in her own church—but for the drama. Revival was the last two weeks in August. The setting was perfect: The huge green barn-like tabernacle down on Overland Avenue, the dirt floor covered with fresh sawdust smelling of pine, the rough green benches, the white-robed choir, black-robed evangelist, the merciless heat, the sweating people waving cardboard fans, and the well known hymns that could make the rafters ring.

After a ten-hour day at the cotton mill Papa was too tired for any sort of meeting, no matter how dramatic, and Becky was too little to stay awake, so Mama and I went alone. I enjoyed it as much as she did. We had simple dinners on revival nights, something that could be served and cleared away quickly. Dinner finished and the kitchen set in order, Mama and I changed our clothes and hurried over to the Fort Bliss car line, as eagerly as ticket-holders catching a taxi to a Broadway hit.

The action started as soon as we got off the streetcar on Yandell Boulevard. The street down to Overland was roped off, and crowds of people emerged from lined-up streetcars, joined together, and walked down the middle of the street, pressing forward towards the tabernacle. Jostled and pushed by the crowd, we passed through the open doors, felt the soft yellow sawdust underfoot, and selected aisle seats offering an unobstructed view of the evangelist. The Reverend Killebrew, the one I remember best, was a commanding figure, adjusting his Bible and other papers on the lectern, but looking up now and then to offer a welcoming smile to the gathering congregation. Later in the service, scores of these hardworking people, the women in cotton dresses, some of the men still in their work overalls, would go forward as tearful sinners, kneel at the alter, and feel Reverend Killebrew's warm embrace as they accepted Jesus as their personal savior.

When Mama and I had settled down on the hard bench, I looked around and found a couple of the cardboard fans which were generously scattered about. One side of the fan had a picture of Christ praying in Gethsemane. The reverse side was an advertisement for McRea's Funeral Parlor.

When the auditorium was more than half filled, Reverend Killebrew motioned to the choir that he was ready to begin. He stepped forward on the platform and raised his long arms majestically, signalling us to rise. The rousing hymn with innumerable verses was irresistible. All joined in:

> Jesus is my captain, I shall not be moved,
> Jesus is my captain, I shall not be moved.
> Just like a tree, planted by the waters,
> I shall not be moved.

Except for supporting rafters, the huge hall was open up to the slanting roof. Reverend Killebrew looked heavenward, raised both arms higher, and shouted "Let the rafters ring!" The choir and congregation responded, repeating verse after verse until the last straggler had settled in and practically every bench in the tabernacle was filled. Reverend Killebrew stretched out his open palms, motioning the congregation to be seated. There was mass coughing, clearing of throats, and the incessant waving of the cardboard fans.

136

I soon learned that Reverend Killebrew had participated in many deathbed scenes. With slight variations, he recounted the always-tragic circumstances. The climax never varied: The dying sinner had waited a mite too long. On his deathbed he begged, "Pray for me, pray for me." Reverend Killebrew, much as he loved the sinner, could only hold the limp hand and weep as the tortured soul slipped away to eternal damnation.

When Reverend Killebrew had to rest his voice a bit, the choir led the congregation in an appropriate song:

> *Oh, Jesus, tell my mother I'll be there,*
> *In answer to her prayer. . .*

Night after night the deathbed scene was repeated, and no matter how often I heard it, it wrenched my heart. People wept openly, and many went forward to kneel at the alter. I recognized some of the kids I knew at school, going forward to ask forgiveness and receive Reverend Killebrew's hand clasp. I wondered what their sins were to make them weep so openly. Sometimes I felt hot tears on my own cheeks, but I turned away, hiding my face from Mama. I knew instinctively that with Mama there was a line I had better not cross.

Reverend Killebrew saved his best sermon for the last night. I let my mind wander a bit as he elaborated once again on the wages of sin, but he brought me back with a theatrical gesture. He pointed to the rough wall on the far side of the hall and called upon us to watch the moving finger writing there. He was persuasive. I watched the imaginary letters form the words: "ME'NE, ME'NE, TE'KEL, U-PHAR'SIN. Thou art weighed in the balances and art found wanting." Reverend Killebrew's voice, at once pleading and condemning, rang out eloquently. Every eye was turned towards the writing finger, and every heart felt guilty for falling short.

The choir began another familiar refrain:

> *Just as I am without one plea,*
> *But that thy blood was shed for me . . .*

On the final night so many people were going down front to be saved that Mama and I finally grew weary, slipped out of our seats, battled our way up the sawdust-covered aisle against the never-ending tide of penitent sinners, and got out into the cool night air. It was a relief.

We were ahead of the crowd, and our streetcar was almost empty. As it rattled along Yandell and on up Copia, the magic lingered in my mind. "Did you think it was a good revival, Mama?"

"Oh, yes. Reverend Killebrew is one of the best. But I'm tired. Two weeks is enough."

"I love the songs. We'll go again next year, won't we?"

"Oh, yes. Why not?"

It was hard to stay awake, but I was too old to go to sleep on the streetcar. I was glad when we reached the Fort Boulevard stop, and the drama was over—at least for that year.

After my triumphant Livingstone speech at the First Church commencement exercises, I just couldn't bear the thought of returning to Auntie Ruth's boring little Sunday School class at Altura. I wanted to start to Miss Clayton's class at First Church immediately; but I had to clear it with Mama and that took a lot of argument.

"No, Mafra, that would hurt Auntie Ruth's feelings," she kept insisting.

Not hurting anyone's feelings was the paramount rule in Mama's code of ethics; but the stakes were high and I was determined. "You don't know how boring Auntie Ruth's class is," I argued. "All we do is read the Scripture in the Quarterly. Both columns on the page, if you can imagine that! One column is the King James Version and the other column is the Revised Version. I guess the elders or whoever is in charge couldn't decide which is right, so we have to do it both ways."

"Well, Auntie Ruth does the best she can. She hasn't had much training."

"She sure hasn't! And not only that: we take turns reading, and Jammie Sue can't even read. She just stumbles along, and I hate it."

Mama didn't answer, and I let her have the clincher: "And that old Inez Trueblood with her chewing gum. She likes to sit next to me and she smacks her gum right in my ear. I hate the whole thing and Beverly does too."

The chewing gum did it. If there was one thing Mama abhorred, it was chewing gum. She didn't give in immediately, but she began to think about it; and pretty soon she said she would explain to Auntie Ruth that I really needed to go to a bigger church with more activities.

Beverly was delighted to make the change with me. "So much more to do at First Church," she said happily, probably thinking of Coach Wyatt-Browne, the croquet games, and the boys we had met, particularly George, and Everett.

Whatever our motives, we were right about the activity at First Church. On the very first day we plunged into an on-going battle the girls were waging to be admitted to Comrades of the Cross.

Harriet Renfro, an outspoken redhead, laid out the problem for us. Why should the club be only for boys? They acted like girls weren't even members of the church, and we gave our money and our parents gave money, and then they just left us out. Someone asked just what the Comrades did, and she told us that in spite of it all being secret, she had been able to find out a few things. At their meetings they all sat in a circle and left one chair empty. That was supposed to remind them Christ was present—his chair, you know. And they all had their badges and gold rings, and Coach Wyatt-Browne even took them on overnight trips to his camp up at Elephant Butte Dam. And what do the girls get to do? Nothing.

Every Sunday we interrupted Miss Clayton's carefully prepared lessons with that kind of talk, and every time we discussed it we got more excited and Miss Clayton got more upset. "Girls," she would say, "now, girls." But she couldn't think of any arguments against our being allowed to join the Comrades of the Cross, except that it had always been a boys' club. She wasn't in the habit of disturbing the status quo. Finally, we protested so persistently, she agreed to take it up with Mrs. Randolph. This seemed to be the logical approach since Mrs. Randolph had actually been the founder of the Comrades of the Cross. Her son, Cecil, had been a charter member, but he was now at Staunton Military Academy in Virginia and only came home on vacations.

Once Miss Clayton started representing us, she went all out. She talked to Mrs. Randolph and even to the session, and they finally hit on a compromise. We couldn't belong to Comrades of the Cross as Mrs. Randolph thought that would ruin everything for the boys, but we could have our own club to be known as Friends of the Cross.

There were nine girls in Miss Clayton's class, and we were to be charter members. Mrs. Randolph was to be our sponsor, naturally. I say naturally, because how else did it come about? They didn't do a lot of voting at First Church. When Mrs. Randolph was involved in something, it was natural for her to be the leader. Coach Wyatt-Browne sponsored the boys, and Mrs. Randolph sponsored us.

We had to wait a few weeks for our white satin badges to be made and embroidered with the red letters: Friends of the Cross. When they were ready, Mrs. Randolph invited us to a twilight initiation tea at her home.

Beverly, Harriet, and I went together to the tea. Mrs. Randolph's home was a beautiful, two-story Georgian brick house on a bluff in Sunset Heights. A Mexican maid in a white apron and perky little cap answered the brass knocker and let us into the foyer, where Mrs. Randolph greeted us. She was wearing a lovely rose crepe dress with a long skirt, and she seemed so majestic I had an awful feeling that my blue wool jumper and embroidered blouse weren't dressy enough, although it was the best I had.

Mrs. Randolph seemed genuinely pleased to see us. "So lucky, you girls are a few minutes early. It will give us a chance to step into the dining room and look at some of the Randolph mementos, especially reminders of Cecil's boyhood—that is, if you can forgive a mother's pride."

She led us into the high-ceilinged dining room. A huge Tiffany chandelier was centered over a long table covered with a lace cloth, obviously to be used for refreshments later on. A silver tea service on a large tray at one end of the table was balanced by a silver bowl holding blush carnations, our club flower, at the other end.

We barely had time to glance at the table before Mrs. Randolph directed our attention to the numerous objects displayed on a broad ledge above the golden-oak wainscoting. "Cecil is at Staunton Military Academy in Virginia now, and of course he will go on to West Point," she repeated. "These are mementos of his boyhood," she added, as she picked up a little lead soldier and held it up for our inspection. "You know Cecil has always loved anything military. See this, one of his Civil War generals." She turned it around so we could admire the details. "It is hand-painted, absolutely authentic. Cecil had both sets, the Confederate generals and the Union generals. Oh, the mock battles he had. But you'll have to excuse me. When I talk about Cecil, I do run on." She put the soldier back on the wainscoting shelf, rearranging the group a little so that the Confederate and Union guns pointed more directly at each other.

While we murmured our admiration for the Civil War collection, Mrs. Randolph directed our attention to another display. "Of course, I've saved absolutely everything. Here is the modern army." She picked up another lead toy, an officer on horseback. "You see the black and gold shoulder insignia. That's the First Calvary Division at Fort Bliss." Mrs. Randolph interrupted herself and pointed towards a little table in the corner, covered with an assortment of photographs. "Of course you all know Cecil. You must have seen him at church," she said, pointing to a series of pictures of a boy in various military uniforms. I stepped up for a closer look. I had seen Cecil only once, and I barely remembered how he looked. The photographs appeared to be a series, each one a year older than the preceding one, probably commemorating birthdays.

Mrs. Randolph had turned back to the toys. "Oh, you must see Cecil's music box. It actually plays reveille," she said, twisting the key. The clear notes tinkled softly. "We played that to call Cecil to breakfast when he was a little fellow, and he loved it." Tenderly, she returned it to the shelf. "Cecil comes by his love of the military naturally—from both sides of the family, you know. My father was a general, retired now, and of course Cecil's father, Colonel Randolph—" She let her voice drop off as she directed our attention to the opposite wall holding a large photograph of a handsome officer in a colonel's uniform.

I recalled that one of the girls had mentioned that Colonel Randolph had been killed in a polo accident or something like that, and I didn't know what to say about the photograph. Mrs. Randolph tactfully changed the subject by pointing to another photograph, this one showing Colonel Randolph astride a beautiful horse. I was relieved when I glanced through the window and saw the other girls and Dr. Poe, the much respected minister at First Church, coming up the front steps.

Mrs. Randolph shepherded us into the living room for the initiation ceremony. Dr. Poe, a large man, slipped on his black ministerial robe and became even more imposing. He stood behind a library table that held another bowl of blush carnations and lighted candelabra. Twilight had fallen and the little dancing flames of the candles were reflected in the beveled glass window panes. Dr. Poe made a little speech about how fortunate and privileged we were to be there together. He said a short prayer expressing gratitude that we, the flower of young womanhood, were about to pledge ourselves to follow in the paths of righteousness during the difficult years that lay ahead.

Next he asked us to raise our right hands and repeat the Friends of the Cross oath:

> I pledge, as much as in me lies, to be worthy of
> the honor and trust this night committed unto my
> keeping, that my thoughts may be pure, my actions
> virtuous, and my price above rubies, so help me God.

After we took the oath, each girl stepped forward and Dr. Poe slipped the badge over her shoulders. Still wearing our badges, we went into the dining room for refreshments. While we had been meeting in the living room, the maid had placed trays of food on the table. I had never seen such tiny little sandwiches, made of soft white crustless bread cut in diamond and oval shapes.

Mrs. Randolph poured tea from the silver pot into almost transparent porcelain cups. She asked me if I took cream. I really liked lemon better, but I was too timid to say anything. I just nodded and took the cream as she suggested. With my cup in one hand I walked around the table, selected one of the little round sandwiches, and tasted it. It was delicious, a very thin slice of cucumber with spicy mayonnaise. After I took a small bite, I held it out and looked to be sure it was cucumber. Mama always served cucumber sliced in a bowl with a splash of vinegar and maybe a sprinkle of celery seeds, and I had never thought of a cucumber sandwich.

The girls were all standing around the table, sipping their tea and talking in monosyllables. Although I knew everybody, I felt terribly self-conscious and ill at ease. I put the rest of the little sandwich in my mouth and felt my throat contract, making it difficult to swallow.

Beverly had been ahead of me in the serving line. Suddenly, she appeared at my side. She held a toothpick with a little boiled shrimp on the end, and while I watched, she dipped the shrimp into a little bowl of pink sauce and plopped it in her mouth. "Have one," she said. "They're delicious." She pointed to the centerpiece, a huge grapefruit, bristling with toothpicks like an overgrown, yellow porcupine, each toothpick holding a little pink shrimp, a tiny brown sausage, or a big black olive. While I watched, she plucked another shrimp and dunked it. She nudged me with her elbow, "Go ahead. You'll like it."

Eyeing Beverly for support, I reached across the table, seized a shrimp, and dunked it as I had seen her do. "How did you know?" I whispered.

"Saw it in a movie," she answered, lightly. "How do you like shrimp?"

"Oh, they're good," I said casually, not wanting to admit even to Beverly that I had never tasted shrimp before. "Have a cucumber sandwich. They're good too."

Beverly and I had come a long way from the ice cream socials at Altura.

After the initiation tea, we served a three-month pledge period, and in early spring we were entitled to receive our Friends of the Cross rings. Mrs. Randolph again invited us to her home for the presentation.

The meeting wasn't quite as formal this time, but anything at Mrs. Randolph's house was impressive. We sat in a circle in the living room—one chair empty to remind us of the presence of Christ. Before presenting the rings, Mrs. Randolph explained that certain members of the session had talked to the jeweler and determined that rings engraved "Friends of the Cross" would require a new mold which would be too expensive. Therefore, although we were to be known as Friends of the Cross, our rings lying there on the table—she pointed to the nine rings—were engraved "Comrades of the Cross" just like the boys' rings.

We were disappointed, but we didn't say anything, at least not to Mrs. Randolph. After she handed each girl a ring, Harriet held out her hand and looked at her ring. "Can you believe it?" she whispered under her breath, not loud enough for Mrs. Randolph to hear. "We can't call ourselves Comrades, but they're too chinchy to make a new ring."

Receiving our rings was such a significant step in our lives, Mrs. Randolph felt she should take the opportunity to say a few words to us. She placed her chair next to that left empty for Christ and started her little speech. She pointed out that we would soon be finishing junior high and going on to high school, and as the director of religious education she felt obligated to give us some guidance for the difficult choices ahead. In an aside she mentioned that even though the Comrades of the Cross had a secret ritual, she felt she would not be violating any trust if she let us know that Mr. Wyatt-Browne— she never referred to him as Coach—was talking to Comrades of the Cross on the same subject. In fact, she and Mr. Wyatt-Browne had shared a book entitled *Preparation for Life*.

She reminded us once again that we were fortunate young women, the flower of American womanhood, or, even better, the flower of Presbyterian American womanhood. Along with our privileges came responsibilities. Now that childhood was behind us and we were going out into the larger, crueler world, she thought it was time to talk to us quite frankly in words that we would understand.

I folded my hands in my lap and looked at my new gold ring. After an eloquent pause, Mrs. Randolph began earnestly. "You have grown up in a capitalistic society, and I don't have to explain to you what happens when goods are hard to obtain. The price goes up." She paused and looked around to be sure we were all in agreement.

"Now, girls, I ask you to imagine a lovely peach tree, loaded with fruit, and a handsome young man is walking through the orchard.

144

The lower branches of the tree are heavy with fruit, bending almost to the ground. In fact, some over-ripe peaches are lying on the ground, and the young man kicks them impatiently aside. Does he pick the fruit on the lower branches, that readily available ripe fruit? No, of course not. His gaze goes ever higher and higher. He wants the topmost peach, the one hard to get."

Mrs. Randolph paused and smiled graciously at our attentive group. "You are a select group, a fortunate group. You each wear the ring signifying that you have taken an oath to live a pure and virtuous life. I leave you with one plea this afternoon: Stay high on the tree. Be desirable. Be hard to get. Some day the right young man will find you, and you will be rewarded, so thankful that you waited for him. He will know you are worthy of his trust, that your price is above rubies."

After the talk we went into the dining room for refreshments. Mrs. Randolph dipped a large silver ladle into the cut-glass punch bowl and poured frosty pink punch into the little cut-glass punch cups. The afternoon sun shone through the beveled glass windows and sparkled on the punch bowl, the cups, and the Tiffany chandelier. Even Cecil's little toys, especially the red-coated soldiers, caught the light.

There were platters of cookies, little iced cakes, and dates stuffed with walnuts and rolled in powdered sugar. Everything seemed warm and friendly. I went back for a refill on the punch and thanked Mrs. Randolph for giving us such a nice party.

Beverly and I left together. We had to take the Sunset Heights streetcar down to Yandell and transfer to the Fort Bliss streetcar. As we settled down on the Fort Bliss streetcar, Beverly opened a package of peppermint Life Savers, and we each took one and started talking about how elegant the Randolph home was.

Beverly was thoughtful for a moment and then recalled all the little lead soldiers and other toys that Mrs. Randolph had shown us on our first visit. "Of course, I don't know Cecil, personally," she said, "but before he went away to Staunton he and George were best friends, and George told me that Cecil doesn't really like all that military stuff. He's handsome in those pictures in his uniform, of course, but George said when you get to know him he is a sensitive sort of guy, I mean not what you'd normally think of as an army officer."

"Well, Mrs. Randolph has really set her heart on his being in the army. I don't think anything short of a general would satisfy her."

"Yeah, that's what George thinks. He said since Cecil's father was a colonel and was killed in that polo accident Cecil won't have any trouble getting into West Point. Mrs. Randolph has it all planned."

Beverly took another Life Saver and offered me one. We were both silent, thinking about Cecil.

I spoke first. "Well, it's natural Mrs. Randolph wants Cecil to follow his father's career, I guess."

"I suppose."

From her tone of voice I sensed Beverly had some reservations. "Say, what did you think of Mrs. Randolph's talk?"

"Oh, the parable of the peaches? Well, I guess she's right that anything that is hard to get becomes expensive. That's really what she said."

"There was more to it than that, Beverly. You just don't take anything seriously."

"I try not to. Romantic as you are, Mafra, well, sometimes I wonder about you. Here, have another Life Saver. Have the whole pack. You're going to need them."

"One more will do." I took one and slipped it in my mouth. The streetcar lurched around the Five Point corners and started straight out Tularosa. I twisted my gold ring on my finger and looked at it. "You like your ring, Beverly?"

She held her ring out at a distance and admired it. "Yes, they're heavy gold, all right. But after they refused to let us be Comrades I think Harriet was right when she said it was sort of chinchy, not giving us our own rings. Oh, well, my price is above rubies. Hey, too bad they couldn't afford a ruby!"

We were quiet, twisting our rings for a while. I had a new thought: "Wonder what Coach Wyatt-Browne told the boys about that book, *Preparation for Life?*

"Probably how to build a ladder."

12

Dianne and I became good friends the summer I gave her the YWCA membership. The membership wasn't actually a gift from me; it was from Mr. Mae, or rather from the Lone Star Cotton Mill. Every year the mill bought several memberships to support the YWCA. This was the first year I was old enough, and Mr. Mae gave Papa two memberships—for Mafra and one of her friends, he had said.

Papa tossed the brochures on the dining-room table, and I didn't have any trouble picking out the activity I wanted: ballroom dancing. Beverly and some of my other friends were already taking dancing from Karma Deane, and I had felt left out because I couldn't afford the lessons. This was a wonderful chance, and right away I decided to give the other membership to Dianne. We could go on the streetcar together, and it would be fun.

I took one of the brochures down to Printz's to show Dianne.

She came out on the porch, and we talked about it. She thanked me and said she had been wanting to learn to dance, so I thought it was all settled. But the next morning she brought the brochure back and told Mama and me she couldn't join the "Y."

"Why not?" Mama exclaimed, clearly perplexed. "Mafra is so pleased to have the chance."

"I know. I would like to do it, and Mama thought it was nice; but Mr. Printz said I can't accept charity."

"Charity? Why does he call it charity?"

"Well, you'd be giving me the membership, and he says that he owns property and he doesn't accept charity from anybody. And another thing, he's afraid there would be a lot of Mexicans down there."

Mama started to answer angrily, but she looked at Dianne's tear-stained face and checked herself. "Oh, my dear, he just doesn't understand. Big companies like the Lone Star Cotton Mill always buy memberships to support the YWCA, and our good friend, Mr. Mae, wants the memberships to be used by representative people."

Mama didn't use that phrase, representative people, very often, but when she did it carried a lot of weight. Once I had been foolish enough to ask her just what it meant. Irritated at my stupidity she had answered, scathingly: "That's a phrase people in Georgia understand perfectly, a very useful phrase. As to what it means, like Humpty Dumpty said in Alice in Wonderland, 'It means just what I choose it to mean—neither more nor less.'"

Whatever the phrase meant, I understood that this time it included Dianne, and was intended to be complimentary. I also realized that Mama was coming to grips with the situation, and we could expect action. She asked if Mr. Printz was at home. Dianne hesitated, obviously afraid of the action Mama comtemplated; but she admitted Mr. Printz was at home. She seemed resigned to the fact there was no stopping Mama.

In a matter of minutes Mama had put on a fresh dress and the three of us were headed down the hill, Dianne and I in front and Mama close behind, her Cuban heels clicking purposefully on the sidewalk. Stiff as a military cadre we turned the barbershop corner, marched up Mr. Printz's walk, climbed the steps and crossed the narrow porch.

Dianne's mother—I always thought of Mrs. Printz as Dianne's mother instead of by her married name—held the door and invited us in. She looked very much like Dianne—the same blue-gray eyes and fair hair, now touched with gray, and the same retiring personality. Obviously surprised, she managed to smile and asked us to sit down, motioning to the seats on the sofa. Mr. Printz, clad in trousers, shirt and vest, but no coat, appeared from the hallway. Mama shook hands with him cordially as though greeting a long-lost friend, and he sat in an armchair facing the sofa. There was a straight chair on my right, and Dianne sat there, completing our little circle.

"I'm so sorry about this misunderstanding," Mama began graciously. In the act of crossing the living room threshold she had laid aside her earlier belligerence like an unneeded outer garment. She leaned forward, radiating charm. "Really, it's all my fault," she went on, "I should have come down myself and explained about the memberships, but Mafra was so excited she just ran down to talk to Dianne. Naturally she didn't make it clear. We didn't buy the memberships ourselves. You know, when the YWCA puts on its annual membership drive they ask civic leaders and the big corporations to buy memberships to be distributed to representative people in different sections of the city—not in South El Paso, of course, there is a different branch of the 'Y' for Mexicans."

Mama paused for breath, and I felt the color rise to my cheeks. I pressed my hand to my mouth, a little embarrassed at that statement. I had no idea if there was a South El Paso branch of the "Y" for Mexicans, and I was reasonably sure Mama didn't know either. It didn't matter. She had neatly disposed of the Mexican objection. "The membership is actually a gift from the cotton mill—not from us personally. Right away Mafra wanted Dianne to go with her. They can ride the streetcar together, and there is no expense at all, except carfare. I presume that's no problem?"

Mr. Printz bristled. "Carfare a problem? No, certainly not," He shifted in his chair and laughed derisively at such a ridiculous notion.

When Mama heard that little laugh she felt the ice was broken and sensed victory. She hastened to wrap it up. "I thought you'd see what a nice opportunity it is for the girls, Mr. Printz. It's really a compliment that they are the kind of girls the 'Y' is looking for."

Hearing no objection, Mama pressed on. "We want to get the two membership forms signed so we can send them back to the YWCA." Nobody answered, and Mama turned to Mrs. Printz, who had not spoken since she invited us to sit down. "Here," Mama held out the form, "if you sign this form, we can turn it in with Mafra's. Oh, just a moment, let Dianne choose her activity."

Mama took the form back and passed it to Dianne, who glanced at Mr. Printz, saw that he was not disapproving, and quickly checked off ballroom dancing for her activity. When she had finished, Mama attempted again to hand the form to Mrs. Printz, but Mr. Printz leaned forward and took it himself.

"I'll take care of it," he said.

We all watched silently while he read the form, took the fountain pen out of his vest pocket, went over to a small corner table, signed and blotted the form, and gave it back to Mama. She shook hands with him again, and we were ready to leave.

As we walked back up the hill Mama looked at the form. Mr. Printz had signed "Edgar Printz, Guardian."

"Is Mr. Printz Dianne's legal guardian?" she asked.

"I don't know. She told me she is still named Mel because she has not been adopted. I think she remembers her real father and doesn't want to change her name. I don't know if Mr. Printz is really her guardian, but he sure bosses her and her mother. No matter, as long as he signed it."

"I purposely gave it to Mrs. Printz," Mama said. "She had been so left out of the conversation that I wanted her to be involved, but she just let Mr. Printz take over. I declare, that woman is so meek. Why didn't she speak up in the first place and tell Mr. Printz that Dianne should accept the membership? It's ridiculous. Everything is done on Mr. Printz's terms." Mama sighed.

Later, after Dianne and I had become good friends, she told me she really appreciated what Mama did for her that morning. We both liked the dancing class. It was a big class, about thirty girls, and I thought Dianne was probably the best in the class—a natural dancer. She always had pretty clothes that her mother made for her, and I especially liked a white linen princess-style dress she wore to dancing class. When I looked across the floor and saw Dianne waltzing around in that circular skirt, the hem embroidered with butterflies, I would miss my own steps, thinking what a picture she made with the bright butterflies fluttering around her slender legs.

Riding home on the streetcar one day, I looked closely at the embroidered butterflies and saw that they were not alike. "Where did you get all the different patterns?" I asked.

"Oh, I just sketched them, and Mama embroidered them. There are always butterflies on Mr. Printz's cacti, and I like to watch them."

Her little clutch-style linen purse that matched her dress was lying on her lap, and I noticed the embroidery on it. "Where did you see such tiny butterflies to copy?" I asked, pointing to some white embroidery on the purse.

"Oh, those are really moths," she explained. "They're on the yucca late in the evening, just before dark. I think it's the only thing that pollinates the yucca. Mama had a hard time with that color. It's not exactly white. I think that's what they call Rembrandt white. Don't you think so?"

I had no idea what she meant by Rembrandt white, but I tried to hide my ignorance. "It is almost white," I said, "but on that white purse it stands out a little bit. How did your mother get that color?"

"We tried different things, and finally she put some little silver stitches underneath where they don't really show, but sort of shine through. I'm lucky: Mama loves to sew for me."

"It's lovely," I said, "and it matches your dress."

The car had reached our stop on Fort Boulevard, and we got off. The sun had already gone behind Mount Franklin, and the welcome shadow had crept across Copia Street. We were tired and walked slowly, not talking much.

In front of Mr. Printz's apartments I told Dianne good-bye, and she ran up the front walk. Not aware that I was watching her, she stopped beside the steps and lightly touched the yucca blossoms which were just coming into summer bloom. She lingered, and I thought perhaps she saw some of the little moths she had told me about. I walked on, but before I turned the barbershop corner I glanced back. She was still there, graceful in her white dress, bending over the yucca blooms. I like to remember Dianne that way.

Without confiding in anyone, not even my best friends, I bolted the conventional wisdom and signed up for public speaking my first year at El Paso High.

"Public speaking? That's a boys' class!" Beverly exclaimed when she saw my schedule. "Why aren't you taking domestic science like all the other girls? We're going to have so much fun in cooking class."

Emmaline was even more distressed: "But, Mafra, what about the cooking apron you made in sewing class last year? All the buttonholes you had to make, and now you won't even be using it!"

They were both right, and the difficult part was I couldn't explain—not without sounding grandiose. But I had pondered Dr. Blevins' message, and in my heart I had made the commitment: "Here am I. Send me." Like David Livingstone I would study, prepare myself, and spread the word among the heathen in darkest Africa; and like Dr. Blevins I would come home on sabbatical and address huge congregations, tell them of my success, and hold them in the palm of my hand with my eloquence. That's why I needed to become an effective public speaker; and choosing public speaking as my elective was the first step along the rocky road ahead.

So the white cambric cooking apron stayed folded in my dresser drawer. Every time I happened to glance at it I remembered Emmaline's consternation when she heard I wasn't going to be in cooking class, and I realized how much I had changed since last spring when the apron seemed so important to me. So many hours of frustrating effort had gone into it: the fitted bodice fastened in back with three buttons and matching buttonholes, the bias tape around neck and armholes, full gathered skirt and two pockets— the triumph I had felt when it was finally finished. And now it just didn't matter. Life certainly had a way of taking sudden changes.

Jeannie M. Frank, Scottish born, was our public speaking teacher. English was her usual subject, but due to some emergency the regular public speaking teacher was gone for a year. Mrs. Frank had taken over the class. El Paso High had a tradition of winning the district declamation contest each year, and Mrs. Frank accepted that challenge as part of her assignment.

She was a large woman but economically structured, a perfect bundle of energy. Her auburn hair was pulled straight up and fastened in a bun on top of her head. Not a wisp escaped. It wouldn't dare. On the first day of class she gave us to understand that she was a teacher at El Paso High not by choice but by a series of adverse circumstances. When she was a young girl, she started to explain, but checked herself abruptly: "Do I hear a snicker on the back row? I once was a young girl—improbable as the notion strikes you—I once was young, and now if I may have your attention, I'll get on with the story."

She had our attention, and certainly no one intended to be the first to snicker. With just the faintest trace of a Scottish brogue she continued: It was some twenty years ago, or maybe more, when, having just been awarded her M.A. degree from Glasgow University, she left Scotland with the intention of visiting America for just a few weeks before returning home to start her teaching career. The sea voyage had made her deathly sick—she spent the entire six days in her bunk, throwing up every bite she'd ever eaten since first she tasted mother's milk. When the ship finally docked and she was assisted down the gangplank in New York, she vowed that never again under any conditions would she set foot on a ship—never. That misadventure, that sea voyage, she explained, was the reason she now found herself a middle-aged teacher at El Paso High. Maybe we hadn't thought of it, but El Paso was just about as far as you can get in America from any ocean.

Mrs. Frank gave us a moment to absorb her story and then brought us back to the present. She didn't know what sort of misadventures may have landed us in this particular class, but she was sure we had our stories. Since we all found ourselves at this crossroad, if she were willing to make the best of the situation, perhaps we would kindly do the same. A bargain? Well, yes, of course. We exchanged cautious glances, wanting to laugh but not knowing how to take this outspoken teacher who was treating us like equals, challenging us to act like grown-ups.

The object of the class was clear: We must win the district declamation contest and then on to the regional. There were twice as many boys as girls in the class, and assignments were gender-oriented: orations for the boys, poems for the girls. The first problem was to fit the selection to the speaker. This meant we had to memorize various selections and try them out before the class. Thanks to this method of teaching, memorizing my own selections and listening to repetitive recitations by others in the class, I made a sort of back-door acquaintance with much of the world's great literature. To this day I can recite from memory reams of poetry and pages of orations that would have slipped by me unnoticed in college and even graduate courses.

Ramón Rodriguez, looking so serious in his khaki R.O.T.C. uniform, was wonderful as the drummer boy responding to his captain's order to beat a retreat:

I cannot beat a retreat. But I can beat a charge!
I can beat a charge that will make the very dead fall into line.
Beat the charge!
And the day was won.

And day after day I heard H.T. Ethridge and others ask and answer the immortal question:

Is life so dear or peace so sweet as to be purchased
at the price of chains and slavery? Forbid it, Almighty
God. I know not what course others may take, but as for
me, give me liberty or give me death!

As to the girls, I conceded on the very first day that Ella Mae Bushong would win the district and probably the regional. She was fifteen—a year or two older than the rest of us. She wore too much makeup and high heels, and she chewed gum, which Mrs. Frank made her remove daily before she recited. But with all that, there was something about the way Ella Mae said those poems that just caught your heart. She was so good that Mrs. Frank had trouble deciding whether she should do something sad or something inspirational. Her first choice was "The Ballad of Reading Gaol":

I never saw a man who looked
   With such a wistful eye
Upon that little tent of blue
   Which prisoners call the sky.

Yet each man kills the thing he loves,
   By each let this be heard
Some do it with a bitter look,
   Some with a flattering word.

Ella Mae said it with such feeling, I would have stopped right there, but Mrs. Frank kept trying other poems. Maybe she just liked to hear Ella Mae recite. She finally decided on "The Bridge of Sighs" by Thomas Hood:

One more unfortunate,
Weary of breath,
Rashly importunate,
Gone to her death!

Take her up tenderly,
Lift her with care;
Fashioned so slenderly,
Young, and so fair!

Alas for the rarity
Of Christian charity
Under the sun!
O, it was pitiful!
Near a whole city full,
Home she had none.

Owning her weakness,
Her evil behavior,
And leaving, with meekness,
Her sins to her savior!

Every time Ella Mae said it I was afraid I would cry. The whole poem was too long—eighteen verses I think they said—but they cut some verses until the poem fit the allotted time, and Ella Mae practiced it every day.

Mrs. Frank, trying to find a poem that suited me, looked puzzled. She said she wasn't quite sure of my style. We tried one poem after another, and she rejected them all. As the rejections mounted, I felt I must be the worst experience that had come her way since that rolling ocean liner. I tried to smile encouragement—surely there was something.

"Hmm," she said, after several days of brain-wracking: "You're rather the gentle type. You like children?"

"Yes, I suppose so. Well, yes," I answered doubtfully. Actually I had never given it much thought.

She gave me a copy of Eugene Field's "Little Boy Blue" and told me to think about the meaning as I memorized it. I was ready the next day:

> The little toy dog is covered with dust,
> But sturdy and staunch he stands
> And the little toy soldier is red with rust,
> And his musket molds in his hands;
> Time was when the little toy dog was new,
> And the soldier was passing fair,
> And that was when our Little Boy Blue
> Kissed them and put them there.

Mrs. Frank looked her disapproval. "You're not thinking about the words, Mary Frances. Did you ever see a little boy playing with his toy soldiers, loving them? Think about it. Express it."

Cecil's toy soldiers that Mrs. Randolph had shown us when we had the tea at her house were as near as I could come. I thought about his collection and tried again, but it didn't work. Mrs. Frank gave me a searching look, determined to fathom the very depths of my soul. "Maybe you're idealistic," she said. "I guess that's the trouble. You're idealistic—moralistic." It didn't sound like a compliment.

She looked over her book of poems again, and finally decided on

"If" by Rudyard Kipling. "For heaven's sake think about the meaning," she said. I felt she had simply chosen it by elimination, and I never read a poem I hated more.

The tryout for district was in early April. There were too many boys in the class, so Miss Frank selected the six best boys; all six girls had to compete. To make it worse, I had to follow Ella Mae's rendition of "The Bridge of Sighs."

The contestants sat on the stage together, and when Ella Mae finished her recitation there was a moment of silence in the big auditorium and then a burst of applause. I was sure she had won. I waited for the applause to die out, stepped forward, and announced I would recite "If" by Rudyard Kipling:

> If you can keep your head when all about you
>   Are losing theirs and blaming it on you,
> If you can trust yourself when all men doubt you,
>   And make allowance for their doubting too;
> If you can wait and not be tired by waiting,
>   Or being lied about, don't deal in lies,
> Or being hated, don't give way to hating,
>   And yet don't look too good, nor talk too wise . . .

That was just the first verse, and there was no way I could get that far without looking too good and talking too wise. I blushed at my own piety, and despite Mrs. Frank's weeks of coaching I slipped into the monotone she hated:

> If you can meet with triumph and disaster,
>   And treat those two impostors just the same,

Some way or other, I got on with it, and shouted the last stanza:

> If you can fill the unforgiving minute
>   With sixty seconds' worth of distance run,
> Yours is the Earth and everything that's in it,
>   And—which is more—you'll be a Man, my son!

Well, it was awful. There were a few more recitations, and the judges announced the winners: Ramón Rodriguez with "The

Drummer Boy" for the boys, and Ella Mae, of course, for the girls. The only surprise was that I placed second, but when I thought about it that was understandable. Except for Ella Mae, there just wasn't any female talent in that class.

Two or three days before the district contest, Ella Mae was not in class. Mrs. Frank, calling the roll, glanced at the empty seat. "Ella Mae Bushong is no longer enrolled at El Paso High," she said, drawing a dark line across the name in her roll book. A hush fell over the class. Mrs. Frank looked directly at me. "That means, Mary Frances, that you will be representing El Paso High at the district declamation contest."

I gasped. "What happened to Ella Mae? Won't she be back?"

"Ella Mae will not be back. We have exactly two days before the contest, and we will practice your poem. You've improved a lot. You'll do very well."

Under normal conditions even faint praise from Mrs. Frank would have felt like a crown of laurel, but this day I hardly noticed it. I hadn't won the tryout, I didn't deserve to be in the District, and, worst of all, I didn't want to take Ella Mae's place. Whatever had happened? I couldn't wait until lunch period to find out.

We met at the cafeteria table as usual: Beverly, Dianne and I together, Harriet next to me, Margaret Williams and some other girls from the church on the other side of the table, Emmaline and even Mary Barnett down at the end. Mary was still as obnoxious as she had been back at Rusk, but she ate with us sometimes—if it suited her.

The rumors were all over school, but Beverly had the inside story, and nobody interrupted when she plunged right in. They were trying to keep it quiet, she said, but Ella Mae had been expelled. She had gone with three boys to that old deserted house out on Newman Road and did it, went all the way with the three boys. Beverly was pretty sure it was three boys, but she didn't know their names, except that one of them was supposed to be a senior.

I forgot to eat my tamale pie and just stared at Beverly, trying to understand what she was saying. Somebody asked how the school found out, and she said one of the boys had written a note, which was pretty stupid, of course. And Coach Wyatt-Browne got hold of the note, took it to Mr. Davis, the principal.

Nobody was eating. Somebody interrupted to ask what the note said. Beverly, maddeningly slow, stirred her own food before going on with the story. It must have happened a whole month ago, she said, because one of the boys was scared and wrote a note saying he hoped the Coke worked.

"The Coke?" I asked. "What Coke?"

"For a douche," Beverly explained, in a confidential whisper. "You know if you do it without meaning to—you know just happen to—well, you can use a Coke douche and maybe not get pregnant."

Well, I didn't know, and I was wondering if it wouldn't really burn, but I didn't want to ask any more dumb questions. I tasted my food which was by now quite cold. Out of the corner of my eye I noticed Dianne had blushed fiery red. She always looked uncomfortable when we talked about sex, and we didn't usually tell jokes or say anything off-color in front of her. We didn't talk about it a lot anyway, but sometimes Beverly liked to tell me little dirty jokes—I don't know where she heard them—like: "Why didn't the big train have a little train? Pulled out on time." Or "Why didn't the pencil have a little pencil? Rubber on the end." From those little jokes I could kind of figure out what she was talking about, but this was the first time we ever said so much in front of Dianne.

The other girls had started talking, and I asked what Mr. Davis did to the three boys, but nobody knew. Ella Mae didn't live with her mother and father. For some reason she lived with her sister, and he had called her sister into the office and explained why they were expelling Ella Mae. Mary Barnett said the Coke might not have worked and wouldn't it be awful if Ella Mae was pregnant. She said it with such a smirk, like that was just what she would expect of someone like Ella Mae, but the other girls at the table were pretty sad about it.

All of a sudden someone pointed to the clock over the door. It was almost time for the bell, and we started gobbling up our food. Harriet remembered another piece of news: "Say, this reminds me of something I was going to tell you, but I almost forgot. You remember when Janet Carter dropped out of school so suddenly last fall, and her little sister Marge spread it around that she was going east to college because her father didn't like El Paso High?"

Of course, we all remembered Janet—popular but stuck-up. We asked Harriet to go on.

"Well, Marge told her best friend what actually happened, and now her friend broke up with Marge and she's telling it all over school. That's how I happened to hear. Anyway, Janet was ready to go out on a date one night, and just as she was leaving she dropped her evening bag on the living-room floor and a rubber—you know, a condom—fell out. Her father saw it, and boy, did he come down on her! He took her back to Boston and got her into some kind of exclusive girls' school. Well, you know the Carters are loaded with money—but imagine Janet at a girls' school."

"I really can't," Beverly answered. "Ha! Wonder if she has to wear a uniform."

"Well, there won't be a girls' school for Ella Mae," Harriet said. "Whatever will she do?"

Nobody answered. The bell rang, and we grabbed our books and rushed to class. Friday afternoons were always slow, but this was endless. I was, sad, mixed-up and really frightened.

When school was finally out on that terrible Friday, Dianne, Beverly and I walked down to Casner's used-car lot to pick up a car. Beverly's father, who was head bookkeeper for Casner's, had taught her to drive the summer before. On weekends if she went by the lot the salesmen would find an old car she could use. The choice of a car always took time because the salesmen liked to tease Beverly, telling her the car was going to break down or she couldn't drive well enough, and all that silly stuff. It was a relief when they finally decided on a battered old sedan.

After flooding the engine several times, Beverly managed to get started, but she had to pull the choke and sort of nurse the old wreck along all the way up Piedras, so we didn't talk much until we turned on to Fort Boulevard where it was level and the car started running better. Once the driving got easier, we started talking about Ella Mae. After we hashed over everything we already knew, Beverly said we were so close to Newman Road we might as well drive out to see the little house where it all happened. "Scene of the crime," she called it.

In no time we were out in the open desert. There on the right side of the road, just as we remembered it, was the little, weather-beaten house, probably the deserted home of some old home-steader who had been forced by wind and drought to abandon his dreams of a productive ranch. Creosote bushes crowded the front steps, and most of the windows were broken.

Beverly slowed the car down as we passed, found a wide place in the road, and turned around. As we came by the second time, the whole scene looked so dreary and godforsaken, we didn't feel like talking about it any more. Beverly stepped on the gas and said she wished we hadn't come—it was a dumb idea. I agreed, and Dianne, who had been even more quiet than usual that day, opened up to say she had sat next to Ella Mae in typing class and liked her. She wondered what would happen to her.

Beverly said she sure hoped the Coke douche worked. Dianne and I had no answer. Beverly went on, sort of musing to herself, "Sometimes if a girl gets in trouble, depending, of course, on who she is, she might get an abortion at that women's clinic down on Yandell, the one we pass every day on the streetcar."

I remembered seeing the clinic sign but until that moment hadn't given it a thought. Beverly drove in silence for a moment and then went on with her monologue, "But, gosh, you can be sure that clinic isn't going to do anything for Ella Mae. She's nobody, hasn't got any money, and they'd want at least a hundred dollars."

"How do you know?" I asked, surprised at Beverly's sophistica-tion.

"Oh, I just hear things. Different girls talk about it. Don't you remember that sort of cute girl, Isabel Wright, in our gym class at Austin? I heard she got pregnant and went to that clinic. They messed her up so bad her mother finally took her to California to get her patched up. She's back in school now, but she looks awful. Anyway, Ella Mae never had a hundred dollars to her name, so let's just hope the douche worked."

For the second or third time that day I repeated that it wasn't fair—something should have happened to the boys, too.

Beverly took her eyes off the road long enough to look at me in exasperation. "Of course, it's not fair. It's just different, that's all. With boys, nobody cares. I'm not going to do anything myself. I mean I'm not going all the way, not until I get married. But, gosh, when I get married—well, heck, I don't care about the boy. What I mean is I sure don't want anybody *learning* on me."

Beverly's statement met a stunned silence, and I think she knew she had gone too far. Dianne stared straight ahead, and I had to do a double take myself, not knowing what to say. It was crazy to talk that way in front of Dianne. Why, she was so *innocent* she wouldn't even tell you when she was menstruating. The other girls would say they had the curse, or fell off the roof, or maybe, "I got it but it don't do me no good." But with Dianne you wouldn't even know, unless you happened to be in her gym class and noticed she was taking her three-day excuse.

I was relieved when we turned up Mountain Avenue and reached the barbershop corner. Dianne got out, still looking embarrassed and not saying anything except to thank Beverly for the ride.

When we stopped at my house, for the first time I remembered to tell Beverly I had to take Ella Mae's place in the district declamation contest and I hated to do it. After we talked about it a while, she said it was funny: Ella Mae getting in trouble and me ending up in the Declamation Contest. After all the tension of the day we both agreed maybe the joke was on me.

As soon as I got in the house and dumped my books, I started telling Mama the events of the day. She was upset, as I knew she would be, about Ella Mae, but as for me being in the contest she seemed rather pleased and, like Mrs. Frank, thought I could do it very well.

It would be nice if I could report that as a result of this ugly affair I suddenly matured, rose to the occasion, recited my poem with passion, and carried old El Paso High to glory. But it didn't happen that way.

Ramón Rodriguez won for the boys; but, although I tried my best, I didn't even place for the girls. I was glad when it was finally over and wanted to slip off the stage without having to confront Mrs. Frank, but I had to look for my family—they had come in spite of my protests—and she followed me down the aisle, so I not only had to face her, I had to introduce her to my family. As we walked towards them, I told her I was glad Ramón had won and sorry I didn't even place.

She put her hand on my shoulder and said, "My dear, it was very gracious of you to fill in at the last minute, and I thought you did quite well."

"But you wanted so much for El Paso High to win."

"Doesn't matter. El Paso High was well represented. How many times did I tell you during the year to think of the words you were saying? How did Kipling say it? 'Meet with triumph and disaster, and treat those two impostors just the same.' I appreciate your helping out at the last minute, and you have improved so much this year, Mary Frances, you should really take another class in public speaking. It's done so much for you."

The unexpected praise from Mrs. Frank was almost as good as winning the contest. She and Mama had some further conversation, and I heard Mrs. Frank confess that she may have pushed the class too hard, even bullied us a little, but she always tried to bring out the best in her students. She left us then, and as I watched her go through the crowd, her tidy little top-knot of auburn hair held tightly in place by the brown celluloid hairpins, I realized how much she had done for me and how much I had come to like her. In a bittersweet sort of way, she probably was my favorite teacher.

Driving home in the car, Mama turned from the front seat and said, "I was really surprised, Mafra, when you selected that course, but you certainly had a good teacher. I think you must have learned a great deal."

I was in the back seat, the wind in my face. "Yeah, I sure did."

13

The Samuel H. Kress Foundation has been generous to El Paso. The famous Kress art collection containing at least fifty-nine European masters is now housed in the El Paso Museum of Art. I had bittersweet memories when I visited that museum a few years ago. Although I have never been properly thanked—unless I am included in one of the "anonymous donor" signs—I made a distinct contribution to the amassing of the vast fortune necessary to create the priceless collection.

My role in this worthy enterprise dates from a Saturday morning in May 1929. I stood on the sidewalk beneath the huge red and gold "S. H. KRESS & COMPANY" sign and gazed at the window filled with a conglomeration of merchandise: toothpaste, shaving cream, rayon hose displayed on shapely leg molds pointing skyward, toy windmills, chocolate-covered peanuts, and dominoes— all a meaningless blur before my frightened eyes. To the annoyance of other pedestrians I had stopped abruptly, trying to get up my courage. I was job hunting, and S. H. Kress and Company was my first stop.

It had sounded so simple. All spring, sitting around the table in the high-school cafeteria, we had talked endlessly about summer jobs, even bragged about working. Sure, we would earn money for our EPHS sweaters: black with the big orange emblem on the left sleeve, ten dollars at Popular Dry Goods and an absolute must for football games. We would buy other school clothes and even start saving for college. In the noisy cafeteria, all of us talking at once, all planning to outdo each other, it had sounded so natural, the thing to do. Well, the time had come to do it, and here I was, all alone on the sidewalk, clutching my purse and wondering what happened next. I let the crowd jostle me through the open doors, and stopped again.

Counters running crosswise of the store displayed jewelry, lace, ribbons, and cosmetics. The candy counter, on my left as I came in, was twice as long as the other counters and ran lengthwise from the front doors all the way to the frosted windows at the rear. Customers walked purposefully, sales girls were busy, cash registers clanged. Maybe I should try to find a floorwalker.

I scanned the vast, noisy area and suddenly cited a vaguely familiar figure at the cosmetic counter. I looked again. Yes, Sadie Lou, Old Sears from Rusk School! She had moved from the neighborhood years ago—I had almost forgotten her—and here she was working at Kress. Her once-braided hair was cut short and set in deep marcel waves, but it was Sadie Lou all right. Walking towards her counter, I remembered that afternoon at Rusk when she had scotched our swimming party. At least I hadn't joined in when the others laughed at her. Maybe she would help me now.

"Sadie Lou," I exclaimed, "I wasn't sure I recognized you. Remember me?"

Well, of course, she did and seemed genuinely glad to see me. We chatted a minute about her leaving home, moving in with her sister, and getting this job. She had been working here more than a year, made ten dollars a week, and liked it. The floorwalker started our way. Sadie Lou saw him out of the corner of her eye and

166

whispered, "Snoopy's coming." She picked up a jar of cold cream and pretended to wait on me.

I took the hint, looked critically at the cold cream, and blurted out: "I'm looking for a summer job. Do you think I could get on here?"

"Yeah, why not?" she asked, obviously pleased with the idea. "But they're already hiring for the summer. You better apply right away."

"What do I do?" I asked, putting the cold cream back on the counter as though I had rejected the sale.

Sadie Lou pointed to the stairway at the back of the store next to the frosted windows, and told me to go upstairs and talk to Mr. French. I had just stepped away from the counter when she called me back. "Psst, Mafra. Tell him you're sixteen."

"But I'm fourteen. I'll tell him I'm going to be a junior."

"Doesn't matter. Say sixteen, or he won't talk to you."

"Won't he know?"

"No, just say sixteen."

Old Snoopy had spotted us again. Sadie Lou turned back to straighten her counter, and I made my way to the back of the store. I hesitated again in front of the Information Desk. I looked up the long flight of stairs that cut diagonally across the back wall, took a deep breath, and went up. At the top of the stairs I entered a short hall. The office door stood partly open, and I saw a bald-headed man sitting at the desk behind a brass nameplate reading "Lamar French, Manager."

He looked up before I spoke. "Good morning. I'm Mary Frances King, and I'm looking for a summer job."

"Summer job? You're in high school? What grade?"

"I'll be a junior."

"How old are you?"

"Sixteen." Flat, just like that I said it. My voice sounded far away, like it belonged to some stranger. I stood perfectly still, conscious of a prickly feeling in my scalp and an involuntary curling under of my toes in my Cuban-heeled pumps; but outwardly things remained the same: the ceiling fan whirling over Mr. French's desk didn't stop, the windows didn't crack, the secretary working at another desk didn't stop typing. One word and it was done.

Mr. French handed me a two-page application and a pencil. I sat at a table and filled it out. Having already said I was sixteen, it was easy to write the number again in the appropriate blank. The arithmetic problems were easy. I double checked and handed the application back to Mr. French. He read it and said, "When can you start?"

"June first, as soon as school is out."

"All right. You know the hours? Eight to six, an hour for lunch, ten dollars per week. You'll be filling in for vacations, so I could use you at the lunch counter or at toys. Girls at the lunch counter get a thirty cent lunch free, and uniforms are furnished. Lunch counter or toys, either one."

Free lunch and uniforms—boy, I could save almost everything I earned. I took the lunch counter.

Mama and Papa had said I was too young for a summer job, but being convinced I wouldn't be hired, their opposition to my plans had been rather passive. When I reported I actually had a job, I was surprised how easily they accepted it. Becky was more concerned. Now that she was old enough to have a "Y" membership she wanted me to go swimming with her.

"Well, I can't help it," I said, feeling very important. "I have to work to make money for my EPHS sweater and other school clothes and even start saving for college. Everybody's getting jobs."

"Is Beverly going to be with you?"

"No, she can't work because her mother's sick and she has to help at home, but her father will buy her an EPHS sweater. Harriet is working at Ye Ole Town Pump. That's lucky, because it's a drive-in and she'll be outside, you know, serving hot dogs and stuff to cars. Even Dianne will be working part time, making posters for the "Y" although she probably won't buy an EPHS sweater. She doesn't like football."

On the first day of June I arrived early at the store. The time clock where I was supposed to clock in was in the hall just outside the office door. I stood awkwardly to one side, envying the girls as they nonchalantly punched their numbers and hurried downstairs to their counters. It was almost eight o'clock, and I was wondering how long I should just stand there when a plump Mexican woman—she was in her late twenties and more matronly than most of the girls—came running up the stairs. She paused, puffing from the exertion. "Hey, you're Mary Frances King?" she asked.

"Yes, but they call me Mafra. I'm new, and I don't know where to go."

She apologized for being late, said her name was Della and she was supposed to show me around. She ushered me into a cloak room and handed me a clean uniform. "Here, quick, put on your uniform before you clock in. The green smock first, then your white apron, inside out until noon, then turn it over and it'll be clean when you start waiting on customers."

I followed the instructions, hung my street dress on a hook on the wall, and without a mirror tried to adjust the white head band. At the time clock Della dug into her purse and came up with a crumpled slip of paper. "Here's your number, sixty-three. Don't forget it. Here," she swung the big metal arm around and located my number, "you punch it yourself. It's against the rules to punch for anybody else. You get fired for that, and you never know who's watching."

The center of the clock was a disk, a big red-orange circle, bright as the morning sun coming up over the Hueco Mountains. I used both hands to steady the metal arm and punched my number. Daybreak, I thought. The sun's up—my day starts here. That big red-orange circle—that's my sun now. I felt an unreasonable tightening around my heart, almost a panic. How irrevocable it was, punching the clock, committing myself. Just one click of that big metal arm and I had signed away all my freedom, all my daylight hours. Easy as that I had sold my long vacation to S. H. Kress and Company.

"You're on the clock, now," Della explained, as though she had read my mind. "And you punch out at noon and in again after lunch." She punched her own number. "Hurry, or we'll be late to the counter, and Dale will be on us." I walked beside her, my right hand on the big brass rail as we descended the stairs.

We had a good view of the first floor. The front doors were not yet open for business, and the aisles were still empty. Rotary fans, suspended from the high yellow ceiling, were beginning to turn slowly, one at a time, like different sections of an orchestra tuning up—one here—one there—faster, faster, until the single blades became only a whir. The girls in their beige uniforms were checking their registers, counting change supplied for the day, and slamming the drawers.

At the foot of the wide stairs Della and I stopped at the Information Desk, told the girl our numbers, and left our purses. "Never take money with you to the counter," Della warned. "You can be fired for having as much as a dime in your pocket."

We started down the lower flight of stairs. The basement ceiling was low and the lights were dim. Holding to the little iron banister, I had the sensation that I was going down, down, down, far underground. The freshly oiled floors smelled of linseed. Counters, covered with long green cloths, seemed to be closer together down here, and the narrow aisles were cluttered with flat wicker baskets filled with merchandise: pots, pans, china plates, glassware. By means of short ropes attached to the handles, the girls pulled the baskets across the oiled floor, folded up the green counter cloths, and began to sort out the merchandise and restock their counters.

From the stairs Della and I picked our way through the maze of counters and baskets towards the distant lunch counter. She exchanged greetings with some of her friends, and I wondered how she could plunge down into this gloomy cavern and sound so cheerful. The low ceiling pressed down upon me, the air was heavy and stale, and I felt as though the walls of an endless tunnel were tightening around me. I had lost all sense of direction except that each step seemed to be taking me farther underground. At last we reached the lunch counter, the corner better lighted than the rest of the basement. Della lifted up a hinged section of the white counter top so we could pass through and led me on through an open door into the kitchen.

A tall woman was standing by the sink. "Hi, Dale," Della said. I soon learned Della was the only employee who addressed Mrs. Dale so familiarly. "Here's Mafra—is that it, Mafra?"

I nodded.

"Okay, Mafra, your boss, Mrs. Dale."

Mrs. Dale set down the cup of coffee she had been enjoying and looked down at me. Her platinum blond hair, marred by a telltale black streak along the part, was pulled back and braided into a bun at the nape of her neck. Large white earrings matched the whiteness of her hair, and she wore rouge and heavy lipstick. "Hello, Mafra," she said, in a surprisingly gruff but pleasant voice. "Is that your real name?"

"Mary Frances, actually. But that's what they call me."

She took another sip of coffee and shrugged. "Okay, Mafra, we need you. We're shorthanded, like always. Della will show you your duties, get you started."

Della picked up four big loaves of Betsy Ross bread from the center work table, held them against her full breasts, and with her right shoulder pushed opened a door at the back of the kitchen. I followed her, wondering how many doors there were, how deep could we go.

We had entered a big room, apparently a storeroom. Della, still hugging the Betsy Ross bread, reached up and turned on a dangling light bulb. In the dimness I could make out stacks of packing boxes piled about the room and a long work counter backed against the wall that separated the storeroom from the kitchen. Della dumped her bread on the counter next to a slicing machine with a round steel blade. Perfectly at ease in this strange place, she hummed a little tune, unwrapped a loaf of bread and slammed it into the metal groove that fed into the slicing blade.

"Turn it like this," she said, giving the blade a quick whirl. "You'll be working here in the storeroom in the mornings. Later, you'll be out at the counter waiting on the customers, but you start here slicing the bread and working on the salad." She stopped the machine, picked up the sliced loaf by pressing on each end, and placed it on the counter. "I'll get the veal and chicken," she said, and disappeared into the kitchen.

In a moment she returned, carrying a big black pan holding boiled chicken and veal. "For the salad," she said.

"What do I do with it?"

"Chop it up for the chicken salad. We mix it all together. Veal is cheaper than chicken, and it all tastes the same in the salad. Now, you have to work fast. Dale will chop the celery and other stuff, and she likes to mix the salad herself. But you get things ready and give it to her before the customers start coming."

While she talked she unwrapped a second loaf of bread and placed it in the slicer. "You speak some Spanish, Mafra?"

"Not much."

"Well, you need to know *ensalada.* That means salad, and that's the way the Mexican customers ask for a chicken salad sandwich. It costs fifteen cents. That's *quince.* If they ask *cuanto,* they mean how much, and you say *quince.* Or if you can't remember that just do it with your fingers." She flashed ten fingers and five more. *"Sabe?"*

"Yeah, I think so."

"Okay, slice the bread and chop the chicken and veal. I'll be inside, helping Dale."

The kitchen door clicked shut behind her. I was alone in this huge, semi-dark room. What to do first? The small light, suspended by a cord from the ceiling, cast my shadow in grotesque proportions across the counter. I looked at the loaf of bread Della had placed on the slicer, turned the handle as I had seen her do, and watched as the sliced bread miraculously emerged on the right side. Using both hands to press the heels together, I lifted the loaf. Without warning it slipped out of my grasp and scattered over the counter and concrete floor. Bending over to pick the slices off the floor, I felt squeamish, faintly nauseated. I straightened up and clutched the side of the counter. Noises from the kitchen sounded far, far away. I brushed the bread slices off on my apron and placed them straight on the counter, Nobody would know I had dropped them, but I didn't care if they knew or not. It was all too horrible. I couldn't go on—not in this awful, black hole. I looked at the next loaf of Betsy Ross bread, but I couldn't unwrap it. I trembled and held to the counter's edge, trying to steady myself. How still it was, how oppressively quiet. I closed my eyes, pressed the back of my hand against my closed lids, trying to block it all out, not to look at the walls of this horrible dungeon.

But I had to look again, and it was all there. Brown cartons piled against the wall, labeled in black print letters: "Octagon Soap," a corner filled with galvanized wash tubs, one on top the other, bundles of rag mops. I looked back at my counter and the slicing machine. I was supposed to be working—slicing bread.

The day had hardly started. Nine hours underground, nine hours to go. Six days in the week, a total of fifty-four hours. But I had wanted the job so much. All my friends were working. I thought about Harriet out at Ye Ole Town Pump, out in the sunshine! How lucky she was. She would be telling me how much fun it was. I couldn't tell her I didn't like my job and had to quit. I couldn't do that. I couldn't tell Mama I had quit.

Oh, God, I was so sick I thought I would faint. Suppose I just stretched out on the floor—would anybody ever come down into this hole and find me? I must stop thinking that way. Maybe I was going crazy. Concentrate on something else, I thought, frantically. The EPHS sweater, black with the orange sleeve patch—how much I had wanted to work for that. Or better still, think of something beautiful—the way the golden poppies blow in that field at the foot of Sugar Loaf. Summer will pass, and fall will come, and I will gather seeds for Mama and Mrs. Pope. It was a mental trick I had made up long ago: in a crisis think of something lovely. It usually worked, but not this time.

I was imprisoned in this dark, clammy hole. No, it was impossible. I couldn't last one day, not until six o'clock that night. I couldn't even last until lunch time, not another minute. How could I get out? Could I run back through the kitchen and through that field of wicker baskets cluttering the basement aisles? I pictured it all. I would kick the baskets aside, jump over them, just run. Up the narrow back steps and up the wider steps with the brass rail to punch the time clock with the horrible red ball. No, no, I didn't care about the time clock. Smash the hideous red-orange ball. Just get outside, out into the sunshine. I was faint, and my eyes were smarting with salty tears.

Two loaves of bread were still wrapped up. I pushed them to the back of the counter, and wondered if I should tell Della or Mrs. Dale I couldn't stay, that I was quitting. I was just turning towards the kitchen door, when suddenly I heard a harsh grating sound and a shaft of sunlight brightened the concrete floor. Unnoticed by me, two Mexican workmen had entered the storeroom from a side door and had raised two overhead iron doors which covered a freight elevator.

My eyes blinked in the sudden brightness. I stepped closer to the elevator for a better look. Of course, the elevator opened on the sidewalk! I should have known—I was working under the sidewalk! The Mexican workmen were hoisting the flat freight elevator up to the sidewalk above. Other workmen on the sidewalk were preparing to load cartons from a truck onto the lift. How many times had I walked on that sidewalk of square glass bricks and stepped aside for those open doors, never realizing there was a storeroom below, maybe some girl just like me slicing bread. The Mexicans on the sidewalk yelled down to the men in the storeroom: *"Arriba, arriba,"* and *"Cuidado,"* and a lot more than I couldn't understand.

Ignoring the workmen in the storeroom, I moved towards the shaft so that I could look directly up into the sunlight. I took a deep breath of the clean air, letting it rush over me like a fresh desert breeze. I looked straight up the shaft to the blue sky. What a wonderful bright blue. "That little tent of blue that prisoners call the sky." I laughed to myself, thinking of poor Ella Mae. How blue it must have looked from some prison cell—how blue it looked now from the storeroom under the sidewalk. I wanted to laugh aloud with sheer joy.

I had moved too near the lift. One of the workmen by a jerk of his head indicated I was in the way. I went back to the slicing machine, and started cutting the bread. It was easy to do! I finished slicing the bread, trying hard not to laugh aloud.

Della came back to help me finish. I couldn't share it, couldn't tell her what a fool I had been. She would think I was crazy calling the sky "that little tent of blue." I tried hard to think of something friendly and commonplace to say. "I was sure surprised when that elevator opened," I finally managed.

"Yeah, it's a messy workroom but it's all the space we have. You'll be working here every morning, and you'll have errands back and forth for supplies all day. You'll get used to the elevator. Shouldn't bother you."

"Oh, no. It's fine. I kind of like to hear the click of heels on those glass bricks in the sidewalk. I didn't notice it at first, but it lets in some daylight."

There were two other girls at the counter: Josephine, a rather quiet Mexican, and Dessie, a freckled-faced redhead from Mississippi. Dessie was garrulous, and her southern drawl seemed almost as foreign to me as the Spanish phrases that Della and Josephine bantered back and forth. Dessie didn't bother much with verbs. "You rather work here or pick cotton?" she asked.

Not qualified to pass on the rigors of cotton picking, I turned the question on her. "What about you?"

"Better here, except for the shoes. Oh, God, my roasten-ears are howling." I didn't translate that one until later in the afternoon when she kicked off her shoes and through her rayon hose showed me corns on her toes.

Her curiosity about me was insatiable. "You in high school, Mafra?

"Yes, I'm a junior."

"Well, then, you know Spanish."

"No, not much."

"They teach Spanish in high school?"

"Yes, but I take Latin."

"Whatever for? They don't never come in here talking Latin."

How to explain to Dessie that I was taking Latin because it was a good background for college and that I was going to college to become a missionary? I tried to ignore her "don't make no sense to me" conclusion. When she poured disinfectant into the sink where we washed the fountain glasses, she never measured, just slopped in a generous amount. It was so strong my hands were always rough, almost bleeding. Even Mrs. Dale couldn't make her do it right. During my first week at the counter I had sadly concluded that what Dessie didn't already know, she wasn't likely to learn.

Besides asking me endless questions, Dessie had another passion: the music blasting forth from the Victrola at the music counter. Unfortunately for Dessie, the music counter was across the basement from the lunch counter, and when business was brisk, the ringing cash registers and other noises of the trade drowned out the music. But when things got slow, we could hear every note. Dessie's favorite was "Million Dollar Baby from the Five-and-Ten-Cent Store," although "Walking my Baby Back Home" was a close second. The girl at the music counter accepted requests, and Dessie put in her share. When one record finished, Dessie would wave to the salesgirl, who already knew what Dessie wanted, and in a moment Dessie's favorite song would start and Dessie would keep time and sing along under her breath:

> If you run into a shower,
> Step inside my cottage door,
> And meet the million dollar baby
> From the five-and-ten-cent store.

One morning, about three weeks after I had started work, Della told me that we all had to work on the double because Josephine was sick.

"What's the matter?" I asked. "She was in here earlier."

"Well, she has to lay down for a while. She's up in the lounge, and she'll be down later."

"I hope it's not the flu."

"No, it's morning sickness."

"Morning sickness?" I had heard Mama talk about that with some of the neighbors. "She can't be pregnant. Married women don't work here."

"Well, Mafra, that's nice to know. I'll tell Josephine, and she'll sure be relieved."

Della couldn't wait to share the joke with Mrs. Dale. They kept laughing. I tried to join in, but I didn't think it was all that funny. "Kress doesn't employ married women," Della would chuckle, and with a significant look at me, "or girls under sixteen."

I felt my face flush, and I worked on the sandwiches silently for a while. When Josephine came back, Mrs. Dale made her some dry toast, and Della repeated my ridiculous statement in Spanish to Josephine. Josephine managed to smile wanly, and I felt better when Della patted me on the shoulder and said "Okay, Mafra, we have our little jokes. Josie's not pregnant, you're not under sixteen, and I'm not a wetback coming across the bridge every morning. But right now I've got to fill the steam table. There are customers at the counter, and Dessie, like always, is way behind washing the fountain glasses. You better get out there and sell some chicken salad."

A Mexican woman, her head covered with a black shawl, was sitting at the counter. *"Ensalada, por favor,"* she whispered timidly.

I passed the sandwich to her. *"Quince centavos,"* I said, proud that I didn't have to use sign language. I rang up her money, took a cloth, and wiped off the end of the counter.

It was almost noon, Thursday, the last week in June. Since my first day on the job I had carried a calendar in my head, marking off each day, and getting through the boring hours by trying to calculate how much I was earning. At ten dollars a week, fifty-four hours figured something less than nineteen cents an hour, maybe eighteen and a half. This afternoon and two full days left in this week, then just eight weeks, forty-eight days, to go, I reflected. No, better than that. There was one holiday coming up. Fourth of July was a holiday. Think of it: we got paid a full day without working. *Subtract the holiday and it's only the rest of this week and forty-seven days to go, and I'll be free. I'll punch the time clock for the last time and go outside and live in the sunshine.*

God, how I hated that seemingly endless summer. I was trapped by the sameness of it all: the greasy leg of veal and soggy chicken to be pulled off the bones, the rows and rows of dirty glasses, the hot steam table and constant smell of chili. My hands burned from disinfectant, and I wanted to stop my ears against Dessie's boring monologues. I made excuses to dash back into the storeroom to feel that rush of fresh air and small splash of sunshine on my face, to look up the open elevator shaft to that "tent of blue that prisoners call the sky."

The work wasn't too hard. I really liked Della, and Mrs. Dale was a good boss. The awful part was the loss of freedom.

14

The *El Paso Times* and the *Post* carried bold headlines covering Black Tuesday, October 29, 1929, the day the stock market crashed. A few people on Mountain Avenue may have read the long columns under the headlines, but it's doubtful if anyone on our street comprehended the significance of the crisis. Our idea of a successful economy was a household where the paycheck could be made to stretch to the end of the week. As for credit, there were charge accounts at Quinn's, but what did Wall Street have to do with that?

Moreover, we had our own grief to deal with that October, and it had nothing to do with the economy. Kerry Quinn, driving the truck home from Juarez in the wee hours of the morning, hit a telephone pole on Fort Boulevard, was thrown out, and instantly killed. That tragedy rated a four-column story with accompanying pictures of the demolished truck in both papers.

Becky and I, with tears splashing all over the papers, read every word, examined the pictures, and couldn't believe it. We said it was so crazy: all those years Mrs. Quinn had been warning Kerry that he was going to be caught smuggling liquor at the bridge and have the truck confiscated; and now the reality was so much worse. Kerry, young, tap-dancing with Clarabow on his shoulders; Kerry, picking me up after my bicycle crashed against the store; Kerry in his white butcher apron; Kerry—well, Becky and I had a thousand images. We kept telling each other we couldn't believe it, not even when we saw the white chrysanthemum wreath on the locked double doors of the store. Since we lived on Mountain Avenue, Quinn's Grocery and Market had never been closed on a business day.

The funeral was at McRea's Funeral Parlor. Mama, Becky, and I went with Mrs. Pope in her car. We sat on the third or fourth row, and Mrs. McCabe sat directly in front of us. She was dressed in black and wore a hat with a wide brim decked with shiny red cherries. She kept turning her short, fat neck from side to side, probably making a mental note of who was there, and the cherries bobbed up and down so that I could scarcely see the minister or the flower-covered casket. When the short service was over, we managed to leave the funeral parlor without talking to Mrs. McCabe, but the next day she came by to see us, and there was no escape.

Mama was trimming the Virginia creeper and didn't stop to ask Mrs. McCabe to sit on the porch. Mrs. McCabe, standing on the sidewalk, ignored the slight, licked her lips, and plunged into the juicy subject: "I just can't get it off my mind, Mrs. King. I mean, doesn't it just break your heart to think Kerry went to meet his Maker with liquor on his breath?"

Mama clipped a dainty tendril with enough savagery to fell an oak. After a moment when she could control her voice: "We'll miss Kerry—such a loss to the whole neighborhood."

Again Mrs. McCabe ran her tongue over her lips. "Well, of course, I knew all the time it just had to happen. With his wild ways, you have to admit he brought it on himself."

This charge was answered with silence and such a clipping of Mama's shears I feared for the very life of the Virginia creeper. Mrs. McCabe, finally realizing she was making no progress, gave a pious toss of her head and said she needed some things at the store. She might as well go on down and see how the Quinns were taking it.

Becky and I, speechless in our fury, watched her out of sight and then told each other she had no right to say that: she didn't really *know* Kerry.

But, of course, life went on. The Quinns took the wreath off the door and opened for business. The newspapers continued the daily stories of bank failures, foreclosures, lost fortunes and even suicides. The economic chaos was spreading, and more sober heads in El Paso began to take notice and seek reassurance. We could rely on the uniqueness of El Paso, we told each other. We were a health resort. Our wonderful climate, "Where Sunshine Spends the Winter," would carry us through. The sick would always come. And another thing, we were diversified. We had the military, farming, ranching, the smelter, the cement plant, the cotton mill. Not only that, we could count on Washington to do something about it. President Hoover had called the industrial leaders to a conference—Ford and all those big shots—and they had pledged not to cut wages, not to repeat the panic of 1893. Papa read that aloud in the *Post* and said that was something we could count on. Mama said she wished we had a Democrat in the White House.

In spite of our brave talk, there was a difference even on Mountain Avenue that we could no longer ignore. With so many rental houses, we were accustomed to some turnovers, but not to long vacancies. Now houses stood vacant for weeks and even months. Tumbleweeds piled high in fence corners; dry winds swept across the open porches, piling ridges of brown sand against doors and window sills; even the rampant Virginia creeper showed neglect, broke its supports and straggled on the ground. Once well-tended Bermuda lawns turned brown and gave way to devil-horn stickers and cone-shaped ant hills. It happened in one yard after another.

When I walked up the hill on my way to Beverly's, I passed the "For Rent" sign in front of Kerry's house. I still thought of it as Kerry's house, although he had been dead for months and Gladys and Clarabow now lived with the Quinns in their house next to the store. The black letters on the sign were pock-marked by the winter sandstorms, and though we were well into spring no prospective tenants came to look at the house.

On up the block, the Jacksons' house had remained vacant since Mrs. Jackson's death a year ago. The girls and Auntie Ruth were back in St. Louis, and only the tattered canvas on the front porch reminded us of their unhappy years on Mountain Avenue.

Mrs. Pope, working in her own flower bed next to the Jacksons' yard, stopped me to reminisce. She pushed her wide-brimmed straw hat back on her forehead, glanced at the vacant house and said, "I do miss the Jacksons. I had a Christmas card from Ruth back in St. Louis, but no real news about how they are getting along." She looked reproachfully at the neglected yard. Yellowish-green coxcombs and tiny bronze-colored, misshapen marigolds had straggled onto the unkept lawn. "Everything's going to weeds over there," she said with a shrug. The year before she had tried to give Auntie Ruth some native plants, but Uncle Horace—the girls always talked about Uncle Horace back in St. Louis—had sent lily-of-the-valley bulbs and Auntie Ruth planted those, saying it would remind Mrs. Jackson of "back home." Of course, they didn't live. "Well," Mrs. Pope continued more briskly, "to tell the truth, the Jacksons always wanted to be in St. Louis. Except for her being sick, they never belonged here at all." She knelt at her flower bed and began pulverizing the soil for some seeds she intended to plant.

Her big hat concealed her face from my view, and I turned to look again at the Jacksons' house. It was true: the Jacksons had never liked El Paso, never even tried to like it. Judy and Jammie Sue had never walked on the desert, never hiked up McKelligon Canyon or gathered wild flowers, never gone on a wiener roast up at the reservoir and watched the North Star come out over Sugar Loaf, never skated down to the bottom of the hill, never gone swimming at Washington Park. When I thought of the Jacksons, the whole family, the one scene that came to mind was Mrs. Jackson's bed on the canvas-covered porch with the fashion magazines, patterns, and dress material strewn on the counterpane. Refusing to be trans-planted, the Jacksons had tried to bring their St. Louis styles and habits with them to the desert. And now Auntie Ruth and the girls had gone back to some world I couldn't even imagine. They had taken nothing of the desert with them. They had left no roots. I had a terrible sense of futility—not grief for Mrs. Jackson because I hadn't really known her that well—but sadness that our paths had crossed and it had made so little difference.

I jerked myself back to the present and asked Mrs. Pope what she was planting.

"Poppy seeds—the ones you gathered for me last fall up near Sugar Loaf. Really, I'd rather call them amapola del campo. Isn't that a lovely name? And once I get them started, they'll spread all over the neighborhood. Native plants—that's my legacy to Mountain Avenue. Yours, too, Mafra. You gathered the seeds."

The vacant houses were disturbing enough, but even worse was the change I noticed in Mama. She had always made a dollar go as far as she could, but it had been a natural way of life, something she did without much comment. Now the uncertainty seemed to bear down on her. Papa's hourly wages weren't cut, but his total hours were cut—so much for the promises of the big financiers to hold the line on wages. There were no orders to fill. Bales of denim and Osnaburg piled up in the warehouse, and Papa complained that there was no more room to stack them. The mill abolished Saturday work and then the second shift, so there was no more going back in the evenings to check on the dye house. Having no operating capital, the mill stopped running except to fill specific orders. Some days when it was closed, Papa went in "to check things out" even though there was nothing to do. Better to walk through the silent mill than just sit around the house. He hated sitting around. His work-life had been so time consuming, he had never even considered developing outside hobbies.

Mr. Mae confided in Papa that he was thinking of putting his home in Austin Terrace on the market. In response to Mama's prodding, Papa admitted that Mr. Mae really meant his mortgage was about to be foreclosed. Everybody knew there were no buyers. We could sympathize. Our own mortgage payments were sometimes a whole month late.

One Saturday in late spring I helped Mama work in her rock garden. She was planting slips of lemon verbena that Mrs. Pope had given her. As she arranged the rocks around the long slender leaves a lemon-like aroma filled the air. I loved that fragrance and watched silently as Mama's brown fingers pushed each plant firmly into place, willing it to grow.

It seemed like a good moment to bring up the dream that I had been secretly nourishing. "Mama, do you think there is any possibility I could go to Park College and study to be a missionary?" For some reason that I didn't understand Mama had never been willing to discuss my wish to be a missionary. She had not actually opposed the idea, but she assumed a wait-and-see attitude, something I couldn't really argue with. Now, having brought the matter out in the open along with my dream of attending Park College, I waited anxiously for her reply.

Mama hesitated. She seemed to be searching for words as she carefully sorted another batch of verbena. I helped make more holes for the new plants and without much hope pursued my suggestion, "When Dr. Blevins was here he told some of the older kids that most of the students at Park work their way through. If you work you can make it on three hundred dollars a year."

Mama finished her planting, stood up and dusted her hands on her garden apron. "Well, college is still a year away for you," she said. "Something could happen, but you know Papa's hours are cut and right now we can barely put food on the table and meet the mortgage payments. It doesn't make much sense for you to plan to go away to college, Park or anywhere else. But to be practical about it, I saw in the paper that by next year the College of Mines right here in El Paso expects to offer a regular four-year degree course. The important thing is to get started, and that looks like your best chance. You do think you can get on at Kress again this summer?"

"Oh, I think so," I answered. I looked down at my empty hands as though I could see Park College slip right through my fingers. Instead of dreaming about going away to college, I had to think about getting on at Kress again and saving for my tuition at College of Mines. I sighed, but deep down I wasn't too disappointed. I guess I had known all the time that Park College wasn't possible. Of course, I could still become a missionary—still follow in the footsteps of David Livingstone and Dr. Blevins. That was the important part, the dream I must hold tight.

The next week I went to see Mr. French and he hired me for another summer at the lunch counter. Once more on the first of June I punched the time clock, dedicating all my daytime hours to the greedy red-orange circle on the clock which monitored my life like the sun. It was easier this time, not so terrifying. Now I realized that summer, even at the lunch counter, wouldn't last forever.

With the exception of Josephine, the lunch counter crowd was the same. Della told me Josephine had managed to stay on until Christmas to get her thirty dollar bonus, ten dollars for each year she had worked at Kress. Now she had a baby boy, eight weeks old. Luz, another Mexican girl, had taken her place at the counter.

Dessie was exactly the same except that her favorite song, "Million Dollar Baby," had been replaced by "Ramona." She hummed it constantly as she haphazardly splashed uncertain amounts of disinfectant into the fountain sink or kicked off a shoe and raised a stocking-clad foot to massage her "roasten-ears." Worse than the song, she had seen the movie, *Ramona,* and she insisted on explaining it to me scene by scene. She stayed romantically involved all summer.

In two weeks I had earned twenty dollars and was ready to open a bank account, saving for college. Papa was determined to go with me to the bank. "No trouble at all," he had said, "I can meet you at noon in front of the First National Bank. No trouble at all."

We met there Monday noon and approached the saving accounts window together. I handed the teller the two ten dollar bills, and Papa with his hand on my shoulder leaned close to the teller's window and explained that I was his daughter Mary Frances, that I had worked at Kress to earn the money, and that I was now opening a bank account for college. The teller kindly congratulated Papa on having such an exemplary daughter. I wriggled my shoulder free from Papa's grasp and wished the polished marble floor would crack just enough to let me fall through and disappear.

Out on the street, Papa gloated that I now had money working for me. He suggested we celebrate with a soda at Warner's, but I knew we couldn't afford it, so I made the excuse that I had to hurry back to work. When I appeared at the lunch counter without having eaten lunch, Mrs. Dale told me to grab a chicken salad sandwich and take it out to the storeroom to eat. Although there were no workmen in the storeroom the freight elevator shaft was open. I walked over to the opening and let the sun strike my face directly. Munching my chicken salad sandwich, I watched the pedestrians overhead picking their way around the open elevator shaft. I smiled as though I were greeting a long lost friend: "that little tent of blue that prisoners call the sky." How I loved it.

Before quitting at the end of summer I asked for part-time work during the school year. In late September Mr. French called me to come work as an extra at the toy counter until Christmas. The toy counter was easier than the lunch counter, but all those hours, after school and Saturdays, cut me out of attending football games, and I even had to quit working on the *Tatler,* the high school paper. In my junior year I had taken a course in journalism under Mrs. Frank, and as a senior I would have been an associate editor of the *Tatler.* I hated giving that up.

The days passed, but the cotton mill business didn't pick up. With so few orders to fill there was no need for a manager, and Mr. Mae was let go. The mortgage on his house out in Austin Terrace was foreclosed, and he and Mrs. Mae "headed south," the way he described it to Papa. He didn't have any definite prospects of work, but if he went back where the mills were close together, at least he could look for work. "There's nothing here, not another mill within two hundred miles," he had said. But of course Papa knew that.

When Mr. Mae left Papa really seemed to lose heart. We talked about the Depression quite frankly now. In fact, at home we didn't talk much about anything else. When Becky and I were studying at the dining-room table at night, we could hear Mama and Papa talking in the living room. Papa said he knew the mills were in a slump everywhere, but maybe Mr. Mae had the right idea. Maybe he could do better back in Georgia. Mama considered it seriously, but to my relief she always concluded: "You know those little mill towns, not a good high school for Becky and no college at all for Mafra. Let's hang on here as long as we can. Surely things will improve."

15

Hueco Tanks, a gigantic formation of basaltic rock some twenty miles east of El Paso, was a favorite picnic spot and a natural selection for the end-of-year celebration that the Comrades and Friends of the Cross gave in honor of the graduating seniors.

Our group met at the church and in six or seven cars caravaned out, everyone eager to climb the rocks or hike the narrow trails, sure of finding some new pinnacle or craggy cliff to explore. We scrambled out of the cars in the narrow parking lot, but before we could start on our various expeditions, Coach Wyatt-Browne, serious about his duties as a chaperon, rounded us up for a short visit to the caves to look at the Indian pictographs on the rock walls. We had all seen the caves before, and there was a little grumbling at the delay, but I always liked to look at the inscriptions. Archaeologists dated them as far back as 1500 B.C. Every time I went from cave to cave examining the curious hieroglyphics I felt I was treading on sacred ground. Actually, the so-called caves were misnamed. They were not subterranean caverns, but more like alcoves or three sided rooms, open to daylight on the fourth side and protected from the elements by overhanging cliffs. I didn't mind at all when Coach urged us to linger and, as he put it, "show a little respect for the ages."

After leaving the shady caves, we came out into the sunshine and walked around some of the tanks, oval hollows the size of bathtubs in the reddish rocks. The water in the tanks was warm from the desert sun, and some of the kids took off their shoes, splashed away the tadpoles, and waded in water almost to their knees, while Coach asked us to visualize what such a supply of water would have meant to wandering Indian tribes. From time to time some tribes must have taken up permanent residence. You could still see mortar holes where the women ground corn, or *masa*.

Coach ended his brief guided tour with the reminder that we shouldn't hike too far. We must be back before sunset to gather mesquite for the wiener roast.

At church parties Beverly and I had been pairing off with George and Everett since the summer at Vacation Bible School when we were croquet partners. We naturally started out together, and today Dianne was with us. She wasn't actually a member of Friends of the Cross—Mr. Printz wouldn't let her leave Altura and come to First Church with Beverly and me—but I often invited her to church parties, and she was especially welcome today on this graduation party.

The five of us hadn't even reached the first bend in the trail when our attention was attracted by a red car raising a cloud of dust on the road below. With a blast of the horn and a screech of brakes it came to a stop in the parking lot, and a tall boy with short-cropped blond hair jumped out. He spotted us on the trail, waved his arms, and called for us to wait. Immediately George and Everett recognized the newcomer. "Hey, it's Cecil Randolph," they shouted in unison and rushed down the trail to meet him. They greeted each other with such hand-shaking and back-pounding that it was obvious they were in a world of their own and had forgotten all about the three of us waiting rather impatiently on the trail. Beverly and

I filled in the time telling Dianne what we knew about Cecil: that he had been friends with George and Everett since grade school, that he was graduating from Staunton Military Institute in Virginia, and that he had an appointment to West Point and would start this summer. We also told her about his mother, Mrs. Randolph, how she doted on him, and I think we even mentioned his little toy soldiers she had shown us at the initiation tea.

At last the boys climbed back up the trail and made the introductions. Cecil had probably never heard of us before, but he acted as though this was the very moment he had been living for. He had that kind of charm. As we started up the trail once more, he explained that when he had arrived in town about noon, his mother—"the Mater," he called her—told him it was too bad he had just missed our picnic. The minute he heard about the picnic he was determined to join us.

He started walking with Dianne, and in his presence she seemed to lose her usual shyness. The trail was steep and we soon spread out: George and Beverly ahead, Everett and I in the middle, and Cecil and Dianne lagging behind. We were out of earshot, but now and then I could look down over the hairpin turns and see that Cecil and Dianne were getting on well together. In fact, Everett noticed it too and said it was a lucky thing Cecil had been able to catch up and make the hike with us.

We had climbed an hour or more, when George and Beverly found a wide rock ledge and waited for the rest of us. After the unusual exertion, it was pleasant to stretch out on the warm rock. The sun was sinking, and the crag where we were resting had already thrown its shadow over the ravine in front of us. It was so still and quiet that even our ordinary conversation carried across the ravine and echoed against the opposite crags. After we had rested and caught our breath, we stood up and shouted hallos, and the words echoed back as clear as we sent them out. After a while we just sat still, enjoying the stillness, the pungent aroma of the few knotty cedar trees that struggled in the rocky crevices, while the shadow crept ever higher up the far side of the ravine. Suddenly in the distance we heard high, sweet, musical notes and realized one of the other hikers had brought a flute. The notes, so true and clear in the rare mountain air, struck against the high rocks and came back to us, echo on echo on echo. It was so lovely that we all fell quiet, drew in our breath, and just waited for more. To our delight, it was repeated again and again.

Somebody, I think it was Cecil, said, "Listen, it's the 'The horns of Elfland faintly blowing.'" Then we all remembered parts of the poem we had learned in English class, and whispered the refrain:

> Blow, bugle, blow, set the wild echoes flying.
> Blow, bugle, answer, echoes, dying, dying, dying.

The flute continued to blow, and I kept thinking of the words:

> Oh, hark, oh, hear, how thin and clear,
> And thinner, clearer, farther going . . .

But at last the flutist finished his concert, the shadows creeping up the ravine had turned the crags from pinkish red to somber purple, and our own rocky ledge had suddenly become chilly. The exquisite moment had faded. It was twilight, and we had to hurry down the trail.

After the wiener roast, when we were sitting around the campfire singing cowboy songs, Coach Wyatt-Browne proposed the camping trip to Elephant Butte Dam. He belonged to a fishing and boating club that owned some cabins up there, and he wondered if we would like to go to the cabins for a three-day camp.

Well, of course! Especially when those who had been to the dam before started talking about all the fun we could have: diving and swimming in ninety-foot water, the little sail boats, speedboats racing over to the island, everything.

It took the rest of the evening to make all the plans. Coach reminded us the camp-out would not be an official church party. The session refused to take the responsibility, so we were going as his guests. Cecil immediately saw the advantage of it not being a church party. "Hey, we can dance," he said. "I'll bring my Victrola and everybody bring records, and every night we can dance on the wharf." Presbyterians didn't approve of dancing and would not permit it on church property or at church parties, but if was a private party, the church had no authority. Presbyterians we were, but we did a lot of dancing.

While the others were cleaning up, putting things back in the cars, and stomping out the fire, Cecil called me to one side and said he had a favor to ask. The date of the camp, it so happened, was exactly when he would be in town, between his graduation from Staunton and his entering West Point Military Academy. He dearly loved to go to Elephant Butte and wouldn't miss the camp for anything, but it would be so great if Dianne could come. He knew Coach wouldn't care, so would I please invite her as my guest?

"Well, she's one of my best friends, and I'd love for her to come," I said, a little surprised at the request. "Why don't you invite her yourself?"

"Well, you know the Mater."

That was the second time I heard him refer to his mother that way. Looking back, I suppose it was a feeble attempt to strip Mrs. Randolph of some of her authority, but at the time I just found it amusing. "Yes, I know your mother. What about her?"

He stepped closer and assumed a more confidential tone: "She'll make a scene. I like Dianne. I know I've just met her, but I feel like I'd always known her. I guess you could tell, the way I was talking to her all afternoon. She is so *genuine*, you know, so understanding."

"Yes, she is." I answered. "And I think she likes you."

"Well, you see how it is, Mafra. The minute the Mater knows I'm interested in a girl, she finds some way to put a stop to it. She's so afraid something will interfere with the military career she has planned for me—let's not go into all that."

He stopped and looked away, as though he needed to reassemble his thoughts. Watching him, I had a fleeting thought—nothing that lingered—but just for a minute I thought he wanted to say something deeper, something about himself. But the instant passed, and he was his laughing self again. He put his arm companionably around my shoulder, saying he was sure I would see it his way and help him out. "You will ask her, Mafra? It'll just make everything so much smoother."

Of course I would. The way he put it, I not only wanted to help, I felt honored he had asked me. The others were already at the cars and called to us to hurry. Cecil grabbed my hand so we could shake on the bargain. "You're a damn good sport, Mafra. I knew I could count on you."

On the drive back to town it occurred to me Cecil's scheme had another advantage he hadn't thought about. Mr. Printz would be much more likely to let Dianne go on the camp, if the invitation came from me.

❦

Elephant Butte Dam takes its name from a humpbacked mountain vaguely resembling the profile of an elephant. The mountain once stood free, but when the dam across the Rio Grande was completed the reservoir waters slowly rose, covering first the elephant's knees, then its thighs, and finally most of its belly, reducing the free-standing mountain to a small barren island in the middle of the emerald green lake. Over the years the gentle waves lapping against the elephant's ribbed sides washed out two or three sandy beaches broad enough to furnish moorings for the little boats of vacationers who frequently came ashore to climb the stony crags and have their pictures taken as they perched precariously on the elephant's trunk.

Our cabins and the assembly hall were arranged in a semicircle atop the bluff on the eastern shore of the lake. Standing in front of the cabins and looking across the lake we had a clear view of the elephant's profile and his half submerged body forming the island. The distance from the foot of the bluff across the water to the island was well over a mile, although in the rare desert air it appeared to be much shorter.

Far to the left of our cabins but still visible, the white concrete dam enclosed the southern or lower end of the lake. Starting at a low promontory on our side of the lake, the dam stretched across the deep ravine to a similar promontory on the southwest bank. Below the dam and hidden from view, unless one walked along the narrow road on top of the dam and peered over the railing, a carefully monitored volume of clear water escaped, coursed rapidly through the narrow gorge, and at a more serene pace wandered out across the plains as it went about its official business of irrigating the arid farmlands of eastern New Mexico, western Texas, and even Mexico.

From our cabins on the bluff a narrow footpath zigzagged through patches of blackfoot daisies down to the lake's eastern shore, broken at that point by a wide wooden wharf and pier. The wharf held several picnic tables and also furnished moorings for a couple of rowboats and several little catboats whose white sails flapped in gentle harmony with the lapping of the tiny waves against the rocky shore.

The wharf's most important function, at least as far as we were concerned, was to provide a dance floor. Every evening after dinner the boys carried the Victrola and a stack of records down to the wharf, and from early twilight until well past midnight we danced to the strains of our favorite songs. The full moon, suspended in the sky high over the sleeping elephant's head, was bright enough to cast shadows on the water and rendered the lanterns that our chaperones had hung about the wharf quite superfluous.

The pier, extending out from the wharf some thirty feet across the water, was popular for sun bathing and provided a diving platform. We spent many daytime hours in the water—diving from the rough planks into the clear water and descending as far as we could, though never disappearing from view, surfacing and swimming to the rope ladder fastened to the far end of the pier. We pulled ourselves up the rope ladder and rested a moment on the pier, where the bright sun dried our cool bodies so quickly there was no need for towels.

The three cabins below the assembly hall were assigned to the girls and the three above to the boys. The chaperones, Coach and Mrs. Wyatt-Browne and their friends, Mr. and Mrs. Hamilton, had rooms attached to the assembly hall, which also held the dining room and kitchen. The cabins were rustic and weather beaten, the lower portion enclosed by rough pine boards and the upper portion open except for screen panels topped by rolls of heavy white canvass to be let down in the unlikely event of rain. The desert breeze, heavy with the aroma of sage, wafted continuously through the cabins so that with no effort on our part everything seemed to be fresh and clean. Each cabin had four bunks with straw mattresses. Beverly and I shared a cabin with Dianne and Harriet.

By a strange vagary of fashion this was the summer, the very moment, that some unseen designer, maybe as far away as New York, had decreed it was permissible for girls to wear beach-pajamas. We had never worn slacks—too risque for nice girls—but suddenly this free-flowing garment with a fitted surplice waist and long full legs was acceptable. We adopted it wholeheartedly. Every girl on the camp had at least one pair of beach-pajamas. We wore them on early morning hikes when we followed the shore line down to the end of the lake and walked across the top of the dam. We wore them speeding over to the island in the noisy motorboats and skimming across the water in the catboats with their little taut sails, and we even wore them in the evening for dancing on the wharf—practically all the time except when we were wearing our bathing suits. How chic we felt, how sophisticated and free from bondage.

Most of the beach-pajamas were dazzling crazy-quilt colors. Mine were bright pink and black broken plaid. Becky and Gwen—they were now in junior high—had pooled their resources and bought them for my graduation present. Beverly's were orange and green, colors that set off her brown hair and eyes. Dianne's were powder blue, and when I said they were pretty she said her mother had made them and all the time she was sewing them they had referred to them as a wrap-around, because Mr. Printz would have considered anything called pajamas strictly taboo. Anyway, she'd had enough trouble getting his permission to come, and it was only because the invitation was from me that he had finally consented.

From the first day at the camp most of the boys and girls had paired off in couples. Sometimes Everett and I made a foursome with George and Beverly, but Everett liked to sail and more often he and I went by ourselves in one of the catboats. We sailed along the shore and up into the quiet coves. He talked about his plans to be a counsellor at a boys' camp at Ruidoso during the summer and then to enter the University of Texas at Austin and study engineering. I said I hoped to work again at Kress during the summer—Mr. French had told me to come back the first of June to see if he could use me—and in the fall I hoped to start at the College of Mines. As the hours went by we got to know each other pretty well, and he asked if I would write to him during the summer when he was at camp at Ruidoso. I promised, with the caveat he needn't expect any earth-shaking news—not if I was working at Kress.

From the moment of arrival at camp, Cecil monopolized Dianne. Once, I think it was the first day, he caught me alone and gave me a hug for inviting her, but that was about the only conversation I had with him. Like Everett, he loved to sail, and he and Dianne spent hours in one of the little catboats, going up and down the coast or even over to the island where they landed on the beach and walked around. Looking across the water I could identify Dianne by the big straw hat she always wore in the sun.

The time slipped by so fast it was hard to believe on the third day that camp was almost over. After a morning of swimming and boating we were resting in the cabin. Beverly and Harriet were doing their nails, and I was reading an Edna Ferber novel someone had left in the cabin when Dianne said she was going over to the camp laundry to wash and iron her beach-pajamas so they would be fresh for the evening dancing. She asked if anyone wanted to go with her, but we were too lazy, and she went alone.

After she left, I grew tired of reading and lay still on the bed with my eyes half closed, musing that by tomorrow afternoon I would be back in the hot city. The first thing I had to do was see Mr. French about my summer job, but I tried not to think about it. No use spoiling my last day at camp. Through half closed eyes I looked at my beach pajamas hanging on a nail across the room. That crazy pink and black broken plaid, I thought, that's the way I am thinking. The lines are all broken, nothing comes together, nothing fits. If I can't get a job this summer, what will I do? The summer before I had saved enough money for tuition in the fall, but if we can't pay the mortgage—well, what's the use? Beverly and Harriet were talking about their nails—what polish they liked—and one part of my mind heard them as though from a great distance. It sounded so childish, but they didn't have so much to worry about. Beverly never worked in the summer, and she planned to enter the College of Mines in the fall to start working on her two-year teacher's certificate: "Just in case nobody wants to marry me," she had explained, "well, then, I could be a teacher."

"Popular as you are, not much chance of that," I had reassured her.

Harriet was lucky, too. She had already been rehired for her old job at Ye Ole Town Pump, and she was going to the University of Texas in the fall. Even Dianne was going to work part-time at the "Y" this summer, making posters and doing a little office work. She had finished the secretarial course at high school with honor grades but had not been able to get any job interviews. Prospective employers shrugged away her high school credentials—she must have job experience, they said. It seemed like an insurmountable obstacle until the office manager at the "Y" offered her part-time work. "Just enough to pay my carfare and give me experience to list on job applications," Dianne told me. "And I'll make posters," she added, happily. "You know, sketch pictures of the activities: kids swimming, tumbling, and dancing. They want posters for the membership drive, and that will be fun."

Well, I thought, returning to my own problems, *I'll have to talk to Mr. French again. Surely, as hard as I had worked there—never being late or missing a day—surely he would take me on.* But I wasn't sure. I turned over with a sigh and was glad when Dianne came back carrying her freshly ironed beach pajamas over her arm. It was time to shower and get dressed.

We were having a cookout on the wharf for our last evening, and the sun was just setting across the lake as we came out of the cabin and started down the hill. Halfway down the zigzag path Dianne stopped and picked a small clump of the little white daisies growing between the rocks. She held them to her face a moment, sniffing their fragrance, and, feeling the back of her head, with one hand she loosened her barrette, slipped the daisies under the white enamel and snapped it closed, the flowers a lovely accent for her pale blonde hair.

Cecil was waiting at the foot of the path. He noticed the daisies immediately and whirled Dianne around for a better look. "Oh, wildflowers," he exclaimed, sighing in mock relief. "For a minute I thought some city slicker was trying to beat my time and had sent you a florist's corsage up here. On you it looked like a florist's corsage. How does that poem go?" He thought a moment:

> If she stuck a piece of heather
>   In her hat,
> You'd think it was a feather.
>   She's like that.

Cecil had such a casual manner—you couldn't be sure if he was joking—so he could say the most sentimental things without sounding affected. Dianne, usually so timid, didn't mind at all. She smiled up at him, and for a moment they looked into each others eyes, quite unmindful that they were the center of a noisy crowd.

Dancing that evening we all felt nostalgic. One after another we played our most sentimental records: "Springtime in the Rockies," "Always," and, most popular of all, "Among My Souvenirs." We knew each other so well by now that most of us changed partners a lot, except for Cecil who scowled off anybody who tried to tag him for a dance with Dianne. Watching Dianne, I recalled our dancing lessons at the "Y" when she had always been the best in the class. Even though she hadn't danced much since those days, she followed Cecil quite naturally in all sorts of fancy steps.

The chaperones had gone up to the kitchen to refill the punch bowl when I noticed Cecil and Dianne waltz off down to the end of the wharf, climb into the little catboat tied there, and shove off. We had been cautioned by Coach Wyatt-Browne that it was dangerous to sail at night, but it wasn't quite dark so I supposed it would be all right. Anyway, I was having so much fun myself that I shrugged and quickly forgot about it.

Around midnight Mrs. Wyatt-Browne announced that even though it was our last night we should quit early because tomorrow we had to make that long hot trip back to El Paso, a hundred and twenty miles, she kept repeating. Every time she said it somebody would wind the Victrola and plead for one more dance, and so it went on and on. I was dancing with George when I suddenly realized that Cecil and Dianne had been gone the whole evening, and I was seized with a horrible premonition. Maybe something had happened: could they have capsized? When the music stopped, I asked George. He looked around, verified that they were not dancing, and then laughed at my concern. "Poor old Cecil," he said, shaking his head in mock sorrow. "He sure hates to leave. Most guys would be excited about going to West Point, but not Cecil."

"What do you think he wants to do?" I asked.

"Oh, I don't know. Write poetry—and he's good at it, too. Anyway, he's just not the military type, and now Dianne is making everything worse."

"I guess it's too late—about West Point, I mean. It's all decided?"

"Oh, sure. As Cecil says—the Mater." He made a grimace, but we didn't go on with the conversation. There was the soft scraping sound of wood against wood and the little sailboat came to rest against the wharf. The music started again, and in a moment Cecil and Dianne waltzed into view. I don't think anyone else had even missed them.

It was midnight or later, and Mrs. Wyatt-Browne's patience was finally exhausted. Standing by the Victrola she selected "Auf Wiedersehen" and said, "This is positively the last record."

I danced that piece with Everett, and when the music stopped Cecil and Dianne were close to us. Dianne raised her hand to smooth her hair and touched the daisies in her barrette. They were wilted. She released the clasp, slipped the flowers out and dropped them into the lake. Cecil pulled her close, put one arm around her waist, and kissed her. I realized I was staring, and I turned away self-consciously and followed the crowd heading for the path. Before I reached the edge of the wharf, Everett grabbed me and kissed me brusquely on the lips. "Auf Wiedersehen," he whispered.

I thought he was as surprised at his actions as I was. "Auf Wiedersehen." I answered. "It's been such fun. We'll never forget."

Nobody had brought a flashlight, and we stumbled up the crooked path, helping each other as we climbed. When we reached the top and separated towards our own cabins, I stood alone outside for a moment. The noise of settling down, muffled voices, doors slamming and water running gradually died out. I walked over to the top of the bluff and looked out across the lake. The full moon about to sink below the western horizon silhouetted the island, throwing a dark shadow on the still water. The little waves lapped against the rocks, and the breeze laden with aromatic sage stirred the white daisies at my feet. Farther down the path a cricket chirped, was quiet, and chirped again.

The lights in the cabins were going out, one at a time. I wasn't ready to go inside. I wanted to hold the moment, remember it forever. The refrain of an almost forgotten song, something we used to play on the Victrola so long ago, ran through my mind:

Good-bye, sweet day. I have so loved thee . . .

I heard a door creak open, and one of the girls in our cabin called softly, "Come in, Mafra. We want to turn out the light."

"Coming," I answered.

I turned and walked slowly towards the cabin where the single light burned. Inexplicably, a wave of sadness deeper than nostalgia swept over me. I looked back at the lake and sleeping elephant. Involuntarily, I pressed my open palm against my mouth as one does when apprehending a sudden danger. Still the old song lingered in my mind:

Good-bye, sweet day. I have so loved thee,
But cannot, cannot hold thee,
Fading like a dream . . .

I shivered in the warm desert air. Something too fragile and delicate to hold had slipped through my fingers, vanished forever. Never again would we be so young, never again so happy.

16

My interview with Mr. French was brief. Kress was not taking on any summer extras. His voice was kind but firm. Fearing I would cry, I avoided meeting his eyes, stared directly at the "Lamar French, Manager" sign on his desk, mumbled my thanks, and walked out.

In the hall I paused a moment before the mammoth time clock. The hideous red-orange sun, once the cruel usurper of my summer days, had cast me out. I had no number, no uniform. I was an outsider. I didn't belong.

On the main floor by the Information Desk I hesitated a moment. Should I go down to the basement and tell Della and the others? No, I couldn't do it. They would know soon enough. I felt a tear slide down my cheek and wiped it away with my sleeve. Walking towards the front doors, I passed Sadie Lou's counter. She was busy. Good. I didn't have to explain.

Out on the sidewalk the iron doors of the freight elevator were raised. Workmen were unloading bundles of mops from a nearby truck and stacking them on the elevator. I walked around the open shaft, my heels clicking on the little glass bricks. Who would be working in the storeroom, slicing bread, chopping veal off the bone? Who would notice my heels on the glass bricks overhead? Who was down there in my place? I had worked so hard—two summers at the lunch counter, and Saturdays and after school at the toy counter. I had never complained, never been absent or late. It made no difference. "Not hiring." That's all they had to say.

I hated to go home. Aimlessly, I let myself be jostled along by the crowd. Maybe some other stores were hiring. I would try Grants, right next door to Kress. No use. A "Not Hiring" sign in the window saved me the trouble of going in. I walked a couple of blocks to Woolworth's—another "Not Hiring." I was just wasting shoe leather. I walked back to the Plaza and caught the streetcar.

At home I threw my purse on the sofa and went back to the kitchen where Mama was ironing. I think she knew, even before she saw my tear-stained face. She tried to comfort me, saying Mr. French couldn't help it, even Kress couldn't help it. It was just the horrible Depression. All over the country millions were suffering. I stopped crying, but I didn't feel philosophical about it. Angrily, I beat my fist on the kitchen table, deploring the whole wasted, boring, summer that stretched ahead of me.

Mama always had a firm grip on reality, and she was thinking way beyond me. Yesterday the *Post* had carried an article about the College of Mines summer school. Since I couldn't get a job and had tuition money in the bank, why not summer school? While she talked, she tilted over the kitchen trash can and retrieved the newspaper. Yes, there it was. She spread the paper on the kitchen table, and we both pored over the article: twenty-two dollars for two courses, catalogues could be picked up at the library, and starting with the fall semester in addition to the mining engineering degree the college would offer a four-year liberal arts course.

I read the details a couple of times, and all the disappointment of the morning vanished. I was going to college! It was a Friday afternoon, too late to do anything, but Monday morning I would go to the bank and take twenty-two dollars out of my savings account—I had a total deposit of ninety-two dollars. Book money could be withdrawn a little later when I knew exactly what I had to buy. After going to the bank, I would pick up a catalogue and decide what courses I would take. I couldn't wait to get started, but there was still the weekend ahead—plenty of time to persuade Beverly to enroll with me.

Actually, Beverly, already bored with the do-nothing summer, needed no persuasion. Her father thought it was a great idea and was able to get her a used car for the summer. On registration day she picked me up early. The college was way around on the west side of the mountain, so we had a long drive: downtown and then out Mesa Avenue a mile or more, then a left turn, across a wide arroyo on a rickety wooden bridge with an overhead arch reading "Texas School of Mining and Metallurgy" and on up a gravel road to a building marked Main. In spite of our long drive we were among the first arrivals.

Neither of us had been on the campus before. Beverly leaned forward for a better look at Main, a three story building of beige stucco, surrounded by white, rocky soil, not landscaped but dotted with a few native plants—creosote, mesquite, rabbit brush, and even devilhorns. She raised her hand to shield her eyes from the glare reflected off the bare stucco walls. "Mafra, this is college? I mean it's so *bleak!*"

I was willing to admit it wasn't Ivy League, but she wasn't going to dampen my enthusiasm for going to college. I had studied the catalogue, and I started explaining the architecture. At first glance Main looked like a rectangle, but if you looked carefully you noticed the walls sloped, tapering in towards the top. According to the catalogue this was authentic Bhutanese style, exactly like build-ings you would find on the Tibetan Plateau.

"Tibet? Hey, aren't we still in Texas?"

"Well, sure. Can't you still see the whitewashed "M" on the mountain? By the way, that "M" is about to become part of your life. Every fall, according to the catalogue, it's a custom for fresh-men to cut class on "M" day, and carry water and lime up the mountain to repaint the letter—a tradition started by the mining engineers.

Beverly, after a reassuring glance at the "M," turned her attention back to the campus. Showing her some illustrations in the catalogue, I started explaining how the Bhutanese architecture was introduced to Texas. Back in 1914, the year Beverly and I were born, the wife of the college dean, a woman named Kathleen L. Worrell, happened to be flipping through a *National Geographic Magazine* and admired the Bhutanese architecture in Tibet. She thought it would fit perfectly into the Texas landscape. Her husband, Dean Worrill, liked the idea and so Main was built. Two or three other buildings later copied the style. In addition to the sloping walls, other Bhutanese features were the red brick border around the top, the round prayer wheels on the corners, and those deep-set windows to close out the sandstorms, a practical idea for West Texas.

Beverly was intrigued by the red circular prayer wheels on the upper corners of the building. Thinking it might take a lot of prayers to get her through this place, she wondered how they worked.

I was sorry to explain the wheels she was looking at were only an imitation. In Tibet real prayer wheels spin, and they're lower down on the buildings where people passing by can reach them. You write your prayer on a piece of paper, stick it in the wheel, and everybody who passes gives the wheel another whirl so the prayer is constantly wafted to heaven. But for now, back here in Texas, I admitted reluctantly, study might be more appropriate than spinning prayer wheels. Anyway, it was time to join the line forming in front of Main.

Registration took most of the morning. We both signed up for freshman English, an eight o'clock class, which meant we could ride out together. Beverly's second class was educational psychology, required for the teachers' certificate and scheduled right after English. My second class was college algebra, scheduled at eleven o'clock, so we couldn't go home together. I would have to take the bus back to Yandell Boulevard and transfer there to the Fort Bliss streetcar. At least that was the way I planned it.

As it worked out, Cliff Powers, a ruddy-faced, dark-haired boy who sat next to me in algebra class, struck up a conversation on the very first day and after class offered me a ride to town. He had an open-topped car, not new but not as ancient as the ones Beverly usually drove. As we left the campus and clattered over the wooden bridge, he explained he couldn't take me all the way home because he was working his way through college delivering papers up to Las Cruces and he had to go pick up his papers.

Before I got out of the car on Yandell, he said he could give me a ride every day and maybe sometime I would like to go on the route with him. I said I would, and, waiting for my streetcar, I watched him drive away in the traffic. He seemed so sophisticated: his own car, making his own way through college, so self-assured and at least in his twenties, certainly older than most of the boys I knew.

The streetcar clanged to a stop in front of me. I got on, but continued my reveries. Summer school had started well. It was going to be fun.

Calvin Willett was our English professor. A young man with reddish blonde hair and bright blue eyes, he greeted our class with enthusiasm. On the first day he laid out the course. Our chief task would be to write a term paper on our favorite historical character. The summer session was short, just eight weeks, he cautioned, and we had better choose our subject and begin our research at once. Even before he finished explaining the assignment, I decided that I would write on David Livingstone.

The college library stood on a hill above Main. Recently discovered letters and other evidence about Livingstone had excited public interest, and the library had a good selection of new books on the subject. A little surprised at the titles, I checked out *Livingstone, the Myth,* and *Livingstone Revisited.* Studying at home on the dining-room table, I turned over page after page of startling revelations. This was certainly not the Livingstone that I had idolized. At first I was indignant, determined not to believe such malacious gossip about a once-trusted friend.

I made an appointment to talk to Dr. Willitt. Instead of being daunted by the conflicting facts I was uncovering, he was delighted.

He assured me conflict was the essence of research. I should find all I could on both sides of the issue, make my own conclusions and carefully document my reasoning. Still dubious, I returned to the library, but the newly discovered evidence was overwhelming. As I read on, unraveling one duplicity after another, I began to feel a bitter satisfaction in the shattered dream. Many afternoons I worked alone in the college library. Summer school at College of Mines was not academically demanding; and I would sit motionless for minutes at a time, staring out the window and trying to realize how completely I had been misled.

The Livingstone personal journals, an original source I had once relied on, implied that throughout his youth Livingstone had been too absorbed in his religious studies to take time to fall in love, but recently published love letters disclosed that the girl he wanted to marry turned him down. He later married the daughter of a missionary but his family life had also been misrepresented. At one point he actually deserted his wife and children, leaving them in England without funds, and returned to Africa alone. His wife, desperate for money, finally followed him to Africa and died there of alcoholism.

The slave trade was another item. True, as a great communicator Livingstone had been instrumental in bringing horrible facts of the slave trade to public knowledge, and that information gave great weight to the abolition movement. However, in reality, he had lived among the Arab slave traders for many years, and—the inference was unavoidable—he could not have survived without the cooperation of the slave traders.

The truth seemed to be that as an explorer Livingstone had expanded British colonialism and for that reason was a British hero, but as a missionary he was a total failure. More than one book claimed to have it on good authority that he had made exactly one convert, but even that one soon became a backslider and denied the faith.

There was also a satirical twist to the story which the *New York Herald* had run about sending its roving reporter, H. M. Stanley, to Africa to find the lost Livingstone. There had been some excitement when Livingstone first disappeared from public view, and for the sake of a scoop the *Herald* planned to send Stanley to find him. While Stanley's expedition was being readied, Livingstone inconveniently surfaced in Zanzibar, thereby killing the story. Undaunted, James Bennet, Jr., proprietor of the paper, told Stanley to hold off a year because Livingstone was sure to disappear again. Bennet's hunch was correct. Livingstone did disappear again, and about a year later Stanley "found" him and the *Herald* had its story—the "Doctor Livingstone, I presume," story that I had proudly used in my Livingstone speech.

At the core of this new material was the description of Livingstone's death and burial. I remembered all too well that I had once described how the natives, instructed to transport his body to the coast so it could be shipped to England, delayed long enough to remove his heart and bury it in his beloved Africa. The brutal facts, I now discovered, were that in that tropical climate when a body had to be transported it was first eviscerated, the vital organs including the heart removed and buried on the spot, because only the salted cadaver could be shipped. There was no sentimental decision to keep the heart in his beloved Africa.

There was even more. An inscription on Livingstone's tomb in Westminster Abbey purports to be Livingstone's last words. Condemning slavery, he was quoted as saying: "All I can add in my solitude is, may heaven's rich blessing come down on everyone, American, English, or Turk, who will help to heal this open sore of the world."

Every book that I now checked—there were four or five of them—stated quite clearly that Livingstone's last words were recorded in his diary April 27, l873: "Knocked up quite, and remain—recovery—sent to buy milch goats. We are on the banks of the Molilamo." So even the epitaph on his tomb was false.

Still a little bewildered by the conflicting accounts, I had to go back to the church library to check again the books I had first studied. Mrs. Randolph was alone in her office, and she followed me into the library. While I looked for the Livingstone books, I explained I was doing a term paper on Livingstone and I had found some interesting new material, quite a different point of view.

She wasn't interested in anything new about Livingstone, but she did ask about my plans to study to be a missionary. I tried to explain that I was at College of Mines summer school but the Lone Star Cotton Mill where my father worked was about to go under, so I didn't know what would happen after summer school. She failed to grasp the problem but simply assured me that I was such a good student she was sure it would all work out. Then she turned the conversation to Cecil, asking if I knew he was at West Point.

"Yes, I know," I answered. "Or at least I knew he was going. What do you hear from him?"

"Oh, he's not allowed to communicate except in case of emergency for six weeks—orientation, you know. But he's used to military school, and I'm sure he will manage beautifully."

I agreed with her that wherever Cecil was he was sure to do well. While we talked I had found the Livingstone books I needed, and said I would sign them out so I could take them home to use in my theme.

"Yes, dear," she said. "It's wonderful to see young people choose their goals so early in life. Fortunately, Cecil has always been dedicated to a military career. He just never wavered from childhood. And you, of course, emulating Livingstone. Indeed, it is refreshing."

She went back into her office and closed the door. I signed the cards, picked up the books, and left by way of the sanctuary so I wouldn't have to go through her office and talk to her again. She didn't listen to a word I said.

17

After that ride to town on the first day of summer school, Cliff took me along on his route to Las Cruces several times, and we started having weekend dates, particularly on Friday nights when the feature changed at the Plaza Theater.

Wonderful Friday nights! The theater was new: air conditioned, soft, plushy seats, a ceiling that looked like a sky full of stars with soft white clouds drifting across, and a series of breathtaking films that went on to become classics: *All Quiet on the Western Front, Dr. Jekyll and Mr. Hyde, Grand Hotel.*

On such an evening in late July we had arrived early before the feature, and I was barely listening to the Pathé News—Hoover talking about economics or something like that—when the camera shifted to the gates of West Point Military Academy with the Gothic granite buildings in the background. A voice made some remarks about the incoming class, and we saw a group of freshmen still in civilian clothing, plebes they called them, entering the gates. Suddenly I recognized Cecil in the midst of the group. His blond hair, his walk, his military posture—all unmistakably Cecil.

"I know that boy!" I gasped. "That's Cecil Randolph. Look, Cliff, look! I know him!" I was so excited I sat on the edge of my seat, my eyes glued on the screen.

Cliff cautioned me to be quiet, not to shout it to everybody in the theater. Indeed, heads were turned towards me, and I managed to lower my voice to a stage whisper, but I couldn't stop talking. "Look, how real it is. It's Cecil!"

The camera focused on a later time and place. The plebes, now in uniform, were chatting in front of the barracks, and then, maybe a day later, they were taking the oath of allegiance which concluded with the pledge to serve in the army at least three years after graduation.

That was all. The newsreel switched to something else, but my mind was racing ahead. I would have to tell Dianne; she would have to see Cecil at West Point. Then the feature came on and I tried to concentrate on it, but I still had my mind on the West Point scenes. Before leaving the theater I checked in the lobby: tomorrow, Saturday, the matinee started at two o'clock. I had to tell Dianne.

On Saturday morning right after breakfast I ran down to Printz's Apartments. As usual Dianne came out on the porch to talk instead of inviting me in. At first she refused to believe I had actually seen Cecil on the screen. Was I sure I recognized him?

"Sure thing, he's there!" I repeated. "You have to see him. Tell your mother and Mr. Printz. Maybe they'll want to go with you."

"They never go to the movies."

"Well, but they'll want to see Cecil. You know they will."

"They don't know anything about Cecil."

"Dianne, why not? Didn't you tell them?"

"What's to tell?"

I was astonished that she hadn't even mentioned Cecil to her mother and Mr. Printz, but I quickly changed my tactics. "Well, just say it's a good show, Greta Garbo in Grand Hotel, and we want to go together."

She brightened at once. If I didn't mind seeing the show again, she said, she could easily get permission to go with me; and so we agreed to go to the matinee.

The news that Cecil Randolph, a hometown boy, was on the newsreel had spread, and I recognized several people from First Church waiting for tickets. Someone said Mrs. Randolph had been told and was planning to see the evening show. Dianne and I took seats in the middle of the theater and waited impatiently for the Betty Boop cartoon to finish. When the newsreel started and we had our first glimpse of Cecil, Dianne grabbed my hand and we sat there breathlessly watching every flicker. When the feature was over we stayed through the tiresome Betty Boop cartoon again so we could see Cecil a second time.

On the streetcar going home we went over every tiny scene. "He looked older on the screen, don't you think?" Dianne asked.

"Yes, I guess, but quite sure of himself. He managed to be the center of the action. You know he just does that without trying."

"Yeah, I suppose he does, but I think he looked happy, especially in that shot in front of the barracks where they were just talking."

"Why shouldn't he look happy, Dianne?"

"Well, he was pretty upset about going to the Academy. He doesn't really want a military life, at least that's what he said. You know, Cecil acts self-assured, and all that military training and having the appointment to West Point makes him seem sort of mature, but underneath he isn't so sure of himself. In fact, he's totally impractical. He told me so much about himself that last night at camp when we sailed over to the island. Oh, the plans he can make. . . ."

She let her voice trail off as if she were reliving that evening. After a moment, without any prompting on my part, she continued: "My thoughts just go around in a circle, and I feel sort of funny talking about Cecil, like I was betraying a trust. But you're my best friend, Mafra, and sometimes I feel like I just have to talk to someone."

"Sure, that's only natural. You know I'll never repeat anything you say. What sort of plans did he want to make?"

She was quiet a while, fingering her little clutch bag, and I wondered if she was would say anything more. "Well," she began, again, "you remember what a lovely moonlight night it was, our last night when Cliff and I sailed over to the island. There was an old blanket folded in the bottom of the sailboat, and Cecil spread it on the sand. I don't know. Maybe I shouldn't say it."

"Go ahead, if you want. You know you can trust me."

"Well, we were lying there, listening to the little waves lapping on the sandy beach and just snatches of songs floating across the lake from the wharf where you were all dancing, and that wonderful spicy aroma of sage."

"Yes, I remember," I said softly, sharing her mood. "The moonlight on the water and the way the music carried in that little valley. I'll always remember that night myself."

"Yes, and we were lying there together, talking about the things we would like to do if he didn't have to go to West Point and I didn't have to look for a job that I can't find."

"What does Cecil really want to do?"

"Well, first he talked about what he doesn't want to do. His mother is pushing him into a military career. He doesn't want it, but he won't stand up to her. He quoted something from Latin—I didn't take Latin myself, and I didn't understand it—but it was something about each man being given a choice and having great praise for those who follow *other* paths."

"I guess I understand what he meant. It would be awfully hard to stand up to Mrs. Randolph, once she's made up her mind."

Dianne sighed. "Yes, I know, but it makes me so sad to think about other paths or, as Frost puts it, 'The Road not Taken.' We studied Frost in English and I memorized that poem. I think Cecil knows practically all of Frost by heart. He quoted one of the verses I already knew:

> I shall be telling this with a sigh
> Somewhere ages and ages hence:
> Two roads diverged in a wood, and I—
> I took the one less traveled by,
> And that made all the difference.

"What other road, less traveled road, would Cecil like to take?"

"Oh, he has ideas all right, poetic ideas. There was a clump of yucca on the island and it was so white in the moonlight. We could even see those little moths that come in the evening to pollinate the yucca. Usually the moths just fly at twilight, but I guess the bright moonlight made them linger. Anyway, Cecil noticed the yucca because he knew that was the picture I painted—you know, the one that was submitted to the district contest and got a prize. I had told him about that."

"Well, of course. It was something to be proud of."

"Well, about the yucca. I told him how the moths pollinate just that one type of yucca and the yucca receives no other moths, and he said that was such a lovely thought that he wanted to write a poem about it. He wanted to just think about it, and he was sure he could come up with a poem. He said he could write a poem for every picture I painted. Oh, you don't know how crazy he really is."

"That's not so crazy. I think you will be a great painter."

"Well, that's a long way off—if ever. He wanted to start right now, wanted to run away to Mexico City, or Guadalajara, or some place. He said he had some money in the bank, a thousand dollars that his father left him, and he wanted to take it out and buy an old car and run away. Live on love, I guess, and paint and write poetry."

"What did you say?"

"Oh, we dreamed a while, and then I came down to earth and told him it was too crazy, we couldn't do it."

"I think he meant it, that he really wanted to."

"I don't know. Maybe he'll change, but you know—well, calling his mother 'the Mater.' What does that mean?"

"Maybe it's his way of trying to escape her authority."

"Maybe, but actually he never really confronts her."

We were quiet for a while, and I tried to think of something encouraging. "Well," I said, "going to West Point doesn't exactly ruin his life. He doesn't have to stay in the military forever. Did he ask you to wait for him?"

We were already at Five Points. People were getting off and on the car, and we stopped talking until the car swung onto Tularosa and picked up speed. "Yes, he wants me to wait. He thinks we are engaged." She opened her little white clutch bag. "Look, he asked me to wear this." She took out a heavy gold ring. It was on a chain, and she held the ring and chain in her hand.

I bent over, examined the ring and read the Staunton crest. "Oh, Dianne, that's wonderful. That's his class ring, and you are engaged. Why don't you wear it? Gosh, I would. I'd be so proud."

"Oh, I can't wear it. I don't want Mama and Mr. Printz to know, or anybody else except you, Mafra. I put the chain on so I can wear it under my gown at night. Silly, I guess. Nothing can come of it."

"You shouldn't feel that way. He'll be home on vacation, or leave, whatever they call it. Hey, maybe he'll invite you to a West Point dance, June Week. Maybe you can go to June Week!"

"Be serious, Mafra. You know who goes to June Week: girls from those eastern colleges, rich girls like Janet Carter."

"He wouldn't like Janet or any girl like that."

"I think the Mater would. Anyway Cecil will be meeting lots of girls from those big schools—maybe not like Janet, but rich girls. And here I am. Can't even get a job."

"Well, you shouldn't be so fatalistic about it. Lots of people do wait for each other. It can happen."

She was quiet for a moment, but she shook her head sadly and continued. "Sometimes I think you just know. I felt so sad that night when we were in the little sailboat coming back from the island. You were all dancing on the wharf, and I could hear the record playing 'Among my Souvenirs.' It's so sad:

> I count them all apart
> And when the teardrops start
> I find a broken heart
> Among my souvenirs.

"I think I knew right then what it means to have a broken heart. Oh, I hope I never hear that song again as long as I live."

I wanted to be encouraging, but I could feel her despair. "What does Cecil think now? I mean what does he write?"

"Oh, he can't write. He told me before he left that he wouldn't be able to write or receive mail for six weeks. So this newsreel was the first word I've had of him."

The car was climbing rapidly up the Copia hill, almost home. Dianne put the ring back in her purse and snapped it shut. "He looked like he was happy there, that he already has friends. Don't you think he looked happy?" she asked again.

"Just because he's happy there doesn't mean he's forgotten you. Wherever he is, he fits in; but he's in love with you. I'm sure of it. It wasn't just a weekend crush. He fell for you when he met you on the picnic at Hueco Tanks. You remember he asked me to invite you to the camp at Elephant Butte. And at camp he spent all his time with you. He was so proud just to be with you. Everybody at camp knew it. He wanted everybody to know it."

The car stopped on Fort Boulevard and we got off. The shadow from the mountain had crept across Copia, and we walked slowly in the shade, not talking but sharing our silence. When we stopped in front of the apartments Dianne touched my hand. "Thanks for telling me about the newsreel, Mafra," she said, "and, even more, thanks for listening."

I watched her walk up the apartment steps, slowly, with bowed head, as one who dreads to come home.

The July days sped by, and for me any hours not spent with Cliff were wasted. On Friday nights we had our standing date at the Plaza, and during the week we saw other movies if something special was on. Many afternoons we left the campus together, got a quick hamburger at the Pump, picked up his papers and did his paper route up the valley. In the open topped car with the wind blowing against our sun-tanned faces we gave a friendly wave to each waiting farmer as Cliff skillfuly tossed the paper precisely at his feet. We went on through Mesilla Park and finally to Las Cruces where the last wire-tied bundle was deposited at the drugstore for final distribution.

No papers between us now, Cliff turned the car around, I slid across the seat to be closer to him, and we left the busy highway and took the river road home. He drove more slowly now, the sun was low and felt good on our backs, and there was a particular cotton-wood tree, close to the river and hidden from the road by a tamarisk thicket, where he always stopped for a few minutes and held me in his arms, and we kissed and knew we were in love.

Sundays were special: long drives down the valley to Ysleta or even as far as Fabens. The "down-the-valley" road, as it was called, wasn't a busy highway like the road up the valley to Las Cruces. The narrow blacktop started just south of the city and, running more or less parallel to the river, twisted for mile after mile under giant cottonwoods. In spots the trees were so big their branches formed a canopy, casting speckled shadows on the road—most welcome to Cliff and me in his topless car. Instead of the spreading acres of cotton or vegetables that bordered the upper valley road, the farms here were small, often tiny orchards around Spanish-type houses of pink or cream stucco; children at little improvised fruit stands offered early pears or Thompson white grapes for five cents a pound.

The trees stopped at the outskirts of Ysleta, and the Spanish-type stucco homes gave way to flat-roofed adobe huts. Mexican laborers, enjoying their day of rest, lolled about in the shade or stood in doorways framed with long strings of chile peppers turning crimson in the desert sun. Sometimes we walked through the historic Ysleta Mission or stopped at the Tigua Indian Reservation to watch the Indian dancers imploring the Great Spirit to send rain.

One Sunday we had an all-day picnic at Soledad Canyon—a shady spot in the New Mexico mountains where we hiked along a cool stream until it mysteriously disappeared underground. Another Sunday we went with some of Cliff's older friends to White Sands, New Mexico, where we had a twilight wiener roast. The boys had brought wood for the fire—there was nothing to be gathered at the sand dunes—and walking on the dunes was like mushing through snow. When the moon came up, one of the boys who had lived in Colorado said the dunes were as white as snow drifts and made him want to ski.

Suddenly it was August, almost the end of summer school. I had entitled my theme "Livingstone—the Missionary Myth," and after all my reading and note taking I found myself hard pressed to finish it before the semester deadline. On the last day I worked in the college library until almost five o'clock. When I left the campus, quite elated that my work was done, I still had to return two books to the church library. On the bus to town it occurred to me that when I transferred to the streetcar at the church corner I would just have time to dash into the church library, return the books, and still catch the streetcar before the time on my transfer expired.

Not wanting to have to stop and talk to Mrs. Randolph, I entered the church by way of the sanctuary. I laid my books on the big library table, and as I searched for the cards to check them in, I became aware of voices in Mrs. Randolph's office. At first I paid no attention, but Mrs. Randolph's voice, usually well modulated, rose to a strident pitch, and I stopped my search and listened: "My dear, that's absolutely impossible. Of course, I cannot give you Cecil's address. He's not allowed to write or receive mail except in case of emergency—not even from me. The military is very strict about such things, and the military definition of emergency is quite narrow."

I had never heard Mrs. Randolph sound so agitated. What could have upset her so? A voice responded, but a streetcar clanged by outside and I didn't catch all the words. Then suddenly the other voice became quite audible, soft but audible. "It is an emergency. I must get in touch with Cecil." That gentle, familiar voice—why, that was Dianne! Whatever could have brought Dianne to Mrs. Randolph's office? It flashed through my mind that she may have met Mrs. Randolph at church parties, but she didn't really know her. Something terrible must have happened. I sat quite still at the library table, not conscious of eavesdropping but determined to hear all I could.

Mrs. Randolph's voice was quite clear. "Cecil's military career is just beginning, and I wouldn't dream of letting anything divert his attention at this point. Whatever your imagined emergency, it will have to wait."

"No, Mrs. Randolph. It is not an imagined emergency, and it will not wait. I am pregnant."

There was no immediate reply, just heavy silence. On my side of the door I froze, staring stupidly at the blank wall that separated me from Mrs. Randolph's office. Had I really heard it right? Those awful words, "I am pregnant." Had Dianne actually said those three words? I couldn't think at all. Scenes flashed across my mind like an old, silent movie: the last night at the camp, that goodbye on the wharf, Cecil's arms around Dianne's waist, the gentle kiss, the look in their eyes, and later when she talked to me on the streetcar, her refusal to hope, her absolute despair. And now, oh, my God—I stopped breathing—just pressed my hand against my lips and stared at the closed door.

After a bleak interval, Mrs. Randolph found her voice. In clipped, sharp words: "My dear, you may be mistaken. Women, especially young women, are often mistaken about these things."

Another streetcar rattled by, and I lost some words. Then Dianne's voice was soft but distinct. "No, I am not mistaken. I must tell Cecil."

"Tell Cecil! Are you trying to imply—but of course he has nothing to do with this." Mrs. Randolph's voice was now strident. "I don't know what sort of preposterous scheme you have cooked up, but I do know this: you are not going to involve Cecil in your sordid affairs. I have no idea what kind of boys—men—you have gone out with. Really, I don't know anything about you, at all. I suggest that if you think you are in trouble you should tell your parents. Really, I can't imagine what possessed you to come here. Cecil is not involved, and I can be of no help to you."

"I thought if you knew you would want to help."

"My dear, there is no way I can help you. You know, you may be mistaken. As I said before, young girls are often mistaken. Anyway, it's a problem you should take up with your parents. Have you seen a doctor? Your mother should take you to a doctor. I'm sure I don't know how these things are handled, but I suppose there is some way. My son has been very carefully raised. He is a gentleman—with all that word implies—and I can trust him implicitly. He is destined for a brilliant career, and I certainly don't intend to see him besmirched by a dirty little scandal right now when he is off to such a splendid start."

There were more street noises. Brakes screeched and a car honked persistently. I missed some words, and when the outside noises ceased everything was quiet in Mrs. Randolph's office. I wondered if Dianne could have left, but then I heard a chair move and I thought perhaps she was standing. "Here," she said, and her voice trembled as though she were holding back tears, "I would like for you to return this to Cecil." I heard her footsteps as though she were approaching Mrs. Randolph, holding out her hand.

"His Staunton ring!" Mrs. Randolph exclaimed. "Where did you get his ring?"

"He gave it to me. He wanted us to be engaged. In fact, he thinks we are engaged."

"Engaged? My dear this is utterly ridiculous. Cecil is just eighteen years old. How old are you?"

"Seventeen. Please return the ring to him. I think he will understand."

There was another long silence. I could picture Mrs. Randolph standing there, staring at the ring. After a moment I heard the outside office door close, and I knew Dianne had gone. Woodenly, I rose from the table. I had forgotten all about my Livingstone books and the cards spread on the table. I must run after Dianne, tell her I would help. We would talk to Mama. She would help, think of something to do. I rushed through the sanctuary and vestibule. From the top of the church steps I looked across the street and saw Dianne waiting for the streetcar. I ran down the steps, but it was rush hour and before I could cross the street a Fort Bliss streetcar came. Dianne got on and was gone.

At that hour the cars ran close together. In a minute or less another Fort Bliss car stopped and I got on. My transfer had probably long expired, but the conductor didn't look at it. Crazy, I thought, how could something like a transfer cross my mind when nothing else was making sense. The streetcar was crowded. I stood in the aisle near the front of the car, hanging to a strap. The cars were so close together I thought maybe I could catch up with Dianne when she got off on Fort Boulevard and Copia and have a chance to talk to her. As we clanged along Yandell, stopping at every corner, through the front window I watched her car. Sometimes we were right next to it, sometimes it went on ahead. Standing, I couldn't see out the side window, but when we stopped for traffic I stooped over to see where on Yandell Boulevard we were. There, just outside the window and hurrying down the sidewalk, was Dianne. I leaned lower to get a full view. Why had she gotten off her streetcar on Yandell Boulevard? It was a rundown neighborhood, old houses converted to small businesses, a beauty shop, home laundry, things like that. Where could she be going? The conductor on my car impatiently clanged the bell, but the car was blocked by traffic and stood still. Dianne walked quickly, purpose-fully. Half way down the block she turned up the steps of one of the renovated houses. The sign over the front door read "Female Clinic, Gynecology a Specialty." Oh, my God—that was the place that Beverly had told us about way back when Ella Mae was expelled. Beverly had said that a girl from junior high—what was her name—Isabel Wright, had gone to that clinic for an abortion and had almost died. And now Dianne! But they wouldn't help her. She had no money. Beverly said you had to have a hundred dollars. All that flashed through my mind as I watched Dianne. She looked so slim, so fragile, in her pale blue linen dress with her little embroi-dered clutch bag under her arm. The door opened and she entered. My car jerked forward and rumbled down the street.

I felt sick and swayed with the lurching car. A man sitting near me stood up and offered me his seat. "You better sit down," he said. "You look faint." I tried to thank him with a nod. I couldn't get my thoughts together. I should have gotten off the car and followed Dianne into the clinic. But what could I do there? Oh, God, what could she do?

I had not straightened out my thoughts at all out when we reached my stop on Fort Boulevard and I got off automatically. Not until I was walking along Copia did I remember that nobody would be at home. It was Wednesday night church supper at Altura. Mama was helping in the kitchen, and Papa and Becky would be there too. Mama had told me to come to the church for supper or, if I were late, to just fix something for myself at home.

No use in going by the church. Not a chance to talk to Mama in all that crowd, better just go on home. As I turned up Mountain Avenue I was a little surprised to notice our car parked against the curbing. Of course, I had forgotten. The battery was weak, and Papa didn't like to drive at night. They would have walked to church. That meant they would walk home and be even later than I had imagined. I went into the empty house and walked from room to room. I was crying, and I couldn't sit down or rest. After a while I fixed myself a glass of iced tea, but I didn't drink it.

About an hour later, it was practically dark, I walked down to the barbershop corner, hoping to see Dianne walking from the car line, but the street was empty. A light shown in Mr. Printz's living room. Maybe she was already home, sitting there with her mother and Mr. Printz and not talking. I couldn't ask her to come out or even telephone her. She didn't want them to know. I just had to wait for Mama. She would think of something.

It was after nine o'clock when Mama, Papa, and Becky finally came home. They said they were a little surprised that I hadn't dropped in for the church dinner. Then Mama looked at me closely and asked if I were sick. I shook my head, but she knew something terrible had happened. She hurried Becky off to bed, told Papa goodnight, and led me into the living room. "Whatever is the matter, Mafra? You look awful."

"Oh, Mama, the most dreadful thing." I put my hands over my face and sobbed aloud. "Mama, Dianne is pregnant!"

Mama's face blanched. "How do you know, Mafra? Did she tell you?"

I tried to explain, repeating all I had heard that day and even going back to the camp at Elephant Butte. Of course, I had already told Mama about Cecil liking Dianne so much, so it wasn't hard for her to piece it all together.

"So Dianne doesn't even know that you know?" she asked.

"No, I haven't had a chance to talk to her. I couldn't run into the office when she was talking to Mrs. Randolph, could I? Maybe I should have, but it didn't seem like it was my business. Mrs. Randolph—oh, Mama, how could she deny it? Of course it's Cecil, and what's more Cecil loves Dianne, wants to marry her. I know he does."

"He has to be told," Mama said, trying to grasp the situation. "Let me take one thought at a time. He has a right to know. Let me think about it. That's utter foolishness that he can't be contacted at West Point. There is some way of contacting him, I'm sure. I'll go talk to Mrs. Randolph myself, or maybe we could get directly to Cecil. Any army officer would know how to do it. I know—Colonel Greer down in the next block might help. He's a West Pointer, and he'll know how to get around the red tape and contact a cadet."

"If Cecil finds out—I mean if he knows—he'd have to leave West Point, wouldn't he?"

"I suppose, but before we decide all that, we have to talk to Dianne. She has to know we'll help her. I'll find a way. It's too late to do anything tonight. We don't even know when she got home from that clinic. Oh, poor Dianne. How terrified she must be. But she shouldn't have gone to that clinic. I've heard some awful stories about that place. But we don't need to worry about that. She hasn't any money. They wouldn't even have talked to her. At least we can dismiss that."

"I guess Cecil could even be kicked out of West Point. Probably that's what Mrs. Randolph is afraid of."

"Well, I don't know. I'm sure I don't see how she could fail to believe a girl as sweet and unsophisticated as Dianne. Oh, poor Dianne." Mama stood up and paced the floor, almost as distraught as I was. "If they don't get married, she could go away and have the baby. There are homes for unwed mothers. I can find out about that. Dr. McSpadden, our minister at Altura, should know. She could have the baby and give it up for adoption if she wanted to. She is so young. This is all crazy. Until we talk to Dianne we can't make plans for her. But we will definitely help her. I'm sure of it. I wish she had come and talked to me in the first place. She can't talk to Mr. Printz—that sanctimonious old fool. And her mother is nothing but a weakling, scared of her shadow. Oh well, I wish morning would come so you could go get Dianne to come up here."

"Yeah, I wish it was morning. I forgot to eat any supper. I'm just going to make a cup of cocoa before I go to bed."

Early the next morning, about an hour before daybreak, Dianne shot herself. We didn't hear the shot. It wasn't even light when Mrs. Williamson came up and told us. She said the shot woke her and Mr. Williamson, and then there was an ambulance and the police came. Mr. Williamson went over to find out what had happened. He said Dianne was already dead when the ambulance came. She had died instantly.

18

The organ played softly. Shafts of sunlight penetrated the western windows of Altura Presbyterian Church and came to rest on the plain white coffin covered by a single spray of calla lilies. A funereal sweetness permeated the still air. Behind the coffin, separating it from the pulpit, sprays of white roses, carnations, and Shasta daisies gave eloquent expression to the grief and anguish of the gathering mourners.

We walked slowly to our usual pew, halfway down the aisle. Becky and Gwen, both dabbing their eyes with damp handkerchiefs, slipped in first, followed by Beverly and me, then Mama and Papa next to the aisle. I watched the neighbors arrive. How strange and far away they looked, two-dimensional figures moving awkwardly in a bad dream. Mr. and Mrs. Quinn with Gladys and Clarabow sat in front of us. They must have closed the store. Mr. Wilson, the barber, walked slowly down the aisle and sat alone in front of the Quinns. Funny to see him without his pipe and white barber's coat. Mr. and Mrs. Williamson came with little Edward—not little any more. His round eyeglasses had been replaced by rectangular lenses which gave him a scholarly look. He was wearing a suit with a coat and tie, and he sat in the pew, taller than his mother. All the neighbors from on up the block were there. Some wept openly, but some stared stoically ahead as though an excess of grief might be an acknowledgement of shared responsibility for the terrible tragedy.

My eyes, red from weeping, smarted in the merciless glare of the afternoon sun. Oh God, those awful white frosted window panes. If only they had stained-glass windows and soft light. All those money-raising activities, the ice-cream socials and Wednesday-night suppers, always raising money to buy stained-glass windows, and they still didn't have them.

I had so many memories centered in this little church: those Sunday mornings when Papa was a deacon and tolled the bell; Auntie Ruth's Sunday-school class with all the Scripture reading and memory verses. Dianne had been in that class. Auntie Ruth, Judy, and Jammie Sue were back in St. Louis now—their house on Mountain Avenue still empty. I wondered if they would ever know about Dianne.

The church was filling up. A group of teachers from Rusk School had arrived: sweet, gentle, little Mrs. Wells with her busy ways and happy plans. She had been so sure that wonderful things were going to happen to all of us; Miss Fuller, the art teacher who had always put Dianne's pictures up on the wall. She sat next to Mrs. Wells. They were both crying.

Boys and girls from First Church began to arrive, a big crowd. They must have come together. Some of the girls were crying. The boys looked awkward, trying to appear manly. Coach and Mrs. Wyatt-Browne and the Hamiltons sat together. The whole Elephant Butte Camp crowd was there, except a few like Everett and Cecil who were out of town. I had written to Everett. *Cecil doesn't even know,* I thought for the thousandth time. Oh, God, here we are burying Dianne, and Cecil doesn't know.

The door to the pastor's study opened, and Dr. McSpadden came out, followed by Dianne's mother. She was wearing a black hat and dress, and a short black veil covered her face. Mr. Printz stood close to her, holding her arm. He and Dr. McSpadden escorted her to the first pew. What a fragile little thing she was—but erect. She carried herself gracefully, like Dianne. Mr. Printz in his black suit looked straight ahead, grimly composed. I wondered what sort of thoughts were penetrating his rigid little brain. How could he have been so mean? A man of property he had called himself that day he insisted Dianne could not take the "Y" membership because it was charity. What did he know about charity? If only he had shown a little charity himself. If only he had loved Dianne, made her feel cared for so that she could have turned to him in her terrible anguish. I looked at his trim haircut, his starched white collar and black suit, and I hated him.

But why should I blame Mr. Printz when I myself was just as much to blame? When I was in the church library and heard Dianne talking to Mrs. Randolph, why didn't I rush in and shake Mrs. Randolph's aristocratic shoulders and tell her she had to listen? All that foolishness about ruining Cecil's career. He loved Dianne. I knew it. Well, now his career was dust and ashes. Suppose he did become an officer, I thought savagely—a general—what of that? No matter how many stars on his shoulders he was destined to dream forever of the path not taken. He could say it in Latin: each man has a choice and we have great praise for those who follow other paths. He couldn't make the choice. Dianne knew he couldn't. But that's not fair, I thought. If he had known, if Mrs. Randolph had told him—

I was crying again. I wiped my eyes, and Mama patted my arm gently. She had told me to stop thinking about all the if-onlys. It had happened, she said, and we had to live with it. We loved Dianne, and we thought at the time that we were doing the right thing. Maybe we were wrong. Well, of course, we were wrong. We should have gone to her sooner, but we thought we had time. We had to accept ourselves as being less than perfect. We were wrong, and Dianne was dead, and there was no way to rationalize it.

The music faded, and Dr. McSpadden stood in the pulpit. "Dearly Beloved, we are gathered together—" The church was perfectly quiet—just silent tears and the sun on the calla lilies. He finished the formal part of the service and paused, having trouble controlling his voice. I sat still, my hands pressed together, wondering if he could go on.

After a moment, without notes and with his hands held before him in an open gesture, Dr. McSpadden stepped forward a little and began again. "This is a beautiful world," he said, and stopped and cleared his throat, "but it is a hard world, for along with all the joys of life God has mixed adversity. Some of us are hardened by adversity. We are the fortunate ones. We fight back and are toughened and become the better for it. But once in a while in his infinite wisdom God creates a delicate creature, a lovely girl, surely one of His chosen"—he hesitated a moment, his eyes on the slim white coffin—"one of his chosen who is too sweet, too gentle, too ethereal to fight back. Dearly Beloved, these children of God are the butterflies of this world. On wings as fragile as rose petals they pass through God's garden, but how their gentle sweetness beautifies the landscape—the butterflies too lovely to linger. Such a beautiful girl, Dianne Mel, has passed through our midst. Sunset came early for Dianne. She could not linger. Cherish the memory of this beautiful girl who for one brief moment brightened our lives."

Burial was in the new cemetery near William Beaumont Hospital. When the crowd gathered there the sun had dropped behind Mount Franklin and the soft shadow had passed over the newly dug grave. We formed a semicircle while Dr. McSpadden read more Scripture. When the service was over and the crowd was drifting back to the cars Mama motioned to us to wait so that Mr. and Mrs. Printz would not be the last to leave the cemetery.

The funeral parlor limousine was parked near the grave. Mr. Printz held Mrs. Printz's arm as they walked towards it together. He opened the car door. Before getting into the car Mrs. Printz hesitated, turned, and looked back. Slowly, she raised her short black veil, touched her slim white fingers to her lips, and blew a kiss towards the open grave.

We watched the limousine pass through the cemetery gate and climbed into our car. Waiting for outside traffic, Papa stopped a moment at the gate. The hedge of tamarisk which separated the cemetery from the road was in full bloom, and the tiny flower sprays looked like soft pink feathers in the early twilight. On either side of the open gate clumps of yucca held up spires of creamy white flowers barely touched with streaks of green.

As the traffic cleared Papa turned the car through the gate and out onto the highway. We drove home in silence.

❦

It was mid August, and the short summer session was over. On the last day of class Dr. Willett returned our graded papers. I had worked so hard on my paper I wasn't really surprised when I got an "A" along with the comment it was an excellent paper, but I was a little puzzled when the class filed out and Dr. Willitt asked me to come by his office.

The office which had been so cluttered all summer was now strangely bare. Dr. Willitt was preparing to leave on a short vacation before the fall term, and as he talked he was sorting out various papers and stuffing them into his briefcase. "Just wanted you to know, Miss King, I was quite impressed with your term paper. I don't use the word lightly, but I do believe you have real talent for writing. Yes, I believe that, and you must develop it."

I murmured a polite "thank you," wondering what was coming next.

"The reason I'm making a point of talking to you—of course, I don't know your circumstances, but it is so distressing, the way students are dropping out because of the Depression. Whatever the sacrifice, you must continue your education. Journalism might be a good field for you, if you could go to a bigger university."

I shook my head, implying that was out of the question. He stopped his packing and stepped closer to me: "Yes, Miss King, it's up to you. You've got the talent and the insight. You must develop your writing. I know talent when I see it, and you have already shown great promise."

I thanked him again, said something about enjoying his course, and the interview was over. When his office door closed behind me, I stood for a moment in the deserted hall. Most of the students had left campus, and the recessed Bhutanese-style windows at each end of the building permitted a cool breeze to circulate through the hallway. I stood quietly, holding my theme to my breast and savoring every word Dr. Willitt had spoken: insight, talent, a chance to be a writer. Oh, how I would love to be a writer!

I stuffed my theme into my notebook and made my way slowly down the hall to the single flight of stairs, musing how much I had changed in the eight short weeks since Beverly and I enrolled. In the beginning, when I started researching my theme, I was still saying I wanted to be a missionary. Now, eight weeks later, I never thought of my future that way. To be honest with myself, discovering Livingstone was a great explorer but a complete bust as a missionary had little to do with my change of mind. Somewhere along the line, maybe in high school, maybe while working at Kress, I had simply abandoned the missionary fantasy. And now, I had barely started to college, and I could hardly believe the exciting possibilities Dr. Willitt had suggested.

Out in the sunshine I stood still a moment, waiting for my eyes to adjust to the white glare bouncing off the caliche soil and rocky paths. From a distance I heard the bus rumbling across the old wooden bridge as it made its way to the campus stop. With a few other students I got on; the bus circled around the sunbaked campus and carried me for the last time over the rickety bridge. I glanced at the lettered arch, "Texas School of Mines and Metallurgy," and wondered idly if they would change that in the fall when they instituted the regular four-year college course.

It was almost noon when I got off the car on Fort Boulevard and walked home through the sweltering heat. Hot and sweaty, I intended to flop on the couch and announce I had gotten an "A" on my English course, but Papa was waiting for me. As the screen door banged behind me, he got up from his chair at the dining-room table and thrust the document he had been reading into my hands. "Eviction notice," he said. "Read it for yourself. I never thought I'd see the day."

Wiping my damp face on my sleeve, I held the paper in my hand and glanced at the first paragraph. No need to read the fine print; we had all seen it coming. In spite of the brief spurt of summer work at the mill, our mortgage payments were two months in arrears, and in formal language the bank was giving us thirty days to vacate the premises.

Before I could finish the first page, Papa snatched the paper back, waved it aloft with one hand and pounded the table with the other. "Vacate the premises!" he shouted. "What are they talking about—'premises'? This is my home. This is where my daughters grew up, where my wife cooked our meals, planted flowers: sunflowers all over the yard and all those little blue flowers, whatever she calls them. This isn't premises. This is where I *live!*"

I could hear Mama busy in the kitchen. After a moment she came and stood in the doorway, wiping her hands on her apron, looking at Papa but saying nothing. Apparently the offensive document had arrived some time earlier, and, although she had read it and was just as upset as Papa, she had no patience with his histrionics. Not until he had exhausted himself raving about the injustice of the entire system, including everybody from President Hoover down to the lowliest officer at the bank, did she interrupt to say calmly—certainly not the first time that morning—that, no, the bank had not singled us out individually for eviction. It was happening to everybody. Just look at the vacant houses on the street, all over town, all around the nation for that matter. The Depression was nationwide, even worldwide, and we were just caught up in it. Papa shrugged at this logic.

Becky had slipped unnoticed into the room. She and I exchanged troubled glances, and she pulled a chair up next to me at the table. We didn't speak but kept our eyes on Papa, his work-worn hands folding and unfolding the legal document. When he finally gave an enormous sigh and tossed it onto the table, Becky and I both cringed and drew back visibly as though we were gazing at a coiled rattlesnake.

Mama had gone back into the kitchen. I could hear her as she slammed cupboard doors, poured dried black-eyed peas into a pot for soaking, let the water run. She had chosen not to sit at the table with our little group, but the message from the kitchen was clearer than words. No matter what happened—eviction notice or no—life for the Habersham Kings was going on. She would see to that.

When a long silence indicated Papa had finally simmered down, at least for the moment, Mama appeared again in the doorway. "Well," she said, impatiently, "bad as it is, we are not helpless characters in a novel, waiting for the thirty day notice to expire so they can move our furniture out on the sidewalk. We have to take action."

"Action? Like what?" Papa asked.

"First of all, we have to go back South where there are cotton mills. Of course, some are closed, but some are running, at least part time, and you have a good reputation as a dyer. There you can at least look for work."

It was the same plan they had discussed and rejected many times before, but it was no longer a matter of choice. There wasn't anything else to do.

The discussion went on all afternoon and was continued out on the front porch well into the night. Papa kept repeating the obvious: the Lone Star Cotton Mill had filled its last order, the one that carried it through the summer, and there was nothing ahead. They might even close down and auction off the machinery, and you'd have to go half way across Texas before you could find another mill where he could even ask for work. Mama agreed, and repeated that we had to go back South.

As they talked, I realized Mama had not been taken by surprise. All summer while she had pretended to be optimistic about the mill hanging on, she had known the chances were slim. Over the years she had kept up a vigorous correspondence with her relatives back in Georgia, especially her favorite brother Baxter, a lawyer in Atlanta. Now she admitted that during the summer she had apprized him of the situation at the mill, and he had offered to help. If the Lone Star Mill actually closed, he wanted us all to come stay with him and his wife Sally in Atlanta, and from there Papa could canvass the whole state looking for work.

The idea of staying with relatives was new to Papa, and at first he found objections. For one thing, the car battery was so weak it couldn't make the trip; and, worse than that, we still owed payments on the car, a Ford sedan bought secondhand a year ago, and it was against the law to take it out of the state as long as it had a lien on it.

Mama was ready with the answers. As for the battery, she said

230

we would just park on hills where we could coast off, like we were doing in El Paso, or, if there weren't any hills we could always ask for a push. The matter of it being illegal to take the car out of the state seemed to enrage her. With times as bad as they were, did Papa expect Henry Ford to be standing at the Texas border trying to stop us? Well, if he dared we would just run him down and go on. Later, when Papa got a job, we could send the installment payments back. The dealer would be glad enough to get them.

Although Papa had no alternative plan, he still wasn't convinced. For one thing, there was the little matter of gas for the trip. He had been buying a gallon or two at a time, just enough to get to work and back when the mill was running. Becky and I hadn't been able to contribute much to the discussion, but at this point I mentioned the sixty-two dollars I still had in the bank. We could use that, since I wouldn't be going to college anyway. Becky didn't have a bank account, but she offered the three dollars she had been saving for school clothes.

Papa attempted a weak smile and muttered something about all pulling together. After quite a silence Becky asked Mama if she would be going to high school in Atlanta. Mama seemed surprised at the question and answered rather crossly: "Oh, I suppose so." I realized she was pretending to feel a lot more secure than she really was.

It was late when we went in to bed, and even then I couldn't go to sleep. I got up and went to the kitchen for a drink of water. Papa was still sitting at the dining-room table, holding his head in his hands. As I came back through the room I urged him to go to bed, saying it would all look better in the morning. He didn't answer me, just sighed with that beaten expression on his face. Before I closed my bedroom door I heard him mutter to himself:

> Backward, turn backward, O Time, in your flight,
> Make me a child again just for tonight!

I slipped into bed and started crying. Becky turned over, "Are you crying, Mafra?"

"Yes, I can't help it."

"Me neither. Just wipe your eyes on the top sheet. That's what I do."

231

The last of August, the dog-days of summer, dragged slowly by. I thought things couldn't get any worse; and since it was settled that we had to leave, I just wished the grace period would pass and we could be on our way. But I was mistaken. Things did get worse.

We didn't hear it on Mountain Avenue, but there must have been a rumor. Anyway, in the early morning of Friday, September 4, 1931, a line began to form in front of the El Paso First National Bank. At ten minutes before opening time a sign was hung on the plate glass door: "This bank closed for business until further notice."

It had taken a long time, almost two years since the Stock Market crash, but El Paso was deep in the throes of Depression. My money gone—all my Kress wages wiped out just like that. I wasn't going to use it for college—not even for gas. Just gone.

That it was happening everywhere was small comfort. Local businesses and institutions tried to help. The Texas School of Mines and Metallurgy, scheduled to open on September 15, announced it would have to pay its professors in scrip and that any students who had lost money in the bank would be allowed to charge tuition and books. Mama read that aloud from the paper, but it was no help to me. On or before September 15 we had to "vacate the premises."

A few days after the bank failure Mama and Papa went to town to find a furniture store interested in buying secondhand furniture, everything we had, which they thought would bring enough to pay for the trip. Becky and I were sitting in the porch rockers, hashing it all over and hoping they could make a good bargain, when suddenly a Western Union boy on a bicycle came around the barbershop corner and started pedaling up the hill. Western Union deliveries were seldom seen on Mountain Avenue—usually just for death notices—and when he stopped at our walk we both stood up apprehensively. He checked the house number against the envelope he held in his hands, came up the steps, and asked for Mr. Habersham King.

"I'll sign," I said. He took the pencil from behind his ear, handed it to me, and I wrote my name on his pad.

As he coasted off downhill, Becky and I examined the envelope.

No red star—it couldn't be a death notice. We held it up to the light and made out the word New Orleans. We didn't know anybody in New Orleans. What could it mean?

It seemed forever, but Mama and Papa finally came driving up the street. Papa made the U-turn, headed downhill, and parked against the curb. Becky and I ran out and gave him the telegram. He was maddeningly slow finding his pocket knife and slitting through the envelope. We pressed around him on the front walk, but I couldn't see over his shoulder to make out the big capital letters pasted in strips on the yellow paper. Finally he cleared his throat, announced it was from Fred Mae, and read aloud:

> Am authorized offer you job head dyer Lane Mills New Orleans fifty dollars weekly starting immediately. Telegraph acceptance Lane Mills, 4300 Tchoupitoulas Street, New Orleans. Fred Mae.

Mama recovered first. "New Orleans!" she exclaimed. "Just think of it—New Orleans! Oh, Hab, what a wonderful opportunity."

Papa just stood there, looking rather stunned. He didn't even know Mr. Mae had gone to New Orleans, but, of course, he had "headed south," and so it all began to fit together. Mama kept repeating that Papa was such a good dyer, the minute Mr. Mae could send for him, of course he did.

As we walked together into the house Becky volunteered that Mr. Mae really owed it to us: "After all the trouble we had with those pigeons." That broke weeks of tension, and we enjoyed a good laugh.

After many suggestions and several attempts Papa finally wrote the ten-word message: "Accept job head dyer fifty weekly arriving by September fifteenth." Mama gave him two dollars out of the housekeeping money to pay for the telegram, and he stuffed the penciled message into his pocket and started for the front door. "That fellow Mae," he chortled, as he reached the door. "Too bad I was limited to ten words. I didn't have a chance to say thanks."

The next day the secondhand man came and priced the furniture—eighty dollars for the lot. Not much, but it would do for the trip. Beverly and Gwen both came down to hear all the news and say good-bye. In spite of our good fortune, they were inconsolable at our leaving. Becky and I were sorry to be leaving our best friends, but we were too excited to dwell on it. We made promises: we would write, maybe visit each other, and always remember the wonderful times we had shared.

That was sweet sorrow, but I still had to tell Cliff good-bye. All summer he had refused to believe I might not be back at school in the fall, but now the reality was upon us, and I dreaded it.

I wanted things to go well on our last date; but Cliff was glum and resentful as though I were in some way responsible for our moving.

We went to a movie at the Plaza but left early and took the long route home over Scenic Drive. I told him over and over how much I treasured our love, how faithfully I would write to him, and how I had no choice in the matter, that it was all out of my hands. By the time we got home he had cheered up a little.

Papa had braced our overloaded car against the curb—we planned to leave at daybreak—and Cliff parked behind it. The living-room light shown through the open door onto the porch, and when we went up the steps Cliff took my hand and pulled me into the shade of the Virginia creeper. With tender kisses, we promised once again that we would never stop loving each other. It would always be the same. We would write, and he would come to see me, maybe Christmas. No matter what, our summer together had been wonderful. We had found each other, and we would never let go, never.

At last he left, almost running off the porch, and I stood alone in the shadow. A slight breeze stirred the heavy leaves of the Virginia creeper, and the sound of Cliff's car faded in the distance. I pressed my open palms against my burning cheeks, trying to wipe away the tears.

I stood a moment on the top step, looking out at the parked car, on across the empty school ground, the silent desert, Sugar Loaf standing pale in the moonlight.

For a better view I went out and stood on the grass. Above Sugar Loaf the North Star twinkled brightly and over to the left, straight above McKelligon Canyon, the Big Dipper, and lower to the right the Little Dipper. How many times I had stood there with Papa and tried to figure out how to tell time by the Little Dipper as it revolved around the North Star: something about imagining a little man with outstretched arms and legs, the hands of a clock, the latitude and the month.

I breathed in the fragrant, desert air, felt its softness around me. With infinite time I was one. The agonizing wrench of departure had vanished. My roots in the desert and the mountains were deep. I would leave so much of myself, but so much more I would take with me.

Quite calmly, without saying good-bye, I turned and walked towards the house.

❦ ❦ ❦ ❦ ❦ ❦ ❦ ❦

MARY KING RODGE left El Paso in the fall of 1931 and has lived in various parts of the country. She currently lives in Hot Springs, North Carolina. In 1995, at the age of eighty, she earned her second masters degree at the University of North Carolina, Asheville. This is her first book.